Comments from readers of the previous edition of this book…

"This book is truly fantastic (I rarely write reviews but thought this was the exception). All of the other books that I've seen for Excel spend too much time on explanation and not enough on practice. I don't have a lot of free time, so being able to learn quickly without a lot of extraneous reading has been invaluable. I'm a physician, so didn't have to use Excel until I started doing administrative work (I was completely new to the Excel program). I now can produce charts with beautiful graphics and trend data (everyone on my team is amazed -- even the data analysts)! Thank you again for such an amazing book."
– *A reader from the USA.*

"We first bought this book after upgrading, and now get a copy for every new trainee accountant. It is structured in a bite size 'lesson' format that makes it easy to pick up and put down during the day. I describe it as a 'basic to intermediate' guide but even advanced users of Excel have been able to pick up tricks and tips."
– *A reader from the UK*

"The book is well laid out. It walks you through all the ins and outs of Excel and can have you producing professional looking spread sheets in no time at all. I very much recommend it."
– *A reader from Canada*

"Mike Smart continues to pave the way for excellence in teaching Microsoft Excel. His approach is well anchored in behavioural principles and consistently results in students learning more, faster. I would highly recommend the book and approach to all those interested in mastering the software and moving on to using it productively."
– *A reader from New York, USA*

"When asked if I could use Excel, I was one of those people who would always say, 'Sure, I use it every day.' Well, after using this book, I found out I really wasn't using Excel. I can now do things with Excel, that a couple of weeks ago, I didn't even know this program could do."
– *A reader from the USA*

"Mike Smart is the best teacher I've ever known. He is concise and precise, showing everything you need to know about this wonderful spread sheet. Even though English is not my mother tongue, I can understand every single word of it."
– *A reader from the USA*

"I bought this book because I consider myself a basic user of Excel and wanted to expand and improve my skills. I can honestly say that this is the best book I have ever bought and has helped me so much. Each section takes about an hour to complete and with only seven sections, this book can be completed very quickly. The layout is easy to follow and has some great tips, and various examples which are very easily downloadable from the website. I always thought I was fairly good on Excel but this book has taught me some stuff I never knew you could even do."
– *A reader from the UK*

Who Is This Book For?

If you need good Excel skills for your work, or want to add Excel skills to your CV, you've found the right book.

If you've never used Excel 2013 before, this book will give you all of the skills you need to be thoroughly competent. By the end of the book your Excel skills will be better than most office workers with many years of experience.

This book is for Excel 2013 users who:

- Need to acquire essential Excel skills quickly.

- Have never used Excel before, or who have only basic Excel skills.

- Want to learn Excel skills from first principles.

- Are moving to Excel 2013 from an earlier version.

Use of this book as courseware

This book is also the official courseware for The Smart Method's *Excel 2013 Essential Skills* course.

Smart Method courses have been taken by a varied cross-section of the world's leading companies. We've had fantastic feedback from the vast number of professionals we've empowered with Excel skills.

This book is also suitable for use by other training organizations, teachers, schools, colleges and universities to provide structured, objective-led, and highly effective classroom courses.

Learn Excel 2013 Essential Skills with The Smart Method

Mike Smart

Published by:

The Smart Method® Ltd
Burleigh Manor
Peel Road
Douglas, IOM
Great Britain
IM1 5EP

Tel: +44 (0)845 458 3282 Fax: +44 (0)845 458 3281

E-mail: info@ExcelCentral.com
Web: www.ExcelCentral.com (this book's dedicated web site)

FIRST EDITION

International Standard Book Number (ISBN13): 978-1-909253-06-3

The Smart Method® is a registered trade mark of The Smart Method Ltd.

4 6 8 10 9 7 5

Contents

Introduction 13

Feedback 13

Downloading the sample files 13

Problem resolution 13

Typographical Conventions Used In This Book 14

Putting The Smart Method to Work 16

Excel version and service pack 16

Sessions and lessons 16

Read the book from beginning to end 16

How this book avoids wasting your time 17

Why our classroom courses work so well 17

How this book mimics our classroom technique 17

Avoiding repetition 18

Use of American English 18

Incremental sample files 18

First page of a session 19

Every lesson is presented on two facing pages 20

Learning by participation 21

Session One: Basic Skills 23

Session Objectives 23

Lesson 1-1: Start Excel and open a new blank workbook 24

Lesson 1-2: Check that your Excel version is up to date 26

Lesson 1-3: Change the Office Theme 28

Lesson 1-4: Maximize, minimize, re-size, move and close the Excel window 30

Lesson 1-5: Download the sample files and open/navigate a workbook 32

Lesson 1-6: Save a workbook to a local file 34

Lesson 1-7: Understand common file formats 36

Lesson 1-8: Pin a workbook and understand file organization 38

Lesson 1-9: View, move, add, rename, delete and navigate worksheet tabs 40

Lesson 1-10: Use the Versions feature to recover an unsaved Draft file 42

Lesson 1-11: Use the Versions feature to recover an earlier version of a workbook 44

Lesson 1-12: Use the Ribbon 46

Lesson 1-13: Understand Ribbon components 48

Lesson 1-14: Customize the Quick Access Toolbar and preview the printout 50

Lesson 1-15: Use the Mini Toolbar, Key Tips and keyboard shortcuts 52

Lesson 1-16: Understand views 54

Lesson 1-17: Hide and Show the Formula Bar and Ribbon 56

Lesson 1-18: Use the help system 58

    Session 1: Exercise 61

    Session 1: Exercise answers.. 63

Session Two: Doing Useful Work with Excel   65

    Session Objectives 65

Lesson 2-1: Enter text and numbers into a worksheet 66

Lesson 2-2: Create a new workbook and view two workbooks at the same time 68

Lesson 2-3: Use AutoSum to quickly calculate totals 70

Lesson 2-4: Select a range of cells and understand Smart Tags... 72

Lesson 2-5: Enter data into a range and copy data across a range... 74

Lesson 2-6: Select adjacent and non-adjacent rows and columns 76

Lesson 2-7: Select non-contiguous cell ranges and view summary information 78

Lesson 2-8: AutoSelect a range of cells 80

Lesson 2-9: Re-size rows and columns... 82

Lesson 2-10: Use AutoSum to sum a non-contiguous range 84

Lesson 2-11: Use AutoSum to quickly calculate averages... 86

Lesson 2-12: Create your own formulas 88

Lesson 2-13: Create functions using Formula AutoComplete 90

Lesson 2-14: Use AutoFill for text and numeric series 92

Lesson 2-15: Use AutoFill to adjust formulas 94

Lesson 2-16: Use AutoFill options 96

Lesson 2-17: Speed up your AutoFills and create a custom fill series....................................... 98

Lesson 2-18: Use automatic Flash Fill to split delimited text.. 100

Lesson 2-19: Use manual Flash Fill to split text 102

Lesson 2-20: Use multiple example Flash Fill to concatenate text 104

Lesson 2-21: Use Flash Fill to solve common problems 106

Lesson 2-22: Use the zoom control 108

Lesson 2-23: Print out a worksheet... 110

    Session 2: Exercise 113

    Session 2: Exercise answers.. 115

Session Three: Taking Your Skills to the Next Level   117

    Session Objectives 117

Lesson 3-1: Insert and delete rows and columns.. 118

Lesson 3-2: Use AutoComplete and fill data from adjacent cells.. 120

Lesson 3-3: Cut, copy and paste... 122

Lesson 3-4: Cut, copy and paste using drag and drop 124

Lesson 3-5: Use Paste Values and increase/decrease decimal places displayed 126

Lesson 3-6: Transpose a range.. 128

Lesson 3-7: Use the Multiple Item Clipboard 130

Lesson 3-8: Use Undo and Redo 132

Lesson 3-9: Insert cell comments 134

Lesson 3-10: View cell comments 136

Lesson 3-11: Print cell comments 138

Lesson 3-12: Understand absolute and relative cell references 140

Lesson 3-13: Understand mixed cell references...142

Lesson 3-14: Understand templates and set the default custom template folder 144

Lesson 3-15: Create a template 146

Lesson 3-16: Use a template 148

Lesson 3-17: Add an App to a workbook 150

Lesson 3-18: Freeze columns and rows 152

Lesson 3-19: Split the window into multiple panes 154

Lesson 3-20: Check spelling 156

Session 3: Exercise..159

Session 3 Exercise answers 161

Session Four: Making Your Worksheets Look Professional   163

Session Objectives...163

Lesson 4-1: Format dates 164

Lesson 4-2: Understand date serial numbers...166

Lesson 4-3: Format numbers using built-in number formats 168

Lesson 4-4: Create custom number formats..170

Lesson 4-5: Horizontally align the contents of cells..172

Lesson 4-6: Merge cells, wrap text and expand/collapse the formula bar 174

Lesson 4-7: Vertically align the contents of cells 176

Lesson 4-8: Understand themes...178

Lesson 4-9: Use cell styles and change themes 180

Lesson 4-10: Add color and gradient effects to cells...182

Lesson 4-11: Add borders and lines 184

Lesson 4-12: Create your own custom theme...186

Lesson 4-13: Create your own custom cell styles 188

Lesson 4-14: Use a master style book to merge styles 190

Lesson 4-15: Use simple conditional formatting 192

Lesson 4-16: Manage multiple conditional formats using the Rules Manager 194

Lesson 4-17: Bring data alive with visualizations 196

Lesson 4-18: Create a formula driven conditional format...198

Lesson 4-19: Insert a Sparkline into a range of cells...200

Lesson 4-20: Apply a common vertical axis and formatting to a Sparkline group 202

Lesson 4-21: Apply a date axis to a Sparkline group and format a single Sparkline 204

Lesson 4-22: Use the Format Painter...206

Lesson 4-23: Rotate text 208

    Session 4: Exercise 211

    Session 4: Exercise answers.. 213

Session Five: Charts and Graphics   215

    Session Objectives 215

Lesson 5-1: Understand chart types, layouts and styles... 216

Lesson 5-2: Create a simple chart with two clicks 218

Lesson 5-3: Move, re-size, copy and delete a chart 220

Lesson 5-4: Create a chart using the Recommended Charts feature.............................. 222

Lesson 5-5: Add and remove chart elements using Quick Layout 224

Lesson 5-6: Apply a pre-defined chart style and color set 226

Lesson 5-7: Manually format a chart element... 228

Lesson 5-8: Format 3-D elements and add drop shadows 230

Lesson 5-9: Move, re-size, add, position and delete chart elements 232

Lesson 5-10: Apply a chart filter 234

Lesson 5-11: Change a chart's source data 236

Lesson 5-12: Assign non-contiguous source data to a chart 238

Lesson 5-13: Understand Data Series and Categories... 240

Lesson 5-14: Change source data using the Select Data Source dialog tools................ 242

Lesson 5-15: Chart non-contiguous source data by hiding rows and columns............. 244

Lesson 5-16: Create a chart with numerical axes 246

Lesson 5-17: Deal with empty data points 248

Lesson 5-18: Add data labels to a chart.. 250

Lesson 5-19: Add data labels from a range 252

Lesson 5-20: Highlight specific data points with color and annotations....................... 254

Lesson 5-21: Add gridlines and scale axes 256

Lesson 5-22: Emphasize data by manipulating pie charts 258

Lesson 5-23: Create a chart with two vertical axes... 260

Lesson 5-24: Create a combination chart containing different chart types 262

Lesson 5-25: Add a trend line... 264

Lesson 5-26: Add a gradient fill to a chart background... 266

Lesson 5-27: Create your own chart templates 268

    Session 5: Exercise 271

    Session 5: Exercise answers.. 273

Session Six: Working With Multiple Worksheets and Workbooks   275

    Session Objectives 275

Lesson 6-1: View the same workbook in different windows.. 276

Lesson 6-2: View two windows side by side and perform synchronous scrolling......................... 278

Lesson 6-3: Duplicate worksheets within a workbook 280

Lesson 6-4: Move and copy worksheets from one workbook to another 282

Lesson 6-5: Hide and unhide a worksheet 284

Lesson 6-6: Create cross worksheet formulas 286

Lesson 6-7: Understand worksheet groups 288

Lesson 6-8: Use find and replace 290

    Session 6: Exercise 293

    Session 6: Exercise answers 295

Session Seven: Printing Your Work   297

    Session Objectives 297

Lesson 7-1: Print Preview and change paper orientation 298

Lesson 7-2: Use Page Layout view to adjust margins 300

Lesson 7-3: Use Page Setup to set margins more precisely and center the worksheet 302

Lesson 7-4: Set paper size and scale 304

Lesson 7-5: Insert, delete and preview page breaks 306

Lesson 7-6: Adjust page breaks using Page Break Preview 308

Lesson 7-7: Add auto-headers and auto-footers and set the starting page number 310

Lesson 7-8: Add custom headers and footers 312

Lesson 7-9: Specify different headers and footers for the first, odd and even pages 314

Lesson 7-10: Print only part of a worksheet 316

Lesson 7-11: Add row and column data labels and grid lines to printed output 318

Lesson 7-12: Print several selected worksheets and change the page order 320

Lesson 7-13: Suppress error messages in printouts 322

    Session 7: Exercise 325

    Session 7: Exercise answers 327

Session Eight: Cloud Computing   329

    Session Objectives 329

Lesson 8-1: Save a workbook to a OneDrive 330

Lesson 8-2: Open a workbook from a OneDrive 332

Lesson 8-3: Understand operating systems devices and Office versions 334

Lesson 8-4: Understand Excel Online 336

Lesson 8-5: Open a workbook using Excel Online 338

Lesson 8-6: Share a link to a workbook 340

Lesson 8-7: Edit a workbook simultaneously with other users using Excel Online 342

    Session 8: Exercise 345

    Session 8: Exercise answers 347

Index   349

Introduction

Welcome to *Learn Excel 2013 Essential Skills With The Smart Method®*. This book has been designed to enable students to master Excel 2013 by self-study. The book is equally useful as courseware in order to deliver courses using The Smart Method® teaching system.

Smart Method publications are continually evolving as we discover better ways of explaining or teaching the concepts presented.

Feedback

At The Smart Method® we love feedback – both positive and negative. If you have any suggestions for improvements to future versions of this book, or if you find content or typographical errors, the author would always love to hear from you.

You can make suggestions for improvements to this book on our support forums at:

www.forums.excelcentral.com

Future editions will always incorporate your feedback so that there are never any known errors at time of publication.

If you have any difficulty understanding or completing a lesson, or if you feel that anything could have been more clearly explained, we'd also love to hear from you. We've made hundreds of detail improvements to our books based upon reader's feedback and continue to chase the impossible goal of 100% perfection!

Downloading the sample files

In order to use this book it is sometimes necessary to download sample files from the Internet. The sample files are available from:

http://www.ExcelCentral.com

Type the above URL into your web browser and you'll see the link to the sample files at the top of the home page.

Problem resolution

If you encounter any problem downloading or using the sample files you'll find detailed help in our support forum at:

www.ExcelCentral.com (click *Support* on the top menu).

You can also post a support request there if necessary and we'll do everything possible to quickly resolve the problem.

Typographical Conventions Used In This Book

This guide consistently uses typographical conventions to differentiate parts of the text.

When you see this	Here's what it means
Click *Line Color* on the left-hand bar and then click *No line*.	Italics are used to refer to text that appears in a worksheet cell, an Excel dialog, on the Ribbon, or elsewhere within the Excel application. Italics may sometimes also be used for emphasis or distinction.
Click: Home→Font→Underline.	Click on the Ribbon's *Home* tab and then look for the *Font* group. Click the *Underline* button within this group (that's the left-hand side of the button, not the drop-down arrow next to it). Don't worry if this doesn't make sense yet. We cover the Ribbon in depth in session one.
Click: Home→Font→ Underline Drop Down→Double Underline.	Click on the Ribbon's *Home* tab and then look for the *Font* group. Click the drop-down arrow next to the Underline button (that's the right-hand side of the button) within this group and then choose *Double Underline* from the drop-down list.
Click: File→Options→ Advanced→General→ Edit Custom Lists→Import	This is a more involved example. 1. Click the *File* tab on the Ribbon, and then click the *Options* button towards the bottom of the left-hand pane. The *Excel Options* dialog appears. 2. Choose the *Advanced* list item in the left-hand pane and scroll down to the *General* group in the right-hand pane. 3. Click the *Edit Custom Lists…* button. Yet another dialog pops up. 4. Click the *Import* button.
Type: **European Sales** into the cell.	Whenever you are supposed to actually type something on the keyboard it is shown in bold faced text.
Press <Ctrl> + <Z>.	You should hold down the **Ctrl** key and then press the **Z** key.

ΣAutoSum ▾

When a lesson tells you to click a button, an image of the relevant button will often be shown either in the page margin or within the text itself.

note

In Excel 2007/2010/2013 there are a possible 16,585 columns and 1,048,476 rows. This is a great improvement on earlier versions.

If you want to read through the book as quickly as possible, you don't have to read notes.

Notes usually expand a little on the information given in the lesson text.

important

Do not click the *Delete* button at this point as to do so would erase the entire table.

Whenever something can easily go wrong, or when the subject text is particularly important, you will see the *important* sidebar.

You should always read important sidebars.

tip

Moving between tabs using the keyboard

You can also use the <Ctrl>+<PgUp> and <Ctrl>+<PgDn> keyboard shortcuts to cycle through all of the tabs in your workbook.

Tips add to the lesson text by showing you shortcuts or time-saving techniques relevant to the lesson.

The bold text at the top of the tip box enables you to establish whether the tip is appropriate to your needs without reading all of the text.

In this example you may not be interested in keyboard shortcuts so do not need to read further.

anecdote

I ran an Excel course for a small company in London a couple of years ago...

Sometimes I add an anecdote gathered over the years from my Excel classes or from other areas of life.

If you simply want to learn Excel as quickly as possible you can ignore my anecdotes.

trivia

The feature that Excel uses to help you out with function calls first made an appearance in Visual Basic 5 back in 1996 …

Sometimes I indulge myself by adding a little piece of trivia in the context of the skill being taught.

Just like my anecdotes you can ignore these if you want to. They won't help you to learn Excel any better!

The World's Fastest Cars

When there is a sample file (or files) to accompany a lesson, the file name will be shown in a folder icon. You can download the sample file from: *www.ExcelCentral.com.* Detailed instructions are given in: *Lesson 1-5: Download the sample files and open/navigate a workbook.*

Putting The Smart Method to Work

Excel version and service pack

This edition was written using the original release version of *Microsoft Excel 2013* running under the *Microsoft Windows 8* operating system. You'll discover how to confirm which versions your computer is running in: *Lesson 1-1: Start Excel.*

If you are using an earlier or later operating system (Excel 2013 can also run under Windows 7, Windows 8.1 and any future Windows version) this book will be equally relevant, but you may notice small differences in the appearance of some of the screen grabs in the book. This will only occur when describing an operating system (rather than an Excel) feature.

This book is written purely for Excel 2013. If you are using Excel 2007 or Excel 2010 you should either upgrade to Excel 2013 or purchase one of the earlier versions of this book: *Learn Excel 2007 Essential Skills with The Smart Method* or *Learn Excel 2010 Essential Skills with The Smart Method.*

Sessions and lessons

The book is arranged into Sessions and Lessons. In a *Smart Method* classroom course a Session would generally last for between sixty and ninety minutes. Each session would represent a continuous period of interactive instruction followed by a coffee break of ten or fifteen minutes.

When you use this book for self-instruction I'd recommend that you do the same. You'll learn better if you lock yourself away, switch off your telephone and complete the whole session without interruption. The memory process is associative, and we've ensured that each lesson within each session is very closely coupled (contextually) with the others. By learning the whole session in one sitting, you'll store all of that information in the same part of your memory and should find it easier to recall later.

The experience of being able to remember all of the words of a song as soon as somebody has got you "started" with the first line is an example of the memory's associative system of data storage.

We'd also highly recommend that you take a break between sessions and spend it relaxing rather than catching up on your e-mails. This gives your brain a little idle time to do some data sorting and storage!

Read the book from beginning to end

Many books consist of disassociated self-contained chapters, often all written by different authors. This approach works well for pure reference books (such as encyclopedias). The problem with this approach is that there's no concept of building knowledge upon assumed prior knowledge, so the text is either confusing or unduly verbose as instructions for the same skill are repeated in many parts of the book.

This book is more effective as a learning tool because it takes a holistic approach. You will learn Excel in the same way you would be taught during one of our *Smart Method* classroom courses.

In our classroom courses it's often the case that a delegate turns up late. One golden rule is that we can't begin until everybody is present, as each hands-on lesson builds upon skills taught in the previous lesson.

I strongly recommend that you read the book from beginning to end in the order that it is written. Because of the unique presentational style, you'll hardly waste any time reading about things that you already know and even the most advanced Excel user will find some nugget of extremely useful information in every session.

How this book avoids wasting your time

> Nobody has things just as he would like them. The thing to do is to make a success with what material I have.
>
> *Dr. Frank Crane (1861–1928), American clergyman and journalist*

The only material available to me in teaching you Excel from a book is the written word and sample files. I'd rather have you sitting next to me in a classroom, but Frank Crane would have told me to stop complaining and use the tools I have in the most effective way.

Over the years I have read many hundreds of computer text books and most of my time was wasted. The big problem with most books is that I have to wade through thousands of words just to learn one important technique. If I don't read everything I might miss that one essential insight.

This book utilizes some of the tried and tested techniques developed after teaching vast numbers of people to learn Excel during many years of delivering *Smart Method* classroom courses.

As you'll see in this section, many presentational techniques are used to help you to avoid reading about things you already know how to do, or things that are of little interest to you.

Why our classroom courses work so well

In *Smart Method* classroom courses we have a 100% success rate training delegates to *Essential Skills* level in one day (the subject matter of this book) and to *Expert* level in a further single day (the subject matter of our follow-on *Expert Skills* book).

One of the reasons we can teach so much in a single day is that we don't waste time teaching skills that the delegates already know. Class sizes are small (six maximum) and the instructor stands behind the delegates monitoring their screens. The instructor will say "Open the sample file *Sales* that you'll find in the *Samples* folder on the C drive". If everybody does this no time is wasted explaining how. If anybody has difficulty, more information is given until all delegates demonstrate success.

Another key to learning effectively is to only teach the best way to accomplish a task. For example, you can save a workbook by clicking the *Save* button on the *Quick Access Toolbar* or you can press the **<Ctrl>+<S>** keys on the keyboard. Because clicking the *Save* button is the easiest, fastest and most intuitive method we only teach this in the classroom. In the book we do mention the alternatives, but only in a sidebar.

How this book mimics our classroom technique

Here's a lesson step:

---

note

You can also use the **<Ctrl>+<S>** keyboard shortcut to save your work.

1 Save the workbook.

When you are editing a workbook the changes you make are only held in the computer's memory. If there is a power cut or your computer crashes, you will lose any work that has been done since the last save. For this reason you should get into the habit of regularly saving your work.

Click the *Save button* on the *Quick Access Toolbar* at the top left of the screen.

If you already know how to save a workbook read only the line: *Save the workbook* and just do it. Don't waste your time reading anything else.

Read the smaller print only when you don't already know how to do something.

If you're in a hurry to learn only the essentials, as fast as possible, don't bother with the sidebars either unless they are labeled **important**.

Read the sidebars only when you want to know everything and have the time and interest.

Avoiding repetition

2	Create a new worksheet and name it *January*.
	This was covered in: *Lesson 1-6: Save a workbook.*

A goal of this book (and our classroom courses) is not to waste your time by explaining any skill twice.

In a classroom course, a delegate will sometimes forget something that has already been covered earlier in the day. The instructor must then try to get the student to remember and drop little hints reminding them about how they completed the task earlier.

This isn't possible in a book, so I've made extensive use of cross references in the text pointing you back to the lesson in which the relevant skill was learned. The cross references also help when you use this book as a reference work but have forgotten the more basic skills needed to complete each step.

Use of American English

American English (rather than British English) spelling has been used throughout. This is because the Excel help system and screen elements all use American English spelling, making the use of British English confusing.

Examples of differences are the British English spelling: *Colour* and *Dialogue* as opposed to the American English spelling: *Color* and *Dialog*.

Because this book is used all over the world, much care has been taken to avoid any country-specific terminology. In most of the English speaking world, apart from North America, the symbol # is referred to as the **hash sign**. I use the term *hash* throughout this book.

Incremental sample files

Many lessons in this course use a sample file that is incrementally improved during each lesson. At the end of each lesson an interim version is always saved. For example, a sample file called *Sales-1* may provide the starting point to a sequence of three lessons. After each lesson, interim versions called *Sales-2*, *Sales-3* and *Sales-4* are saved by the student.

A complete set of sample files (including all incremental versions) are provided in the sample file set. This provides two important benefits:

- When you have completed the course you will want to use this book as a reference. The sample files allow you to work through any single lesson in isolation, as the workbook's state at the beginning of each lesson is always available.

- If you have difficulty with a lesson it is useful to be able to study the completed workbook (at the end of the lesson) by opening the finished version of the lesson's workbook.

First page of a session

1/ The first page begins with a quotation, often from an era before the age of the computer, that is particularly pertinent to the session material. As well as being fun, this helps us to remember that all of the real-world problems we solve with technology have been around for a long time.

3/ The session objectives *formally* state the precise skills that you will learn in the session.

At the end of the session you should re-visit the objectives and not progress to the next session until you can honestly agree that you have achieved them.

In a *Smart Method* course we never progress to the next session until all delegates are completely confident that they have achieved the previous session's objectives.

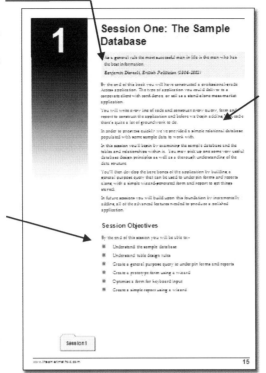

2/ In the next few paragraphs we *informally* summarise why the session is important and the benefits that you will get from completing it.

This is important because without motivation adults do not learn. For adults, learning is a means to an end and not an end in itself.

The aim of the introduction is to motivate your retention of the skills that will be taught in the following session by allowing you to preview the relevance of the material that will be presented. This may subconsciously put your brain into "must remember this" mode—assuming, of course, that the introduction convinces you that the skills will be useful to you!

Every lesson is presented on two facing pages

> Pray this day, on one side of one sheet of paper, explain how the Royal Navy is prepared to meet the coming conflict.
> **Winston Churchill, Letter to the Admiralty, Sep 1, 1939**

Winston Churchill was well aware of the power of brevity. The discipline of condensing information onto one side of a single sheet of A4 paper resulted in the efficient transfer of information.

A tenet of our teaching method is that every lesson is presented on *two* facing sheets of A4. We've had to double Churchill's rule as they didn't have to contend with screen grabs in 1939!

If we can't teach an essential concept in two pages of A4 we know that the subject matter needs to be broken into two smaller lessons.

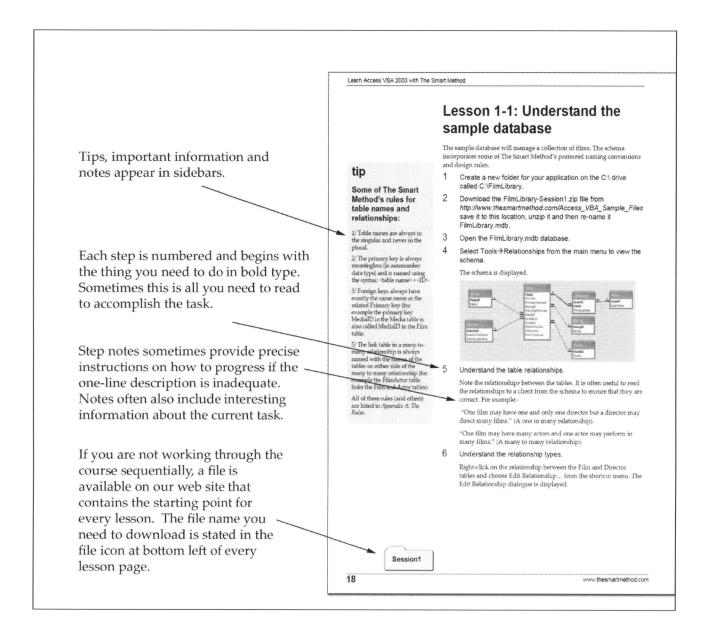

Tips, important information and notes appear in sidebars.

Each step is numbered and begins with the thing you need to do in bold type. Sometimes this is all you need to read to accomplish the task.

Step notes sometimes provide precise instructions on how to progress if the one-line description is inadequate. Notes often also include interesting information about the current task.

If you are not working through the course sequentially, a file is available on our web site that contains the starting point for every lesson. The file name you need to download is stated in the file icon at bottom left of every lesson page.

Learning by participation

> Tell me, and I will forget. Show me, and I may remember. Involve me, and I will understand.
>
> *Confucius (551-479 BC)*

Confucius would probably have agreed that the best way to teach IT skills is hands-on (actively) and not hands-off (passively). This is another of the principal tenets of The Smart Method® teaching system. Research has backed up the assertion that you will learn more material, learn more quickly, and understand more of what you learn, if you learn using active, rather than passive methods.

For this reason pure theory pages are kept to an absolute minimum with most theory woven into the hands-on lessos (either within the text or in sidebars). This echoes the teaching method in Smart Method courses, where snippets of pertinent theory are woven into the lessons themselves so that interest and attention is maintained by hands-on involvement, but all necessary theory is still covered.

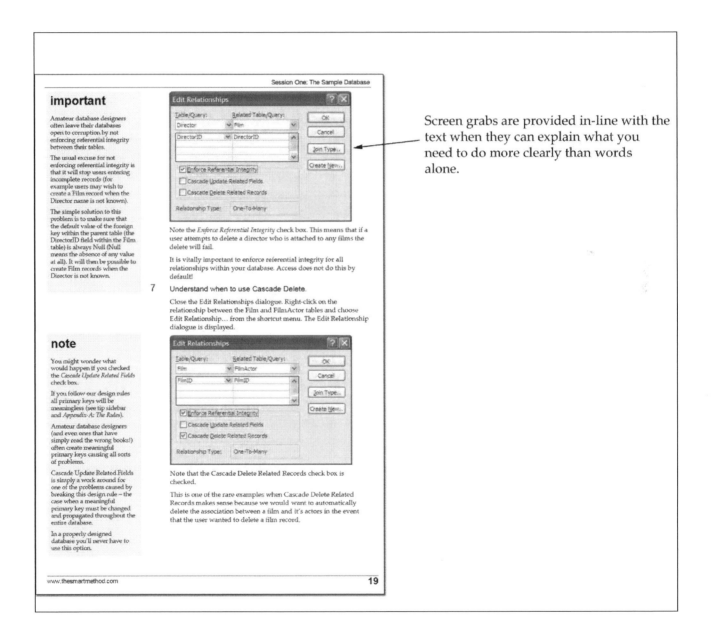

Screen grabs are provided in-line with the text when they can explain what you need to do more clearly than words alone.

Session One: Basic Skills

A bad beginning makes a bad ending.

Euripides, Aegeus (484 BC - 406 BC).

Even if you are a seasoned Excel user, I urge you to take Euripides' advice and complete this session. You'll fly through it if you already know most of the skills covered.

In my classes I often teach professionals who have used Excel for over ten years and they *always* get some nugget of fantastically useful information from this session.

In this session I teach you the absolute basics you need before you can start to do useful work with Excel 2013.

I don't assume that you have any previous exposure to Excel (in any version) so I have to include some very basic skills.

Session Objectives

By the end of this session you will be able to:

- Start Excel and open a new blank workbook
- Check that your Excel version is up to date
- Change the Office Theme
- Maximize, minimize, re-size, move and close the Excel window
- Download the sample files and open/navigate a workbook
- Save a workbook to a local file
- Understand common file formats
- Pin a workbook and understand file organization
- View, move, add, rename, delete and navigate worksheet tabs
- Use the Versions feature to recover an unsaved Draft file
- Use the Versions feature to recover an earlier version of a workbook
- Use the Ribbon
- Understand Ribbon components
- Customize the Quick Access Toolbar and preview the printout
- Use the Mini Toolbar, Key Tips and keyboard shortcuts
- Understand views
- Hide and show the Formula Bar and Ribbon
- Use the help system

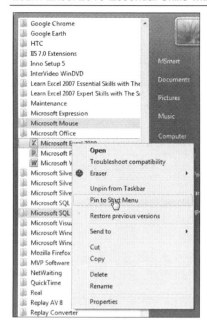

Lesson 1-1: Start Excel and open a new blank workbook

Startup in Windows 7

1   Click the *Windows Start Button* at the bottom left of your screen.

2   Click the *All Programs* item at the bottom of the pop-up menu.

3   Scroll down the list and click on the *Microsoft Office 2013* item.

4   Pin *Microsoft Excel 2013* to the start menu.

You'll be using Excel a lot so it makes sense to pin it to the start menu. This will make it appear at the top of the list in future so you'll be able to start Excel with just two clicks.

To pin to the start menu, point to *Microsoft Excel 2013* in the list, right-click your mouse and then choose *Pin to Start Menu* from the shortcut menu.

5   Left-click *Microsoft Excel 2013* to start Excel.

Excel starts and is displayed on the screen:

Startup in Windows 8

1   Locate the Excel icon on the Windows 8 start screen.

If you can't find the icon see the facing page sidebar for instructions on how to create it.

2   Drag *Excel 2013* to the left hand side of the start screen.

You'll be using Excel a lot so it makes sense to locate the icon on the left-hand side of the Windows 8 start screen. You'll then be able to start Excel without having to search for the icon.

---

note

Can I make Excel start with a blank workbook, like it used to in earlier versions?

Whenever a new version of Excel arrives, many users' first instinct is to try to make it more like the older version it replaced.

The majority of people resist change of any sort (as any politician will tell you).

My opinion is that showing a start-up screen is more intuitive and logical than starting Excel with an open blank worksheet.

But if you long for the "good old days" here's how you can make Excel 2013 mimic Excel 2010 (and earlier versions) at start-up:

1. Start Excel.

2. Click the *Blank Workbook* template to open the main Excel screen.

3. Click:

 File→Options→General

4. Uncheck the *Show the Start Screen when this application starts* checkbox at the bottom of the dialog.

---

note

Potential problems when using templates

Many of Microsoft's templates have been created using some very advanced Excel skills and techniques. If you make use of them there's a danger that you may depend upon a workbook you don't understand and are unable to maintain.

In: *Lesson 3-15: Create a template*, you'll learn how to create your own custom templates.

Templates you create yourself are far more useful. Because you understand how they are built, you will be able to maintain them, and any workbook created from them.

note

If you can't find the Excel 2013 icon in Windows 8

When you install Excel 2013 on a Windows 8 computer, icons are automatically added to the start screen. If you can't find the icon it is likely that it has been accidentally unpinned. In this case proceed as follows:

1. When the Windows 8 start screen is displayed, type: **excel** on the keyboard. You will see the excel 2013 application icon on the screen. If you don't, Excel is not installed on this computer.

2. Right-click the Excel 2013 application icon. A tick will appear next to it:

3. Click the *Pin to Taskbar* icon on the menu bar at the bottom of the screen.

You will now be able to locate the Excel 2013 icon on the start screen (though you may have to scroll to the right to find it).

1. Point to the Excel 2013 icon.

2. Click and hold down the left mouse button.

3. With the left button held down move your mouse towards the left hand side of the screen. The icon will move with the mouse cursor.

4. When you reach the left-hand side of the screen release the left mouse button.

   The Excel 2013 icon is now permenantly positioned on the left-hand side of the Windows 8 start screen.

5. Left-click the Excel 2013 icon to start Excel.

After you've started Excel 2013...

Now that Excel 2013 has started, Excel needs to know whether you want to create a new workbook, or whether you want to open a workbook that was created earlier.

When creating a new workbook, Excel also offers to give you a "flying start" by using a template. Templates are sample workbooks that you can adapt and modify for your own needs. The idea is very good but, in reality, templates are not usually a good choice as it can take longer to adapt them to your true needs than to design from scratch (see sidebar).

In this lesson we'll create a blank workbook.

1 Create a new blank workbook.

Left-click the mouse button on the *Blank Workbook* template.

Note that, from now onwards, I will simply use the term "click" when I mean left-click (the mouse button you will use most of the time) and "right-click" only when you need to click the (less-used) right mouse button.

The Excel 2013 screen is displayed showing a blank workbook:

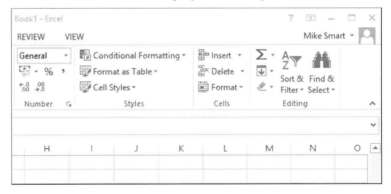

2 Leave the workbook open for the next lesson.

Lesson 1-2: Check that your Excel version is up to date

Updates

When a new product like Excel 2013 is first released it often has many bugs (as do all computer programs of any size).

Microsoft is very pro-active at fixing bugs that are found and regularly releases updates.

Updates normally only fix bugs found in the original program, but Microsoft sometimes take things a little further by including new, or at least enhanced, features with their updates.

I had many emails from readers of my earlier Excel 2010 books suggesting that some Excel features were missing, or that some of the examples didn't work. In almost every case the reader had switched automatic updates off and was using an out-of-date Excel version.

Automatic Updates

Normally Microsoft Office (including Excel) will look after updates without you having to do anything. By default, Automatic Updates are enabled. This means that updates are downloaded from the Internet and installed automatically.

It is possible that Automatic Updates have been switched off on your computer. In this case there is a danger that you may have an old, buggy, out of date version of Excel installed.

This lesson will show you how to make sure that you are using the latest (most complete, and most reliable) version of Excel 2013.

1 **Start Excel and open a new blank workbook (if you have not already done this).**

You learned how to do this in: *Lesson 1-1: Start Excel and open a new blank workbook.*

2 **Make sure that Automatic Updates are enabled.**

1. Click the *File* button ▮ FILE ▮ at the top-left of the screen.

This takes you to *Backstage View.* Backstage View allows you to complete an enormous range of common tasks from a single window.

2. Click: *Account* ▮ Account ▮ in the left-hand list.

Your account details are displayed on screen. Notice the *Office Updates* button displayed in the right-hand pane.

If all is well, and automatic updates are switched on, you will see a button similar to this:

If *Automatic Updates* have been switched off, you will see a button similar to this.

In this case you will need to switch *Automatic Updates* on (see next step).

3 Switch on *Automatic Updates* if necessary.

Click: Update Options→Enable Updates.

4 If there are updates waiting to install, apply them.

Sometimes Excel will download updates but will not install them automatically.

In this case you will see an update button similar to the following:

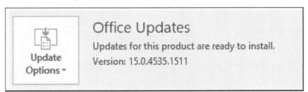

If you see this type of button you should apply the update.

Click: Update Options→Apply Updates.

You may be asked to confirm that you want to apply the update, and to close any open programs in order to apply the update.

5 Click the *Back Button* ⬅ to leave *Backstage View* and return to the worksheet.

6 Click the *Close Button* ✕ on the top-right corner of the Excel screen to close Excel.

note

Themes and Backgrounds affect every Office application on all of your devices

When you set a theme or background in Excel you are actually changing the theme and background for the entire Office 2013 application.

This means that you will have a consistent experience when using other Office applications such as *Word* and *PowerPoint*.

In: *Session Eight: Cloud Computing*, you'll discover that Excel 2013 now includes features that are useful to users with multiple devices (such as a work computer, home computer, laptop, tablet and smartphone).

If you are logged in to a *Microsoft Account*, the theme you select will also magically change on all of your devices.

Cloud computing is a challenging concept that isn't yet widely used, so don't worry if all of this sounds rather confusing at the moment. All will be clear by the end of this book.

Lesson 1-3: Change the Office Theme

If you are coming to Excel 2013 from an earlier version of Excel, you'll immediately notice that the Excel screen now has very little use of color and contrast. A very large number of Excel users (myself included) feel that this lack of contrast causes more eye strain, and is more difficult to work with, than earlier Excel versions.

Fortunately you are able to change Excel's default "White" color scheme to one with higher contrast using the new *Office Themes* feature.

Three *Office Themes* are available to customize the look and feel of Excel.

White

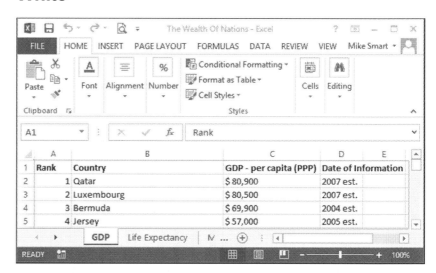

This is the default theme with very low contrast and shading. Some designers feel that this gives Excel a modern and "minimalist" appearance but it has been criticized by some users:

Light Gray

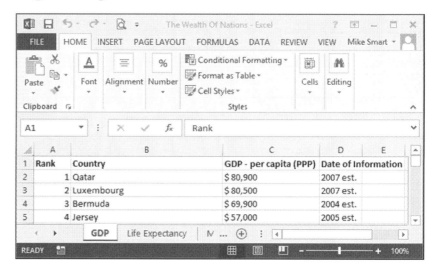

The *Light Gray* theme has a little more contrast that helps to separate screen elements.

Dark Gray

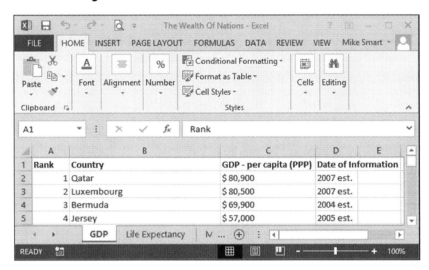

This is my personal preference. I find the higher contrast a lot easier to work with.

1   Open Excel.

2   Change the *Office Theme*.

1. Click the *File* button  at the top-left of the screen.

2. Click the *Options* button at the bottom of the left-hand menu bar.

    The Excel *Options* dialog box appears.

    In the *Personalize your copy of Microsoft Office* section you'll see an *Office Theme* drop-down list. Click the drop-down arrow to see the three different themes available.

3. Click the *Dark Gray* theme.

4. Click *OK* to return to the Excel Screen.

    Experiment with each theme until you discover the one you prefer. All of the screen grabs in this book were done using the *Dark Gray* theme. If you choose a different theme the screen grabs in the book may look slightly different to what you see on your computer screen.

3   Close Excel.

note

You can also personalize Excel by changing the background

Background customization can only be done if you are connected to the Internet and logged into a Microsoft Account. You'll learn more about Microsoft Accounts later, in: *Session Eight: Cloud Computing*.

I personally find the *Background* feature a little frivolous for a serious business application.

For this reason I always leave it set to *No Background*.

Perhaps you feel differently and would like to stamp your own identity onto your copy of Office.

If you are logged into your Microsoft Account you will see another drop-down list (above the *Office Theme* setting) that enables backgrounds to be set:

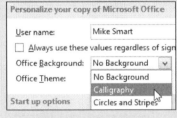

When you choose a background a "tattoo" is added to the area above the Ribbon with your chosen design:

Lesson 1-4: Maximize, minimize, re-size, move and close the Excel window

> The great successful men of the world have used their imaginations, they think ahead and create their mental picture, and then go to work materializing that picture in all its details, filling in here, adding a little there, altering this a bit and that bit, but steadily building, steadily building.
>
> *Robert Collier, American motivational author, (1885-1950)*

The main Excel window has a dazzling array of buttons, switches and other artifacts. By the end of this book they will all make sense to you and you'll really feel really comfortable with Excel.

For now we'll explore the big picture by looking at how the Excel window can be sized and moved. The details will come later.

1   Open Excel.

2   Use the *Blank workbook* template to open a new blank workbook.

> You learned how to do this in: *Lesson 1-1: Start Excel and open a new blank workbook.*

3   Understand the *Maximize, Minimize, Close* and *Restore Down* buttons

> At the top right corner of the Excel window you'll see three buttons.

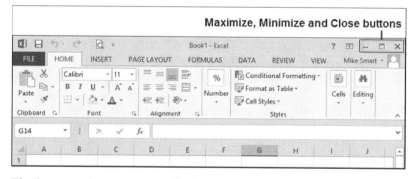

The buttons that you see will depend upon how the Excel window was left last time the application closed down. Normally the Excel screen is Maximized to fill the screen and you'll see:

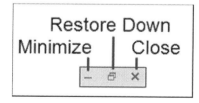

But if you had reduced the size of the Excel window so that it didn't fill the screen you'd see this instead:

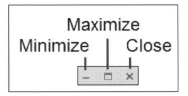

Try clicking the *Maximize, Minimize* and *Restore Down* buttons.

- *Maximize* makes the Excel window completely fill the screen.
- *Minimize* reduces Excel to a button on the bottom task bar.

Click this button again to restore the window to its previous size.

- *Restore Down* makes the Excel window smaller allowing you to re-size the window.

4   Re-size the Excel window

After clicking the *Restore Down* button you are able to re-size the Excel window. Hover over either the side of the window, or a corner of the window, with your mouse cursor. The cursor shape will change to a double-headed arrow.

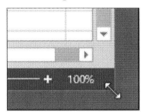 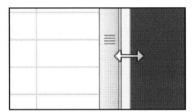

When you see either cursor shape, hold down the left mouse button and move the mouse (this is called *click and drag*) to re-size the window.

Clicking and dragging a corner allows you to change both the height and width of the window.

Clicking an edge allows you to change only one dimension.

note

Other ways to close down Excel

There are two other ways of closing Excel.

1. Double click the Excel button at the top left of your screen.

2. Press the <**Alt**>+<**F4**> keys on your keyboard.

5   Move the Excel window.

Click and drag the *Title Bar* (the bar at the very top of the window) to move the Excel window around the screen.

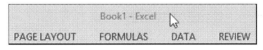

6   Close Excel

Click on the *Close button* at the top right of the Excel window.

This is the most common way to close down Excel

There are also two lesser known (and lesser used) methods of closing Excel (see sidebar).

Excel often provides many different ways to do exactly the same thing.

The Wealth of Nations

Lesson 1-5: Download the sample files and open/navigate a workbook

Excel uses the analogy of a book that has many pages. In Excel terminology we use the term: *Workbook* for the entire book and *Worksheet* for each of the pages. We'll be learning more about worksheets later in this session in: *Lesson 1-9: View, move, add, rename, delete and navigate worksheet tabs.*

1   Download the sample files (if you haven't already done so).

1.   Open your web browser and type in the URL:

www.ExcelCentral.com

2.   Click the *Sample Files* link on the top left of the home page.

3.   Download the sample files for *Excel 2013 Essential Skills.*

Note that we strongly recommend that you click the *Recommended Option* button to download the sample files as a self-extracting .EXE file. This avoids the *Protected View* issue discussed on the facing page sidebar.

2   Open the sample workbook: *The Wealth of Nations.*

1.   Open Excel.

2.   Click *Open Other Workbooks* on the left-hand menu bar.

3.   Click *Computer* in the *Open* menu bar.

4.   Click: *Browse* in the *Computer* menu bar.

5.   Navigate to your sample files. If you downloaded using the recommended option and didn't change the normal file location you will find these in the *C:/Practice* directory.

6.   Open the *Excel 2013 Essential Skills* folder.

7.   Open the *Session 1* folder.

8.   Double click *The Wealth of Nations* to open the sample workbook.

3   Go to Cell ZZ3 using the Name Box.

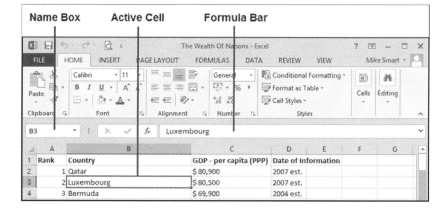

note

Potential problem when downloading sample files

Protected view is a brand new security feature that was first introduced in Excel 2010. It is designed to protect you from potential viruses by treating all files downloaded from the Internet as being suspicious.

Any workbooks that are downloaded from the Internet, or are sent by e-mail attachment, will open in Protected View by default.

The user then has to click an *Enable Editing* button to use the file as normal:

Enable Editing

While some users may find it useful to be reminded about the origin of their files, others may find this feature annoying.

To avoid seeing this message whenever you open a sample file, we recommend that you download using the recommended option:

Download Sample Files
(Recommended Option)

This downloads the entire sample file set as a digitally signed self-extracting executable file.

We also offer an alternative method to download:

Download Sample Files
(Zip file Option)

This has been provided because some companies (or anti-virus products) block the download of executable files.

If you download using the zip file option, you'll have to click the *Enable Editing* button every time you open a sample file.

Excel uses the letter of the column and the number of the row to identify cells. This is called the *cell address*. In the above example the cell address of the active cell is B3.

In Excel 2013 there are a little over a million rows and a little over sixteen thousand columns. You may wonder how it is possible to name all of these columns with only 26 letters in the alphabet.

When Excel runs out of letters it starts using two: X,Y,Z and then AA, AB, AC etc. But even two letters is not enough. When Excel reaches column ZZ it starts using three letters: ZX, ZY, ZZ and then AAA, AAB, AAC etc.

The currently selected cell is called the *Active Cell* and has a green line around it. The Active Cell's address is always displayed in the *Name Box* and its contents are displayed in the *Formula Bar*.

We can also use the *Name Box* to move to a specific cell.

To see this in action, type **ZZ3** into the *Name Box* and then press the **<Enter>** key. You are teleported to cell ZZ3:

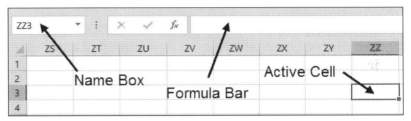

4   Return to Cell A1 by pressing <Ctrl>+<Home>.

5   Go to the end of the worksheet by pressing <Ctrl>+<End>.

6   Use the Scroll Bars.

There are two scroll bars for the Excel window.

The vertical scroll bar runs from top to bottom of the window and allows you to quickly move up and down the worksheet.

The horizontal scroll bar is at the bottom right hand side of the window and allows you to move to the left and right in wide worksheets.

Here's how the scroll bars work:

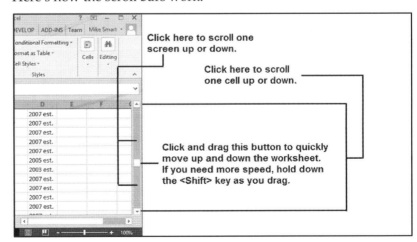

Lesson 1-6: Save a workbook to a local file

1   Open *The Wealth of Nations* from your sample files folder (if it isn't already open).

2   Save the workbook.

When you are editing a workbook, the changes you make are only held in the computer's memory. If there is a power cut or your computer crashes you will lose any work that has been done since the last save.

For this reason you should get into the habit of regularly saving your work.

Even though we haven't changed this worksheet, let's save it now by clicking the *Save* button on the *Quick Access Toolbar* at the top left of the screen.

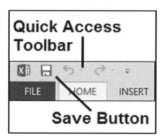

3   Save the workbook with a different name.

1.   Click the *File* button. **FILE** at the top-left of the screen.

2.   Click: *Save As* **Save As** in the left-hand list.

3.   Click *Computer* **Computer** in the *Save As* menu.

4.   Click *Browse* in the *Computer* menu.

The following dialog will appear if you are using Windows 8. The dialog may be slightly different for Windows 7 users but you should easily be able to figure out the differences:

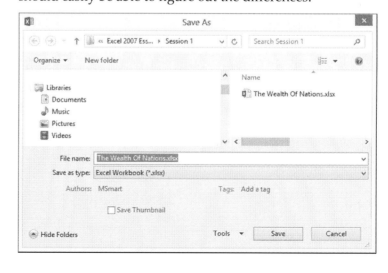

The Wealth of Nations

note

OneDrive and Cloud Computing

You may have noticed that the *Save As* dialog also has an option to save your workbook to a OneDrive:

A OneDrive can be thought of as a "disk drive in the sky".

It is just like the C:\ drive on your computer but exists on a Microsoft server many miles away, accessed via the Internet.

The OneDrive can be very useful when you need to access your files from several different computers.

A OneDrive also provides an easier way to share files with others.

The OneDrive is part of a completely new way of working called *Cloud Computing*.

Support for Cloud Computing is by far the most important new feature of Excel 2013.

Because Cloud Computing is such an involved (and complex) subject I have devoted an entire session to it in: *Session Eight: Cloud Computing*.

I advise you not to jump ahead to the last session, at this stage in your learning, as this session will be difficult to understand until you have completed the earlier sessions.

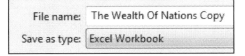

1. Click the drop-down arrow to the right of the *Save as type* drop-down list.

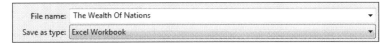

2. A list appears showing a large number of different file types:

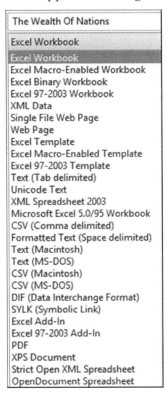

Most of the time you'll want to use the default format: *Excel Workbook* but there may be times when you'll need to save in one of the other formats. You'll learn all about the most important formats (and when you should use them) in the next lesson: *Lesson 1-7: Understand common file formats*. For now we'll stay with the default: *Excel Workbook* format.

3. Click inside the *File name* box.

4. Type: **The Wealth of Nations Copy**

5. Click the *Save* button.

    Notice that the name of the workbook in the title bar (at the top of the window) has now changed indicating that you are now viewing the new workbook that you have just saved.

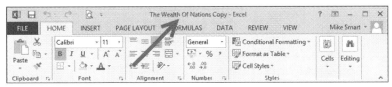

Lesson 1-7: Understand common file formats

1 Open a new blank workbook.

You learned how to do this in: *Lesson 1-1: Start Excel and open a new blank workbook.*

2 View the file formats supported by Excel.

1. Click the *File* button at the top-left of the screen.

2. Click: *Save As* in the left-hand list.

3. Click *Computer* in the *Save As* menu.

4. Click *Browse* in the *Computer* menu.

The *Save As* dialog appears.

5. Click the drop-down arrow to the right of the *Save as type* list.

| File name: | The Wealth Of Nations Copy | ∨ |
| Save as type: | Excel Workbook | |

A list appears showing all of the different file formats supported by Excel (see sidebar).

3 Understand the most important file formats.

Excel Workbook (the Open XML format)

Before Office 2007 was released, every program stored its information on the hard disk in a completely different way. These incompatible formats are called *binary formats*. This made it very difficult to write applications that could be used together.

All of this has changed with the new file format that was first introduced in Office 2007: *Office Open XML*

Microsoft have published exactly how this format works and given it away free to the world's developer community. This allows other programs to easily work with Excel workbook files. For example, Apple's iPhone already supports Office Open XML Email attachments.

Unfortunately the future has to co-exist with the past and there are still some people in the world (though a declining number) using pre-2007 versions of Office (97, 2000, 2002 and 2003). If you save your files in the Open XML format, only people running Office 2007/2010/2013 will be able to read them (but see the sidebar on the facing page for two potential solutions to this problem).

Excel Macro Enabled Workbook

An Excel Macro Enabled Workbook is simply a workbook that has program code (called VBA code) embedded within it. Macros are beyond the scope of this book but are covered in the *Excel Expert Skills* book in this series.

note

You can also use the <F12> key to instantly display the *Save As* dialog.

The Wealth Of Nations

Excel Workbook

Excel Workbook
Excel Macro-Enabled Workbook
Excel Binary Workbook
Excel 97-2003 Workbook
XML Data
Single File Web Page
Web Page
Excel Template
Excel Macro-Enabled Template
Excel 97-2003 Template
Text (Tab delimited)
Unicode Text
XML Spreadsheet 2003
Microsoft Excel 5.0/95 Workbook
CSV (Comma delimited)
Formatted Text (Space delimited)
Text (Macintosh)
Text (MS-DOS)
CSV (Macintosh)
CSV (MS-DOS)
DIF (Data Interchange Format)
SYLK (Symbolic Link)
Excel Add-In
Excel 97-2003 Add-In
PDF
XPS Document
Strict Open XML Spreadsheet
OpenDocument Spreadsheet

The Wealth of Nations

While Macro code is very powerful it can also be destructive as it is extremely simple to write damaging viruses within Excel macro code.

Macro programming (also called VBA programming) is a vast subject of its own and is not useful to the vast majority of Excel users. The Smart Method® run comprehensive classroom Excel VBA courses but they are usually only taken by scientists and engineers who need to add very advanced functionality to Excel.

Versions of Excel before Excel 2007 could potentially allow a workbook to infect your machine with a macro virus because all Excel files were capable of carrying macros. Because the formats are now separate, it is easier to avoid opening potentially infected files.

Excel 97-2003 Workbook

This is the old binary format that allows users with earlier versions of Excel to open your workbooks. Some features won't work in earlier versions and if you've used those in your workbook, Excel will display a warning when you save telling you which features will be lost.

Excel Binary Workbook

An oddity in Excel 2007/2010/2013 is a binary format called: *Excel Binary Workbook*. This is a binary alternative to Open XML but it can't be read by earlier versions of Excel. The only advantage of this format is that it loads and saves more quickly than Open XML.

PDF

If you need to send a worksheet to a user who does not own a copy of Excel, you can save it in PDF (Portable Document Format). This format was invented by Adobe and is also sometimes called *Adobe Acrobat* or simply *Acrobat*.

Adobe provides a free reader program for PDF files and most users will already have this installed upon their computers. If you send a user a PDF file they will be able to read and print (but not change) the worksheet.

XPS

This format is a Microsoft-developed alternative to the Adobe PDF format. It is not as widely used as PDF.

Other formats

As you can see, there are several other less commonly used formats supported by Excel 2013 but the above formats are the only ones you'll normally encounter. The most important thing to remember is that, unless there's a good reason to use a different format, you should always save documents in the default *Excel Workbook* format.

Lesson 1-8: Pin a workbook and understand file organization

tip

Increasing the number of items in the recent workbooks list

Excel remembers the twenty five most recently opened documents.

As you open more documents the twenty-fifth oldest is removed from the *Recent Documents* list unless you pin it.

If you'd like to increase Excel's memory up to a maximum of fifty items here's how it's done:

1. Click the *File* button at the top left of the screen.

2. Click the *Options* button at the bottom of the left-hand menu bar.

3. Choose *Advanced* from the left hand menu bar.

4. Scroll down the right-hand list until you find the *Display* category. You'll see *Show this number of Recent Workbooks: 25.*

5. Change the number to the number of recently opened workbooks you'd prefer Excel to remember (up to a maximum of fifty).

1   Close down and restart Excel.

2   Pin a workbook to the *Recent Workbooks* list.

Notice that there is a list of recently opened documents at the top of the left-hand menu bar.

The list begins with the most recently opened workbook (probably the *Wealth of Nations Copy* workbook saved in: *Lesson 1-6: Save a workbook.*

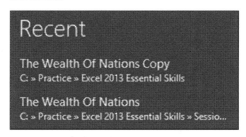

1. Hover the mouse cursor over one of the files in the *Recent* list:

    Note that a pin icon  has appeared next to the workbook name.

    When you hover the mouse cursor over the pin a tooltip is displayed saying: *Pin this item to the list.*

    This can be a great time saver as it enables any workbook that you use a lot to always be at the top of the *Recent Workbooks* list. You won't have to waste time looking for it on the hard drive.

2. Click the pin icon. The item moves to the top of the list and the pin icon changes from unpinned to pinned.

3. Click on *The Wealth of Nations* to open the workbook.

3   Understand file organization.

By default Excel saves all workbooks into your *Documents* folder along with other Office documents (such as Word and PowerPoint

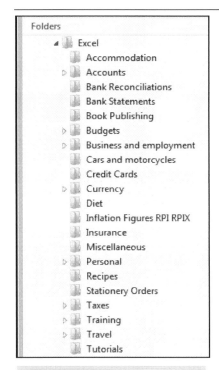

Folders
▲ 📁 Excel
    📁 Accommodation
    ▷ 📁 Accounts
    📁 Bank Reconciliations
    📁 Bank Statements
    📁 Book Publishing
    ▷ 📁 Budgets
    ▷ 📁 Business and employment
    📁 Cars and motorcycles
    📁 Credit Cards
    ▷ 📁 Currency
    📁 Diet
    📁 Inflation Figures RPI RPIX
    📁 Insurance
    📁 Miscellaneous
    ▷ 📁 Personal
    📁 Recipes
    📁 Stationery Orders
    ▷ 📁 Taxes
    ▷ 📁 Training
    ▷ 📁 Travel
    📁 Tutorials

note

How do I create a subfolder?

The concept of folders, subfolders and files is a very fundamental Windows skill rather than an Excel skill.

If you do not have basic Windows skills (an understanding of how Windows organizes files) you would get good value from a Windows book to give you the foundation skills you need to use any Windows program.

Here's how you create a new subfolder:

1. Right-click on the *Documents* folder.

2. Click *New Folder* in the shortcut menu.

A new folder will appear called *New Folder*.

3. You will now be able to type: **Excel** in order to name the folder.

If this doesn't work for you, right-click the new folder and select *Rename* from the shortcut menu. You'll then be able to type: **Excel** to rename the folder.

files). This clearly is going to cause problems when you have a few hundred files.

Better to organize yourself from the start by setting up an orderly filing system.

4   Create an *Excel* subfolder beneath your *Documents* folder.

I create a folder called *Excel* beneath the *Documents* folder. In this folder I create subfolders to store my work. You can see a screen grab of my Excel folder in the sidebar (of course, your needs will be different to mine).

See sidebar if you don't know how to create a subfolder.

5   Set the default file location to point to the new *Excel* folder.

If you take my advice and create an Excel folder you will waste a mouse click every time you open a file because Excel will take you to the *Documents* folder by default.

Here's how to reset the default file location to your new Excel folder:

1. Click the *File button* at the top left of the screen.

2. Click the *Options* button towards the bottom of the left-hand list.

    The *Excel Options* dialog appears.

3. Choose the *Save* category from the left hand side of the dialog.

    During the remainder of the book I'll explain the above three steps like this:

    Click: File→Options→Save.

    This will save a lot of time and forests!

4. Change the *Default local file location*.

    Type: **\Excel** after the end of the current default file location.

    You have to actually type this manually. Microsoft seem to have forgotten to add a browse button!

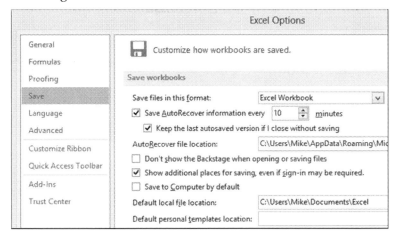

When you click File→Open in future you'll automatically be taken to your Excel folder ready to choose a category.

note

Changing the default number of worksheets created in new workbooks

When you open a new, blank workbook in Excel 2013, one new worksheet is automatically created called *Sheet1*.

In all previous versions of Excel, three worksheets were created called *Sheet1*, *Sheet2* and *Sheet3*.

My opinion is that this is a change for the better as it keeps things neater. Most of my workbooks only need one worksheet.

But if you long for the "good old days" here's how you can make Excel 2013 mimic Excel 2010 (and earlier versions) at start-up:

1. Click:

File→Options→General→ When creating new workbooks →Include this many sheets:

2. Enter the number of sheets required:

Lesson 1-9: View, move, add, rename, delete and navigate worksheet tabs

When you save an Excel file onto your hard disk, you are saving a single workbook containing one or more worksheets. You can add as many worksheets as you need to a workbook.

There are two types of worksheet. Regular worksheets contain cells. Chart sheets, as you would expect, each contain a single chart. We'll be exploring charts in depth in: *Session Five: Charts and Graphics*.

1 Open *The Wealth of Nations* from your sample files folder (if it isn't already open).

2 Move between worksheets.

Look at the tabs on the bottom left corner of your screen. Notice that this sample workbook contains three worksheets. Click on each tab in turn to view each worksheet.

3 Add a new worksheet.

Click the *New Sheet* button (the circle with a plus sign inside it next to *Mobile Phones*). A new tab appears named *Sheet1*.

1. Double-click the *Sheet1* tab.

2. Type the word **Population** followed by the **<Enter>** key.

4 Move a worksheet's tab.

1. Click on the *Population* tab (you may have to do this twice).

2. Hold the mouse button down and drag to the left or right. As you drag you'll notice an icon of a page and a black arrow telling you where the tab will be placed.

3. Release the mouse button to move the tab to the location of your choice.

5 Understand the tab scroll buttons

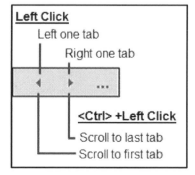

Because this workbook only has four tabs, there's no need to use the tab scroll buttons (in fact, they don't do anything when all tabs are visible). When there are more tabs than will fit on the screen the *tab scroll buttons* are used to move between tabs.

6   Move between worksheets using the keyboard.

You can move between worksheets using only the keyboard by pressing the **<Ctrl>+<PgUp>** and **<Ctrl>+<PgDn>** keyboard shortcuts to cycle through all of the tabs in your workbook.

7   Change tab colors.

1.   Right-click on any of the tabs and choose *Tab Color* from the shortcut menu.

2.   Choose any color.

It is best practice to choose a color from the top block of *Theme Colors* rather than one of the *Standard Colors.*

You'll discover why later, in: *Lesson 4-8: Understand themes* and in: *Lesson 4-10: Add color and gradient effects to cells (sidebar).*

3.   Repeat for the other tabs on the worksheet.

8   Delete a worksheet.

Right click on the *Population* tab and select *Delete* from the shortcut menu.

9   Delete several worksheets at the same time.

1.   Hold down the **<Ctrl>** key.

2.   Click each tab you want to delete in turn. Don't select them all as it isn't possible to delete every worksheet in a workbook.

3.   Right click any of the selected tabs and select *Delete* from the shortcut menu.

Don't worry about the missing tabs. We're going to close the workbook without saving it so you won't overwrite the original workbook.

10   Close the workbook without saving it.

1.   Click: File→Close.

A dialog is displayed:

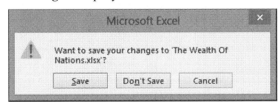

2.   Click *Don't Save* so that you don't over-write the workbook.

Because you haven't saved the workbook it will remain in its original state when you next open it.

Lesson 1-10: Use the Versions feature to recover an unsaved Draft file

Excel 2010 introduced a major new feature called *Versions*. The Versions feature is fantastically useful as it finally solves two common problems that are as old as computing itself:

1. Your computer crashes, there's a power cut, or you close your work without saving... and then discover that you've lost all of your work since the last save.

2. You delete parts of your workbook and then save, only to realize that you deleted something important before saving. Because saving over-writes the old version of the file, you find that you've lost the deleted work forever.

Microsoft has finally figured out how to solve both problems. The Versions feature works like this:

1. Every so often Excel saves a backup of your workbook (called a *Version*) for you. The default time interval for these automatic backups is every 10 minutes (but you can change this to any interval). You'll see the Versions feature at work in the next lesson: *Lesson 1-11: Use the Versions feature to recover an earlier version of a workbook.*

2. If you create a brand new workbook and then close it without saving, Excel will still keep the last automatic backup it made. Excel calls this a *Draft* version. Draft versions are automatically deleted after four days. The Draft feature is the subject of this lesson.

You'll need a watch or clock with a seconds hand for this lesson.

1   Open a new blank workbook.

    You learned how to do this in: *Lesson 1-1: Start Excel and open a new blank workbook.*

2   Set the AutoSave interval to one minute and check that AutoSave features are enabled

    1. Click: File→Options→Save.

    2. Change the *Save AutoRecover information every* box to 1 minute.

    3. Make sure that the other options are set in the same way as in this screen grab (the two check boxes will already be checked unless another user has changed them):

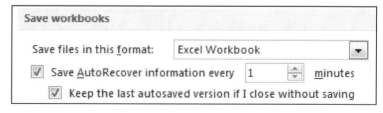

    4. Click: *OK* and check the time on your clock or watch. The first AutoSave will happen one minute from now!

The versions feature will not protect you from a hard drive failure

Carnegie Melon University conducted a study of 100,000 hard drives in 2007. They found that there's a probability of between 1 in 50 and 1 in 25 of your hard drive failing each year.

In an office of 100 workers that means that between two and four unlucky workers will suffer a hard drive failure every year.

To insure against drive failure you need to back up your data to a different hard drive (or other media).

If your computer is part of an office network, the normal solution is to save your files on a shared network drive. The IT department are then responsible for backing this up every night.

For home users (or small companies that only have one computer) you should back up all of your data to an external hard drive (or a memory stick if your files are not very large).

When I write my books it would be a disaster even to lose one day's writing so I save my files onto a special drive called a RAID Array (Redundant Array of Independent Disks). The drive contains two hard drives and automatically writes my data to each drive (this is called mirroring). If one drive fails the other will still have my data.

Cloud computing offers an even better solution to prevent potential file loss after hard drive failure. In: *Session Eight: Cloud Computing,* you'll learn how to use a OneDrive to store your workbook in the cloud.

5. Type the following into cells A1 and A2 , pressing the **<Enter>** key after each line:

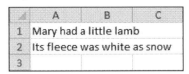

6. Wait for at least one minute. (After one minute Excel will automatically save your workbook).

7. After a little over a minute try to close the workbook. The following dialog will appear:

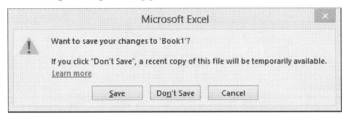

Excel is telling you that it has already saved a draft copy of the workbook.

8. Click the *Don't Save* button.

Even though you told Excel not to save, there's still a draft copy saved just in case you made a mistake and may need the file later.

3   Recover the draft document.

1. Open Excel.

2. Click: *Open Other Workbooks* at the bottom of the menu bar.

3. Click: *Recover Unsaved Workbooks.*

You'll find this at the bottom center of the screen (you may need to scroll down).

4. A dialog appears showing the unsaved document that you were working on:

5. Double-click the document to open it.

The document is now shown on screen (even though you have never saved it).

6. Recover the unsaved file.

Click the *Save As* button in the yellow top information bar.

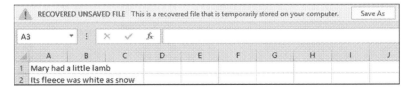

7. Save the file in your sample files folder with the name: **Mary.**

Lesson 1-11: Use the Versions feature to recover an earlier version of a workbook

Excel's ability to automatically backup your document at a chosen time interval was explored in the last lesson: *Lesson 1-10: Use the Versions feature to recover an unsaved Draft file.*

This lesson will show you how to view the automatic backups and to revert to an earlier version if you've messed up the current version.

You can even cut-and-paste sections from older versions of a workbook and paste them into the current version.

You'll need a watch or clock with a seconds hand for this lesson.

1 Open *Mary* from your sample files folder (if it isn't already open).

2 Cause Excel to automatically save a different version of the workbook.

In the last lesson: *Lesson 1-10: Use the Versions feature to recover an unsaved Draft file*, you set the time interval for automatic backups to 1 minute. If you are not completing this course sequentially, you will need to go back to this lesson and make sure that this setting is set to 1 minute.

Add the following text to cells A4 and A5, pressing the **<Enter>** key after each line:

	A	B	C	D
1	Mary had a little lamb			
2	Its fleece was white as snow			
3				
4	and everywhere that Mary went			
5	The lamb was sure to go			
6				

Look at your watch or clock and wait for a little over one minute. Excel should have automatically saved a new version of the workbook.

3 Make sure that Excel AutoSaved the new version.

Some users have reported that Excel sometimes takes as long as ten minutes to AutoSave a file (even when the AutoSave interval is set to one minute). Here's how to check that it performed as it should:

1. Click the *File button.*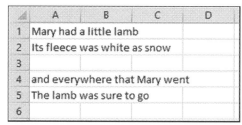

You should see an AutoSave file version alongside the *Manage Versions* button.

Mary

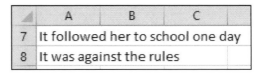

If you don't see the AutoSave version, click the *Back Button* wait another minute and then click the *File* tab again. Don't move on to the next step until it has appeared.

4   Further modify the file and then save it.

    1.   Add the following text to cells A7 and A8 pressing the **<Enter>** key after each line:

    2.   Save the workbook.

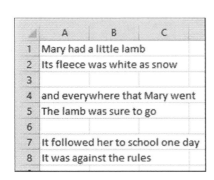

5   View the earlier version that Excel automatically saved.

    1.   Click the *File button.*   FILE

    2.   Click the earlier AutoSaved version.

Versions

  📄 Today, 21:04 (autosave)

The earlier version opens in Excel.

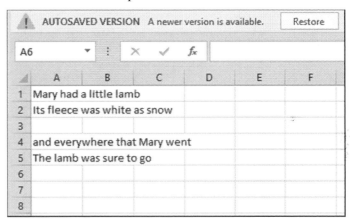

6   Replace the current version of the workbook with the earlier AutoSaved version.

    1.   Click the *Restore* button on the top yellow information bar.

Excel warns that you will over-write the current version of the workbook.

    2.   Click OK.

7   Reset the AutoSave interval to 10 minutes.

You learned how to do this in: *Lesson 1-10: Use the Versions feature to recover an unsaved Draft file.*

Lesson 1-12: Use the Ribbon

The Ribbon provides fast access to hundreds of Excel features.

The sheer breadth of Excel features can seem overwhelming. This book will gently introduce all of the most important features, one at a time.

By the end of the book you'll be really comfortable and productive with the Ribbon.

1 Start Excel and open a new blank workbook.

You learned how to do this in: *Lesson 1-1: Start Excel and open a new blank workbook.*

2 Use Ribbon tabs.

Each Ribbon tab has its own toolkit available to you. By far the most important tab is the *Home* tab which has buttons for all of the most common and useful features.

Click each tab in turn and view the buttons. The screen grab below has the *Insert* Tab selected. Don't worry if the buttons seem cryptic at the moment. Most of them will make complete sense by the end of this book. (And if you later go on to complete the *Expert Skills* course, Excel will have no mysteries left at all)!

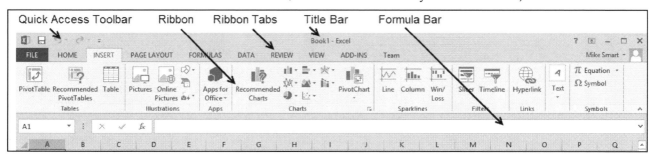

Quick Access Toolbar   Ribbon   Ribbon Tabs   Title Bar   Formula Bar

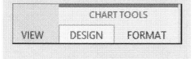
3 Type the word **Test** into any blank cell and then press the **<Enter>** key on the keyboard once.

Notice how the Active Cell moves to the cell beneath.

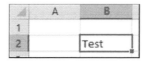

4 Make the cell with the word *Test* into the active cell.

Click once on the word *Test* or use the arrow keys on the keyboard to navigate back to the cell. Be very careful not to double-click, otherwise Excel will think that you want to edit the cell.

5 Click the *Home* tab on the Ribbon and focus upon the Font panel (it's the second panel from the left). Try clicking each of the buttons and you will see the word *Test* change to reflect your choices.

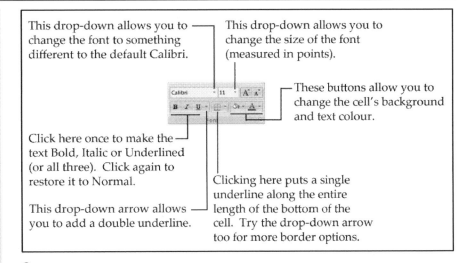

This drop-down allows you to change the font to something different to the default Calibri.

This drop-down allows you to change the size of the font (measured in points).

These buttons allow you to change the cell's background and text colour.

Click here once to make the text Bold, Italic or Underlined (or all three). Click again to restore it to Normal.

This drop-down arrow allows you to add a double underline.

Clicking here puts a single underline along the entire length of the bottom of the cell. Try the drop-down arrow too for more border options.

6 Minimize the Ribbon.

1. Double-click any of the Ribbon tabs except the *File* tab (for example the *Home* tab or the *Insert* tab).

    Notice how the Ribbon is now minimized in order to save screen space (though the *Formula Bar* is still visible).

2. Click once on any tab, except the *File* tab, to temporarily bring the Ribbon back to full size.

    Notice that as soon as you click back onto the worksheet the Ribbon is minimized again.

7 Bring back the Ribbon.

Double-click on any tab except the *File* tab to permanently bring back the Ribbon.

8 Close Excel without saving changes.

1. Click: File→Close or click the cross [×] in the top right corner.

2. When asked if you want to save your changes, click the *Don't Save* button.

Lesson 1-13: Understand Ribbon components

> The whole is more than the sum of its parts.
> *Aristotle, Greek critic, philosopher, physicist & zoologist*
> *(384 BC – 322 BC)*

The Ribbon is made up of several different controls.

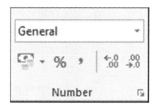

Command group

Similar actions are grouped into a cluster. For example, every control relating to numbers is clustered into the *Number* group.

Normal button

Simply executes a command when clicked. The *Bold* button on the *Home* tab is a good example.

Menu button

This type of button has a little down-arrow on it. It will display a *list*, *menu* or *rich menu* drop-down when clicked.

Split button

This is the hardest button to understand because these buttons look almost the same as the *Menu* button. When you hover the mouse cursor over a split button, the icon and drop-down arrow highlight seperately as different "buttons within a button".

A good example is the *underline* button on the Home toolbar.

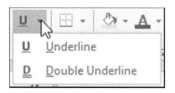

Clicking the icon part of a split button (the U) will perform the default action of the button (in this case a single underline). Clicking the arrow part of the button will display a drop-down list of further choices (in this case the choice between a single and double underline).

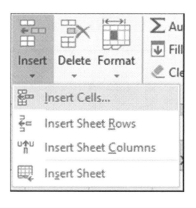

Drop down list

I often shorten this to simply "Drop Down" in this book. A drop down is a simple menu listing several choices.

If you see an ellipsis (…) after a drop down list item, this means that a dialog will be displayed after you click, offering further choices.

Rich menu

The rich menu is a drop-down list with added help text explaining what each item will do.

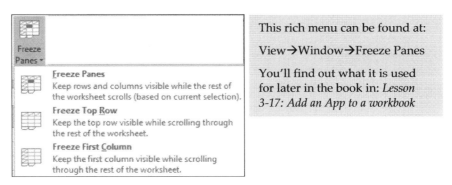

This rich menu can be found at:

View→Window→Freeze Panes

You'll find out what it is used for later in the book in: *Lesson 3-17: Add an App to a workbook*

Drop down gallery

This is a little like a drop down list but has graphics to visually demonstrate the effect of each choice.

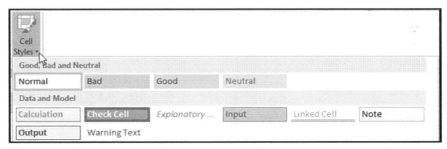

Check box

A little square box that you can click to switch an option on or off.

In this example (from the *Page Layout* Ribbon) you are able to switch the gridlines on and off for the screen display and/or the printout.

Dialog launcher

Dialog launchers appear on the bottom right-hand corner of some command groups. Dialogs offer more choices than it is possible for the Ribbon to express graphically.

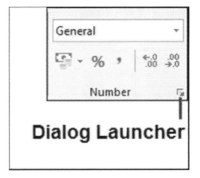

Lesson 1-14: Customize the Quick Access Toolbar and preview the printout

You can customize the *Quick Access Toolbar* to suit your own special requirements. In this lesson we'll add some useful buttons to *the Quick Access Toolbar* to save a few clicks when accessing common commands.

The *Quick Access Toolbar* is one of the keys to being really productive with Excel 2013. This lesson will introduce you to the main features.

1   Open *The Wealth of Nations* from your sample folder.

2   Preview how the *Life Expectancy* worksheet will look when printed.

1.   Click the *Life Expectancy tab* at the bottom of the worksheet.

2.   Click: File→Print.

Backstage View is displayed.

Backstage view displays a huge number of print-related features. A preview of how the page will look when printed is displayed on the right-hand side of the screen..

Notice there's a button to the bottom-left of the preview pane that allows you to cycle through each page:

3.   Click the *Next Page* and *Previous Page* buttons to move through the print preview.

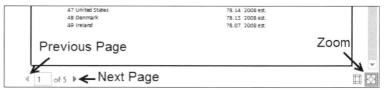

4.   Use the *Zoom* button to magnify the page for a clearer view.

5.   Click the *Back button* 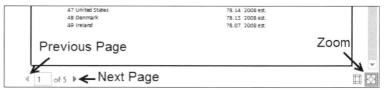 at the top left of *Backstage View* to return to the workbook.

Customize Quick Access Toolbar Button

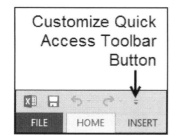

3   Add a *Print Preview* button to the Quick Access Toolbar.

The quick *Print Preview* offered by the *Backstage View* is a very useful feature and you'll probably use it a lot. Every time you use it, however, it is going to take two clicks of the mouse. Wouldn't it be better if you could show a print preview with just one click?

1.   Click the *Customize Quick Access Toolbar button* (see sidebar).

2.   Click the *Print Preview and Print* item in the drop-down list.

A new button now appears on the Quick Access Toolbar. You are now able to *Print Preview* your work with a single click of the mouse.

The Wealth of Nations

note

Some amazing "hidden" Excel features cannot be used at all without customizing the Quick Access Toolbar or the Ribbon

One of my favourite "hidden" features in Excel 2013 is its ability to read the workbook to me via its *Text to Voice* facility.

When I need to input lots of numbers from a sheet of paper and want to check them, I get Excel to read them to me as I tick each off my list. This is much faster and nicer than continuously looking first at the screen, then at the paper, for each entry.

This feature is covered in depth in the *Expert Skills* book in this series.

You can't use this feature at all unless you either add some custom buttons to the Quick Access Toolbar or customize the Ribbon.

tip

The Quick Access Toolbar is one of the keys to being really productive with Excel 2013.

Always try to minimize the number of mouse clicks needed to do common tasks.

If you find yourself forever changing tabs to use a button, change two clicks into one by adding the button to the Quick Access Toolbar.

All of those extra clicks add up to a lot of time over the weeks and years.

4   Add a *Font Color* button to the Quick Access Toolbar.

The *More Commands...* option is available when you click the *Customize Quick Access Toolbar* button. This enables you to add any of Excel's commands to the toolbar. But there's an easier way!

1. Click the *Home* tab on the Ribbon (if it isn't already selected).

2. Right-click on the *Font Color* button ![A] in the *Font Group*.

3. Click *Add to Quick Access Toolbar*.

A *Font Color* button is added to the Quick Access Toolbar.

5   Remove a button from the Quick Access Toolbar.

1. Right-click on the *Font Color* button you've just added to the Quick Access Toolbar. ![A]

2. Click *Remove from Quick Access Toolbar* on the shortcut menu.

6   Add separators to make heavily customized Quick Access toolbars more readable.

When you add many items to the Quick Access toolbar it is a good idea to use separators to split icons into logical groups.

1. Click the Customize Quick Access Toolbar button. ![button]

2. Click *More Commands...* on the shortcut menu.

3. Click the <Separator> item at the top of the *Commands* list.

4. Click the Add>> button.

5. Use the up ![up] and down ![down] buttons to move the separator to the required location.

6. Click the OK button.

Here's a screen grab of my own Quick Access Toolbar. I've added buttons for all of the features I use most often.

This means that I can always access these features with a single click of the mouse:

Separators

The Wealth of Nations

Lesson 1-15: Use the Mini Toolbar, Key Tips and keyboard shortcuts

1 Open the *Wealth of Nations* sample worksheet (if it isn't already open).

2 Select cell B2 (Qatar) on the GDP worksheet.

1. Click on the *GDP* tab.

2. Click on cell B2 (Qatar).

Make sure that you only click once, otherwise Excel will think that you are trying to edit the cell.

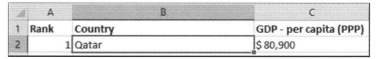

3 Make cell B2 (Qatar) bold, italicized and underlined.

1. Click: Home→Font→Bold.

2. Click: Home→Font→Italic.

3. Click: Home→Font→Underline.

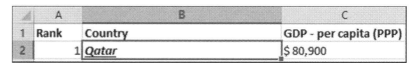

4 Display *Key Tips*.

Hold down the <**Alt**> key on the keyboard.

Notice how *Key Tips* are now displayed on the Ribbon and the Quick Access Toolbar:

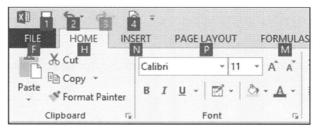

5 Use the *Key Tips* to show a print preview using only the keyboard.

The key tips reveal the key you need to press to simulate clicking any of the Ribbon and Quick Access Toolbar icons.

Hold down the <**Alt**> key and press the relevant number to show a print preview (in the above example this is 4).

NB: Your toolbar, and the number you need to press, may look different to the screen grab above. Note that the print preview button will not be on the Quick Access Toolbar unless you added it during: *Lesson 1-14: Customize the Quick Access Toolbar and preview the printout.*

note

The shortcut menu

If you right-click on a cell, a shortcut menu is displayed.

The shortcut menu doesn't display *everything* that you can do to a cell but Excel's best guesses at the *most likely things* you might want to do.

Because Excel is guessing at the actions you might want to take in the context of what you are doing, the *shortcut menu* is also sometimes referred to as the *contextual menu.*

6   Click the *Back Button* ⊙ to leave *Backstage View* and return to the worksheet.

7   Use the mouse to select the text *Qatar* in cell B2.

    1.   Double-click the cell containing the text.

        You'll see the cursor flashing in the cell. This means that you have entered *Edit Mode* enabling you to change the contents of the cell

    2.   Position the cursor just after the word *Qatar* and hold down the left mouse button.

    3.   Drag the mouse across the complete word until it is highlighted like this:

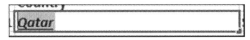

    4.   Release the mouse button but do not move it away from the text.

8   Observe the *Mini Toolbar.*

Provided you didn't move the mouse cursor away from cell B2 you will now see the mini toolbar above the cell:

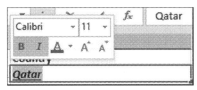

9   Use the *Mini Toolbar* to restore the text to non-bold and non-italic.

Click on the Bold **B** and Italic *I* buttons to remove the bold and italic attributes from the text.

> Qatar

10   Show a bigger Mini Toolbar with a right-click.

Right-click on *Bermuda* (Cell B4). Notice that, as well as the shortcut menu (see sidebar), you now get an even better Mini Toolbar with a few extra buttons.

11   Remove the underline from Qatar using a shortcut key.

    1.   Click on Qatar (cell B2).

    2.   Press the **<Ctrl>+<U>** keys on the keyboard to remove the underline.

But how can you remember cryptic keyboard shortcuts like **<Ctrl>+<U>**? Fortunately you don't have to. Hover the mouse over the underline button **U** (on the Home tab of the Ribbon) and you'll see the keyboard shortcut listed in the tooltip.

Lesson 1-16: Understand views

Views provide different ways to look at your worksheet.

Excel 2013 has three main views. They are:-

View	Icon	What it is used for
Normal		This is the view you've been using until now. It's the view most users use all of the time when they are working with Excel.
Page Layout		This view allows you to see (almost) exactly what the printout will look like. Unlike running a *Print Preview* you are able to edit cells just as you can in *Normal* view.
Page Break Preview		A page break indicates when the printer should advance onto a new sheet of paper. We'll use this view in: *Lesson 7-5: Insert, delete and preview page breaks* to make sure that the page breaks in the right place.

1 Open the *Wealth of Nations* sample worksheet (if it isn't already open).

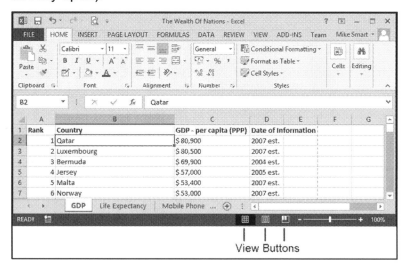

View Buttons

You can change views in two ways:

1. By clicking one of the View buttons at the bottom of the window (see above).

2. By clicking one of the buttons in the *Workbook Views* group on the Ribbon's *View* tab (see below).

The Wealth of Nations

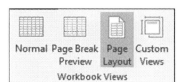

2   View the GDP worksheet in *Page Layout* view.

1.   Click on the *GDP* tab and then select *Page Layout* view.

2.   Click: View→Workbook Views→Page Layout.

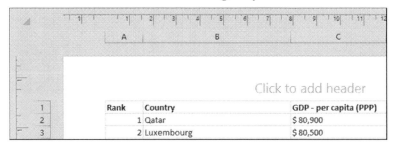

The worksheet is displayed in *Page Layout* view. You are able to see (almost) exactly what will be printed. Headers, footers and margins are all shown.

You are also able to edit the worksheet.

You may wonder why we don't use *Page Layout* view all of the time when editing worksheets. While some users may prefer to do this, most will want to see the maximum amount of data possible on screen and so will prefer the *Normal* view.

3   Select *Page Break Preview* view.

Click: View→Workbook Views→Page Break Preview.

The worksheet is displayed in *Page Break Preview* view (you may also see a help dialog first).

This view shows each page with a watermark to indicate which sheet of paper it will be printed on:

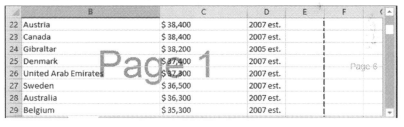

It also shows the break between each page as a dotted line:

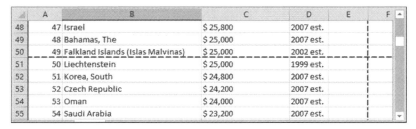

It is possible to click and drag the dotted line to change the place where the page breaks.

Adjusting page breaks using click and drag will be covered later in: *Lesson 7-6: Adjust page breaks using Page Break Preview.*

4   Select *Normal* view.

Click: View→Workbook Views→Normal.

Lesson 1-17: Hide and Show the Formula Bar and Ribbon

Most desktop computers have large display screens. The space taken by the Ribbon and Formula Bar isn't usually a problem.

As you'll discover in: *Session Eight: Cloud Computing,* it is now possible to run Excel 2013 on tablet computers (and even on Smartphones). These devices often have a very small display screen, meaning that the Ribbon and Formula Bar take up too much valuable screen space.

When screen space is limited, you may wish to hide the Formula Bar, Ribbon, or even both, in order to maximize the number of cells visible on the screen.

1   Open the *Wealth of Nations* from your sample files folder (if it isn't already open) and click the *Life Expectancy* tab.

Notice that the *Ribbon* and *Formula Bar* are taking up space that could be used to display the contents of the worksheet.

Consider the screen below:

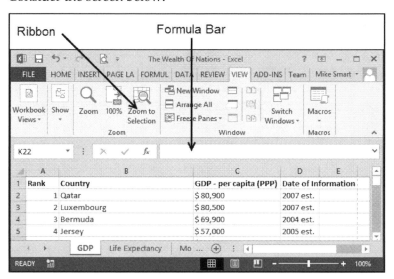

This is the type of smaller screen you might see on a small tablet device or Smartphone.

Only five rows are visible, making the worksheet difficult to work with. Hiding the Ribbon, Formula Bar, or both, will free up some valuable screen space.

1   Hide the Formula Bar.

Click: View→Show→Formula Bar.

The Formula Bar vanishes:

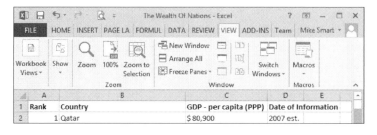

The Wealth of Nations

2 Use the *Ribbon Display Options* to reduce the Ribbon display to only show tabs

In: *Lesson 1-12: Use the Ribbon,* you learned how to hide the Ribbon by double-clicking any of the Ribbon tabs (except the *File* tab).

In this lesson we'll do the same thing in a different way by using the *Ribbon Display Options* button. This is a new feature in Excel 2013.

1. Click the *Ribbon Display Options* button at the top right of the Excel window.

   A *Rich Menu* is displayed showing three different ways to hide the ribbon.

2. Click *Show Tabs* to reduce the Ribbon to a row of tabs.

   The Ribbon now reduces in size to only show tabs. You can still access the Ribbon. It now pops up when you click on any tab and disappears when you click back onto the worksheet.

3 Completely hide both the Ribbon and Ribbon tabs

1. Click the *Ribbon Display Options* button at the top right of the Excel window.

2. Click *Auto-hide Ribbon* on the rich menu.

   This time both the Ribbon, and Ribbon tabs disappear. The worksheet itself fills the entire screen. This is called *Full Screen View*.

   When you are in *Full Screen View* you can temporarily bring back the Ribbon by double-clicking at the very top of the screen. The Ribbon then re-appears but vanishes once again when you click back into the body of the worksheet.

4 Restore the Ribbon and the Formula Bar.

1. Click the *Ribbon Display Options* button at the top right of the Excel window.

2. Click: *Show Tabs and Commands* on the rich menu.

   The Ribbon is restored.

3. Click: View→Show→Formula Bar.

   The Formula bar is restored.

Lesson 1-18: Use the help system

Microsoft have completely re-designed the help system for Excel 2013.

The entire help system is now delivered as a simple search box that works in a similar way to a search engine such as Google.

If you are connected to the Internet, the help system also includes a web page delivered from Microsoft's *Office.com* website. This page adds links to material on the Internet.

1 Click the Help button ⌗ at the top right of your screen.

The *Excel Help* dialog is displayed:

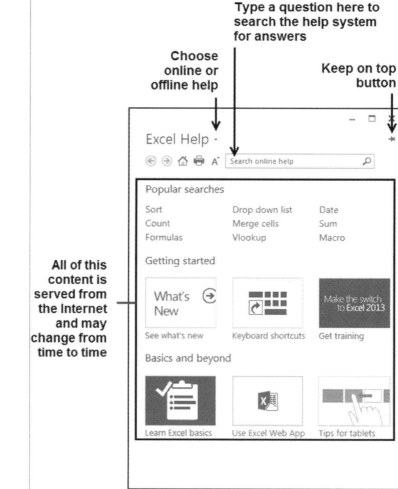

If you are not connected to the Internet you will not see the information shown below the search box. You can also switch off the lower part of the dialog with the *Choose Online or Offline Help* button ⬜ shown above.

2 Type **how do I save a file** into the search box followed by the **<Enter>** key.

The help system provides many potential answers to the question:

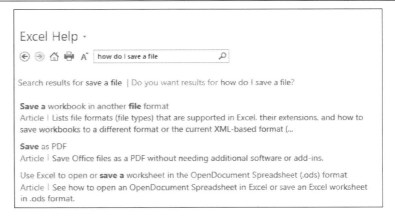

3 Click on the most likely answer to read the help topic.

Some information is displayed about saving files.

4 Get help directly from the Ribbon.

1. Close the *Excel Help* dialog by clicking the close button  in the top right corner.

2. Click the *Home tab* on the Ribbon and hover the mouse cursor over the drop down arrow to the right of the word *General* in the *Number* group.

   If you keep the mouse still, after a short delay a screen tip pops up providing a short description of what the drop-down list is for:

   A *Tell me more* hyperlink is also provided offering more detailed help. This will only work if you are connected to the Internet.

3. Click the *Tell me more* hyperlink.

   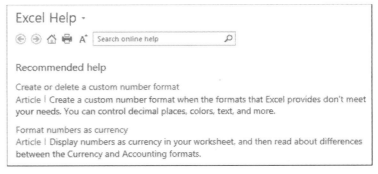

   If you are connected to the Internet, you will see links to pages on the *Office.com* website that have more information about number formats.

   The help screen you see may differ from the above screen grab as Microsoft may have updated the *Office.com* website content since this book was written.

Session 1: Exercise

In this exercise you'll try to remember the name of each of the Excel screen elements. The answers are on the next page so you might want to recap by turning the page for a little revision before you start.

Keep trying until you are able to name each of the screen elements from memory. We'll be using this terminology during the remainder of the book, so it's important that you can correctly identify each element.

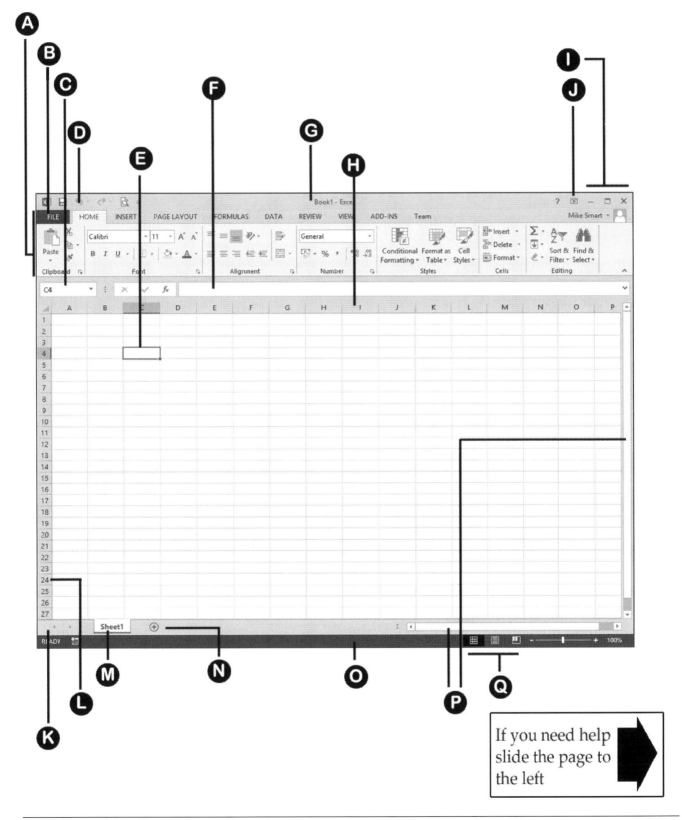

If you need help slide the page to the left

Session 1: Exercise answers

Ribbon

File button (this opens the Backstage View)

Minimize, Maximize and Close buttons

Name Box

Formula Bar

Ribbon Display Options button

Quick Access Toolbar

Title bar

Active Cell

Column Header

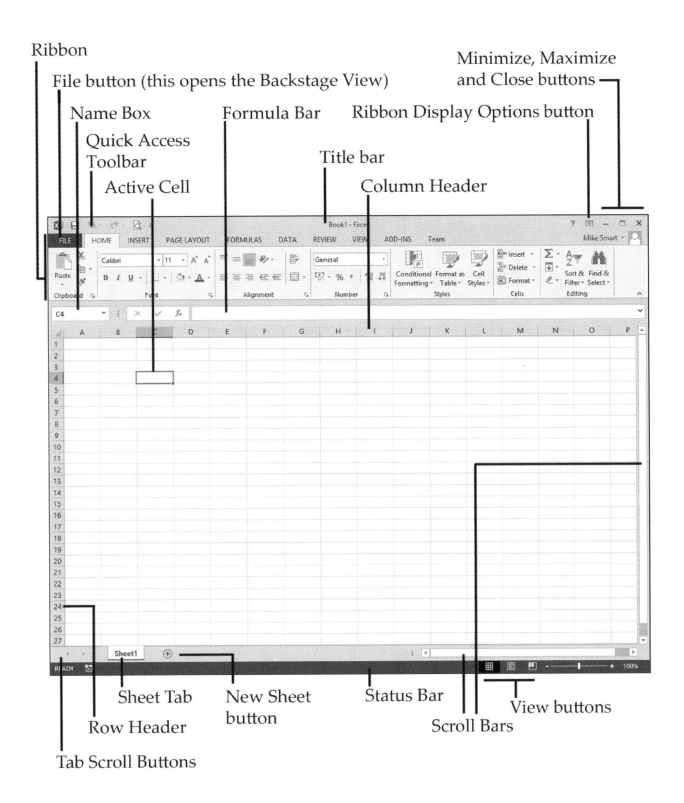

Sheet Tab

New Sheet button

Status Bar

View buttons

Row Header

Scroll Bars

Tab Scroll Buttons

2

Session Two: Doing Useful Work with Excel

> Only those who have the patience to do simple things perfectly ever acquire the skill to do difficult things easily.
>
> *Unknown author*

Now that you've mastered the basics, you are ready to do really useful work with this amazing tool. In this session you will learn to use all of Excel's basic features properly. This will put you way ahead of anybody that hasn't been formally trained in Excel best practice. You'll be doing simple things, but you'll be doing them perfectly!

Even after years of daily use, many users are unable to properly use Excel's fundamental features. They often reach their goal, but get there in a very inefficient way, simply because they were never taught how to do things correctly. By the end of this session you'll be astonished with how well you are working with Excel.

Session Objectives

By the end of this session you will be able to:

- Enter text and numbers into a worksheet
- Create a new workbook and view two workbooks at the same time
- Use AutoSum to quickly calculate totals
- Select a range of cells and understand Smart Tags
- Enter data into a range and copy data across a range
- Select adjacent and non-adjacent rows and columns
- Select non-contiguous cell ranges and view summary information
- AutoSelect a range of cells
- Re-size rows and columns
- Use AutoSum to sum a non-contiguous range
- Use AutoSum to quickly calculate averages
- Create your own formulas
- Create functions using Formula AutoComplete
- Use AutoFill for text and numeric series
- Use AutoFill to adjust formulas
- Use AutoFill Options
- Speed up your AutoFills and create a custom fill series
- Use Flash Fill to split and concatenate text
- Use the zoom control
- Print out a worksheet

Lesson 2-1: Enter text and numbers into a worksheet

Excel beginners tend to reach for the mouse far too often. One of the keys to productivity with Excel is to avoid using the mouse when entering data. In this lesson we'll quickly populate a worksheet without using the mouse at all.

1   Open the sample file: *First Quarter Sales and Profit.*

	A	B	C	D
1	Sales and Profit Report - First Quarter 2008			
2				
3		Jan	Feb	Mar
4	New York	22,000	29,000	19,000
5	Los Angeles			
6	London			
7	Paris			
8	Munich			

2   Notice the difference between values and text.

Cells can contain values or text. Values can be numbers, dates or formulas (more on formulas later).

Excel usually does a great job of recognizing when there are values in a cell and when there is text. The giveaway is that text is always (by default) left aligned in the cell and values are right aligned.

Look at the numbers on this worksheet. Notice how they are all right aligned. This lets you know that Excel has correctly recognized them as values and will happily perform mathematical operations using them.

3   Save a value into a cell.

1.   Type the value 42000 into cell B5. Notice that the mouse cursor is still flashing in the cell.

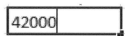

At this stage the value has not been saved into the cell.

If you change your mind, you can still undo the value by pressing the **<ESC>** key at the top left of your keyboard or by clicking the *Cancel button* ☒ on the left hand side of the Formula Bar.

2.   Decide that you want to keep this value in the cell by either pressing the **<Enter>, <Tab>** or an **<Arrow>** key on the keyboard, or by clicking the *Confirm button* ☑ on left hand side of the Formula Bar.

4   Enter a column of data without using the mouse.

When you enter data into a column, there's no need to use the mouse. Press the **<Enter>** key after each entry and the active cell

tip

Entering numbers as text

Sometimes you need Excel to recognize a number as text.

If you type an apostrophe (') before the number, Excel won't display the apostrophe but will format the cell as text. You'll notice that the number is then left justified to reflect this.

When a number is formatted as text you cannot perform any mathematical calculation with it.

First Quarter Sales and Profit

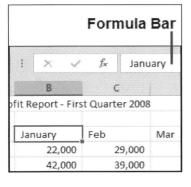

moves to the cell beneath. Try this now with the following January sales data:

1. Type **18,000** into cell B6.

2. Press the **<Enter>** key to move to cell B7.

3. Do the same to enter the relevant values into the next two cells.

	A	B	C	D
3		Jan	Feb	Mar
4	New York	22,000	29,000	19,000
5	Los Angeles	42,000		
6	London	18,000		
7	Paris	35,000		
8	Munich	12,000		

5   Enter a row of data without using the mouse.

You can also enter a row of data without using the mouse.

1. Click in Cell C5.

2. Type **39,000** and then press the **<Tab>** key on your keyboard.

    The <Tab> key is on the left hand side of the keyboard above the <Caps Lock> key. Notice how pressing the <Tab> key saves the value into the cell and then moves one cell to the right.

3. Type **43,000** into cell D5 and press the **<Enter>** key.

    You magically move to cell C6 as Excel assumes you want to begin entering data into the next row.

6   Complete the table without using the mouse.

By using the **<Tab>** or **<Enter>** key in the right place you should be able to complete the table now without using the mouse:

	A	B	C	D
3		Jan	Feb	Mar
4	New York	22,000	29,000	19,000
5	Los Angeles	42,000	39,000	43,000
6	London	18,000	20,000	22,000
7	Paris	35,000	26,000	31,000
8	Munich	12,000	15,000	13,000

7   Change the text in cell B3 to January.

1. Double-click cell B3. Notice that there is now a flashing cursor in the cell.

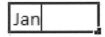

2. Type **uary** on the keyboard to change Jan to January.

3. Press the **<Enter>** key.

8   Change the text in cell B3 back to **Jan** using the formula bar.

Click once in cell B3 and then change the text in the formula bar back to **Jan** (see sidebar).

9   Save your work as *First Quarter Sales and Profit-2*.

Lesson 2-2: Create a new workbook and view two workbooks at the same time

tip

Other ways of creating a new workbook

- Use the keyboard shortcut <Ctrl>+<N>.

- Add a button to the Quick Access Toolbar.

See more details of how this is done in: *Lesson 1-14: Customize the Quick Access Toolbar and preview the printout.*

1 Create a new workbook by opening Excel.

    1. Open Excel.

    2. Click the *Blank Workbook* template to create a new workbook.

       Excel helpfully creates a workbook, unimaginatively named *Book1*. If you already have a workbook open called *Book1*, the new workbook will be called *Book2...* and so on.

       Notice that *Book1 – Excel* is displayed on the *Title Bar.*

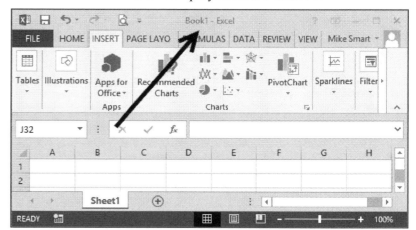

2 Create another new workbook.

    1. Click the *File* button FILE at the top left of the screen and click the *New* button in the left hand menu.

       You are presented with the same familiar dialog you see when you start up Excel.

    2. Click the *Blank workbook* template. A new blank workbook called *Book2* is displayed in the workbook window.

       You could be forgiven for thinking that nothing has happened but you can see that the *Title Bar* now says: *Book2 – Excel,* showing that you are now looking at a different workbook.

3 Use the taskbar to move between workbooks.

    You'll see an Excel icon with two right-hand borders at the bottom of the screen. Hover over this icon with your mouse. A gallery will pop up showing two workbooks: *Book1* and *Book2.*

note

Finding a workbook when many are open

An alternative way to quickly find a workbook when many are open is to click:

View→Window→ Switch Windows

This presents you with a list of all open workbooks.

You can also use the **<Ctrl>+<Tab>** keyboard shortcut to cycle through all open workbooks.

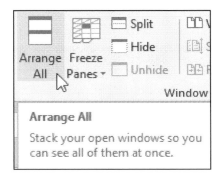

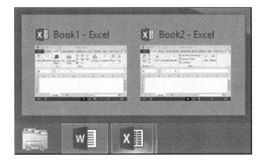

Hover over each item in the pop-up gallery to display each workbook. The only difference you will see is the *Title Bar* changing from *Book1* to *Book2* because both workbooks are empty.

See sidebar for other methods of switching windows.

4 **Display both *Book1* and *Book2* at the same time.**

1. Click: View→Window→Arrange All.

The *Arrange Windows* dialog is displayed.

2. Choose the *Horizontal* arrangement and click the OK button.

Both workbooks are now shown, one above the other. Each window occupies exactly half of your screen:

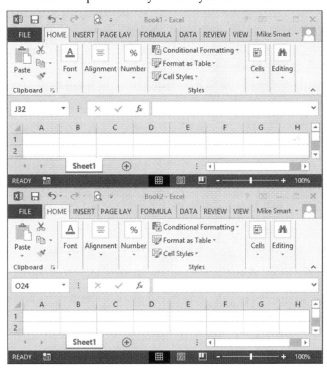

Notice that as you click each workbook window the *Title Bar* and the *Close/Minimize/Restore Down* buttons light up, to show that this is the active window.

5 **Close *Book2* and maximize *Book1* to restore the display to a single workbook.**

If you've forgotten how to do this, refer back to: *Lesson 1-4: Maximize, minimize, re-size, move and close the Excel window.*

Lesson 2-3: Use AutoSum to quickly calculate totals

Excel's *AutoSum* feature is a really useful and fast way to add the values in a range of cells together.

1 Open *First Quarter Sales and Profit-2* from your sample files folder.

2 In cell A9 Type the word **Total** followed by the **<Tab>** key.

The active cell moves to the right and is now in cell B9:

	A	B	C	D
7	Paris	35,000	26,000	31,000
8	Munich	12,000	15,000	13,000
9	Total			

3 Click: Home→Editing→ Σ (this is the AutoSum button).

AutoSum Button

Σ ▾
Sort & Find &
Filter ▾ Select ▾
Editing

Something interesting has happened to the worksheet:

	A	B	C	D
3		Jan	Feb	Mar
4	New York	22,000	29,000	19,000
5	Los Angeles	42,000	39,000	43,000
6	London	18,000	20,000	22,000
7	Paris	35,000	26,000	31,000
8	Munich	12,000	15,000	13,000
9	Total	=SUM(B4:B8)		
10		SUM(**number1**, [number2], ...)		

Excel has placed a *marquee* around the number range that AutoSum has guessed we want to work with. The pattern of dots that marks the boundary of the marquee are called the *marching ants*.

The marching ants surround all of the numbers in the column above, up to the first blank cell or text cell (in this case, up to the word Jan).

=Sum(B4:B8) is your first glimpse of an Excel *Formula*. Formulas always begin with an equals sign. This formula is using the SUM function to compute the Sum (or total) of the values in cells B4 to B8.

4 Press the **<Enter>** key or click the AutoSum button Σ once more to display the total January sales:

tip

Entering an AutoSum using only the keyboard

You can also execute an AutoSum using the keyboard shortcut:

<Alt>+<=>

note

You can also add an AutoSum formula using the Quick Analysis button

Whenever you select a range of cells, a *Quick Analysis* button appears just outside the bottom-right corner of the selected range.

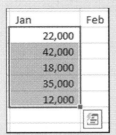

When you click the *Quick Analysis* button, the *Quick Analysis* dialog appears.

One of the menu options on this dialog is *Totals*.

The *Totals* dialog allows you to add an AutoSum beneath a selected range (in a similar way to the AutoSum button method described in this lesson).

	A	B	C	D
3		Jan	Feb	Mar
4	New York	22,000	29,000	19,000
5	Los Angeles	42,000	39,000	43,000
6	London	18,000	20,000	22,000
7	Paris	35,000	26,000	31,000
8	Munich	12,000	15,000	13,000
9	Total	129,000		

5   Type the word **Total** into cell E3 and press the **<Enter>** key once.

The active cell moves down one row and is now in cell E4.

	A	B	C	D	E
3		Jan	Feb	Mar	Total
4	New York	22,000	29,000	19,000	
5	Los Angeles	42,000	39,000	43,000	

6   Use AutoSum to calculate sales for New York.

1. Click: Home→Editing→AutoSum.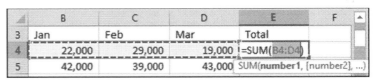

   This time AutoSum correctly guesses that you want to sum the values to the left of cell E4:

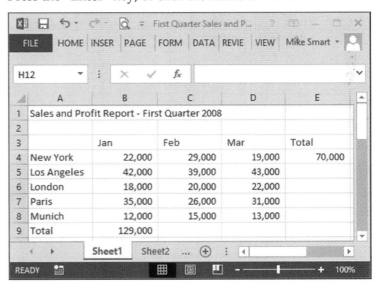

2. Press the **<Enter>** key, or click the AutoSum button once more.

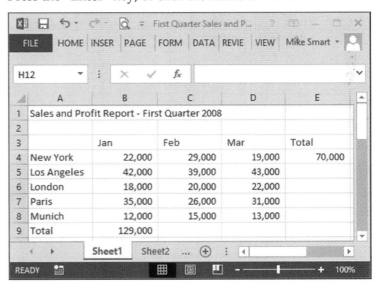

7   Save your work as *First Quarter Sales and Profit-3*.

Lesson 2-4: Select a range of cells and understand Smart Tags

1 Open *First Quarter Sales and Profit-3* from your sample files folder (if it isn't already open).

2 Observe the formula behind the value in cell B9.

Click once on cell B9 or move to it with the arrow keys on your keyboard.

Look at the *formula bar* at the top of the screen. Notice that the cell displays the *value* of a calculation and the formula bar shows the *formula* used to calculate the value:

B9			✕	✓	*fx*	=SUM(B4:B8)
	A		B		C	D
8	Munich		12,000		15,000	13,000
9	Total		129,000			
10						
11			**Value**		**Formula**	

3 Delete the contents of cell B9.

Press the **<Delete>** key on your keyboard.

4 Change the word *Total* in cell A9 to *USA Sales* and press the **<Tab>** key once.

The cursor moves to cell B9.

8	Munich	12,000
9	USA Sales	

5 Select cells B4:B5 with your mouse.

When the mouse cursor is hovered over a selected cell there are three possible cursor shapes:

Cursor	What it does
⬦1.6	The white cross (Select) cursor appears when you hover over the center of the active cell. You can then click and drag to select a range of cells.
1.6 ✚	The black cross (AutoFill) cursor appears when you hover over the bottom right-hand corner of the active cell. We'll be covering AutoFill later in this session.
1.6 ✛	The four headed arrow (Move) cursor appears when you hover over one of the black edges of the cell (but not the bottom right corner).

First Quarter Sales and Profit-3

<table>
<tr><td colspan="2">

note

Selecting cells with the keyboard

To select cells with the keyboard hold down the **<Shift>** key and then use the **<Arrow>** keys to select the range needed.

</td></tr>
</table>

note

Selecting a large range of cells with the <Shift>-click technique

If you need to select a very large range of cells it is sometimes useful to use this technique:

1. Click the cell in the top left corner of the required range.

2. If necessary, use the scroll bars to make the bottom right corner of the required range visible.

3. Hold down the **<Shift>** key.

4. Click in the bottom right corner of the required range.

Beginners often have difficulty selecting cells and end up moving them or AutoFilling them by mistake.

Position the mouse at the center of cell B4 so that you see the white cross (Select) cursor. When you see the white cross, hold down the left mouse button and drag down to cell B5. You have now selected cells B4 and B5 (in Excel terminology we say that you have selected the *range* B4:B5).

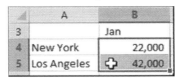

6   Display total USA sales in cell B9.

Because you have selected only the cells containing USA sales, (cells B4:B5), AutoSum can be used to show the value of the selected cells.

Click the AutoSum button $\boxed{\Sigma}$ to display the total value of the selected cells.

USA sales are shown in cell B9.

9	USA Sales	64,000

Notice the small green triangle at the top left of cell B9. This is Excel's way of saying: "I think you may have made a mistake".

7   Inspect a potential error using a Smart Tag.

1. Click once on cell B9 to make it the active cell.

    An *Exclamation Mark* icon appears $\boxed{\diamond}$. This is called a *Smart Tag*.

2. Hover the mouse cursor over the Smart Tag.

    A tip box pops up telling you what Excel thinks you may have done wrong (see below). Of course, in this case, everything is fine. The Smart Tag thinks that perhaps we didn't want to total just the USA sales – but the Smart Tag is mistaken!

8   Examine the remedial actions suggested by the Smart Tag.

1. Hover the mouse cursor over the Smart Tag icon $\boxed{\diamond}$.

2. Click the drop-down arrow that appears.

    A list of possible remedial actions is displayed. In this case you can choose *Ignore Error* to remove the green triangle from the corner of the cell.

9   Save your work as *First Quarter Sales and Profit-4*.

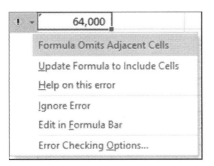

Lesson 2-5: Enter data into a range and copy data across a range

Now that you have mastered the technique of selecting cells, you can use it to speed up data entry.

When you select a range of cells prior to entering data, Excel knows that all data entered belongs in that range. Several key combinations are then available to greatly speed up data entry.

1   Open a new workbook and save it as *Data Range Test*.

2   Select cells B2:D4.

> You learned how to do this in: *Lesson 2-4: Select a range of cells and understand Smart Tags.*

3   Type: **London.**

> The text appears in Cell B2, the top left cell in the range selected.

4   Press the **<Enter>** Key.

> The cursor moves to cell B3 as it normally would.

5   Type: **Paris** followed by the **<Enter>** key.

> The cursor moves to cell B4 as it normally would.

6   Type: **New York** followed by the **<Enter>** key.

> This time something new happens. The cursor doesn't move to cell B5 as you might expect but jumps to cell C2.

7   Type: **150,000** followed by the **<Enter>** key.

> The value appears in C2 and Excel moves down the column again to cell C3.

8 Press the **<Enter>** key without entering a value to leave C3 blank.

Excel moves down the column to cell C4.

9 Type **225,000** followed by the **<Enter>** key.

The cursor jumps to cell D2.

10 Press **<Shift>+<Enter>** twice to change your mind about leaving the value for Paris blank.

1. Press **<Shift>+<Enter>** to move backwards to the value for New York.

2. Press **<Shift>+<Enter>** a second time and you are back to the Paris cell.

	A	B	C	D	E
1					
2		London	150,000		
3		Paris			
4		New York	225,000		
5					

11 Type **180,000** followed by the **<Tab>** key.

<Tab> moves you across the range, to cell D3.

	A	B	C	D	E
1					
2		London	150,000		
3		Paris	180,000		
4		New York	225,000		
5					

You can now appreciate how to use the technique of <Enter>, <Tab>, <Shift>+<Tab> and <Shift>+<Enter> to save a lot of time when entering a whole table of data.

12 Select cells D2:D4.

13 Type **50%** but don't press the <Enter> or <Tab> keys.

The challenge this time is to place the same value into cells D3 and D4 without having to type the value two more times.

14 Press **<Ctrl>+<Enter>.**

The value is replicated into all of the other cells in the selected range.

	A	B	C	D	E
1					
2		London	150,000	50%	
3		Paris	180,000	50%	
4		New York	225,000	50%	
5					

Lesson 2-6: Select adjacent and non-adjacent rows and columns

1 Open *First Quarter Sales and Profit-4* from your sample files folder (if it isn't already open).

2 Select all of column A.

Hover the mouse cursor over the letter **A** at the top of the column. The column header lights up and the mouse cursor changes to a black down arrow:

Click to select the entire column. The column becomes slightly shaded and a green line surrounds all of the cells.

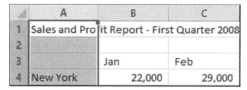

3 Click: Home→Font→Bold to bold face the column.

Because the whole column was selected, all of the values become bold faced.

	A	B	C	D	E
1	Sales and Profit Report - First Quarter 2008				
2					
3		Jan	Feb	Mar	Total
4	New York	22,000	29,000	19,000	70,000
5	Los Angeles	42,000	39,000	43,000	
6	London	18,000	20,000	22,000	

4 Click: Home→Font→Bold once more to change the type in column A back to normal.

5 Select all of row 4.

1. Hover the mouse cursor over the number on the left hand side of row 4. The button lights up and the mouse cursor changes to a black arrow pointing across the row:

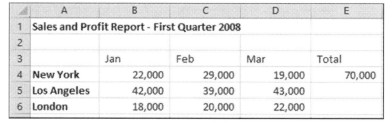

2. Click to select the row.

6 Select columns B and C.

Hover the mouse cursor over the letter at the top of column B until you see the black down arrow. When you see the arrow, click and drag to the right to select columns B and C.

First Quarter Sales and Profit-4

	A	B	C	D
1	Sales and Profit Report - First Quarter 2008			
2				
3		Jan	Feb	Mar
4	New York	22,000	29,000	19,000

7 Select rows 6 and 7.

1. Hover over the number at the left of row 6 until you see the black arrow pointing across the row.

2. When you see the arrow, click and drag down to row 7 to select both rows.

5	Los Angeles	42,000	39,000
6	London	18,000	20,000
7	Paris	35,000	26,000

8 Select columns A, B, C, D and E without dragging the mouse.

Sometimes you will need to select a large number of adjacent columns or rows. You could drag across them, but it is often easier to use the following technique:

1. Select Column A.

2. Hold down the **<Shift>** key.

3. Select Column E.

Columns A to E are selected.

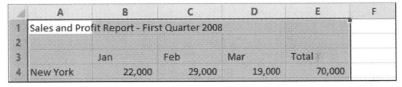

	A	B	C	D	E	F
1	Sales and Profit Report - First Quarter 2008					
2						
3		Jan	Feb	Mar	Total	
4	New York	22,000	29,000	19,000	70,000	

9 Select rows 4 and 6.

Perhaps you need to perform an operation on two non-adjacent rows. To select rows 4 and 6 you need to:

1. Select row 4.

2. Hold down the **<Ctrl>** key on the keyboard.

3. Select Row 6.

		Jan	Feb	Mar
3		Jan	Feb	Mar
4	New York	22,000	29,000	19,000
5	Los Angeles	42,000	39,000	43,000
6	London	18,000	20,000	22,000
7	Paris	35,000	26,000	31,000

Lesson 2-7: Select non-contiguous cell ranges and view summary information

Non-contiguous is a very impressive word! It simply means a range of cells that is split across two or more blocks of cells in different parts of the worksheet.

Non-contiguous ranges can be selected using both the mouse and keyboard. The keyboard method may seem a little involved at first but you'll find it much faster once you have the hang of it.

1   Open *First Quarter Sales and Profit-4* from your sample files folder (if it isn't already open).

2   Select the contiguous range B4:D8 with the keyboard.

When you need to select a contiguous range with the keyboard here's how it's done:

1. Use the arrow keys on the keyboard to navigate to cell B4.

2. Hold down the **<Shift>** key on the keyboard

3. Still holding the **<Shift>** key down, use the arrow keys on the keyboard to navigate to cell D8

The contiguous range B4:D8 is selected.

	A	B	C	D	E
1	Sales and Profit Report - First Quarter 2008				
2					
3		Jan	Feb	Mar	Total
4	New York	22,000	29,000	19,000	70,000
5	Los Angeles	42,000	39,000	43,000	
6	London	18,000	20,000	22,000	
7	Paris	35,000	26,000	31,000	
8	Munich	12,000	15,000	13,000	
9	USA Sales	64,000			

3   Select the non-contiguous range B4:B8,D4:D8 using the mouse.

1. Select the range B4:B8 using the mouse.

2. Hold down the **<Ctrl>** key and select the range D4:D8 using the mouse.

The non-contiguous range **B4:B8,D4:D8** is selected:

	A	B	C	D	E
3		Jan	Feb	Mar	Total
4	New York	22,000	29,000	19,000	70,000
5	Los Angeles	42,000	39,000	43,000	
6	London	18,000	20,000	22,000	
7	Paris	35,000	26,000	31,000	
8	Munich	12,000	15,000	13,000	
9	USA Sales	64,000			

First Quarter Sales and Profit-4

4 Select the same non-contiguous range with the keyboard.

This is a little more involved than using the simple **<Shift>+<Arrow keys>** method used earlier.

Here's how it's done:

1. Use the arrow keys on the keyboard to navigate to cell B4

2. Press the **<F8>** key (it is on the very top row of your keyboard)

3. Use the arrow keys to navigate to cell B8

4. Press **<Shift>+<F8>**

5. Use the arrow keys to navigate to cell D4

6. Press **<F8>**

7. Use the arrow keys to navigate to cell D8

8. Press **<Shift>+<F8>**

The non-contiguous range B4:B8,D4:D8 is selected:

	A	B	C	D	E
3		Jan	Feb	Mar	Total
4	New York	22,000	29,000	19,000	70,000
5	Los Angeles	42,000	39,000	43,000	
6	London	18,000	20,000	22,000	
7	Paris	35,000	26,000	31,000	
8	Munich	12,000	15,000	13,000	
9	USA Sales	64,000			

5 Obtain a total sales figures for January and March using the status bar.

The status bar contains summary information for the currently selected range.

Look at the bottom right of your screen. You can see the average sales and total sales (sum of sales) for January and March:

AVERAGE: 25,700   COUNT: 10   SUM: 257,000

6 View the maximum and minimum sales for January and March using the status bar.

Right-click the status bar and click *Maximum* and *Minimum* on the pop-up menu (see sidebar).

The status bar now also displays maximum and minimum values.

AVERAGE: 25,700   COUNT: 10   MIN: 12,000   MAX: 43,000   SUM: 257,000

7 Close the workbook without saving.

Lesson 2-8: AutoSelect a range of cells

When data is arranged in a block (as it is in the Sales Report used in this lesson) it is referred to as a *Range*.

You will often want to select a row or column of cells within a range, or even the entire range.

You can select ranges by using any of the techniques covered so far but this could be very time consuming if the range encompassed hundreds, or even thousands, of rows and columns.

In this lesson you'll learn how to select range rows, range columns and entire ranges with a few clicks of the mouse.

1 Open *Sales Report* from your sample files folder.

This report contains a single block of cells in the range A3 to E19.

2 Select all cells within the range to the right of cell A7.

1. Click in cell A7 to make it the active cell.

2. Hover over the right hand border of cell A7 until you see the four headed arrow cursor shape.

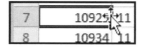

3. When you see this cursor shape hold down the **<Shift>** key and double-click.

All cells to the right of A7, but within the range, are selected.

| 7 | 10929 | 11 March 2008 | Frankenversand | Germany | 1,380.33 |

3 Select all cells within the range except the header row.

1. Click in cell A4 to make it the active cell.

Sales Report

---

note

Other ways to AutoSelect a range

Using the keyboard

Here's how you would select the entire range in the Weekly Sales Report (excluding the header row) using the keyboard method.

Make cell A4 the active cell by navigating to it with the <Arrow> keys.

1. Press: <Ctrl>+<Shift>+ <DownArrow>

   Cells A4:A19 are selected.

2. Press: <Ctrl>+<Shift>+ <RightArrow>

   The entire range (excluding the header row) is selected.

Using shortcut keys

The shortcut keys method is the fastest way to select the entire range *including* the header row.

1. Click anywhere inside the range.

2. Press: <Ctrl>+<A>

   The entire range (including the header row) is selected.

From the Ribbon

The Ribbon method isn't as powerful as the other methods but does provide a way to select the current range (described as the *region* in the dialog).

Make sure that the active cell is within the range.

1. Click:

   Home→Editing→ Find & Select→ GoTo Special...

   The *GoTo Special* dialog is displayed.

2. Click the *Current Region* option button and then click the OK button.

The entire range (including the header row) is selected.

2. Hover over the right hand border of cell A4 until you see the four headed arrow cursor shape.

3. When you see this cursor shape hold down the <Shift> key and double-click.

   All cells to the right of cell A4, but within the range, are selected.

4. Hover over the bottom border of the selected cells until you see the four headed arrow cursor shape.

5. When you see this cursor shape hold down the <Shift> key and double-click.

The entire range (except the header row) is selected.

You can also use this technique to select cells to the left of the active cell or above the active cell.

4   Close the workbook without saving.

Lesson 2-9: Re-size rows and columns

1 Open *First Quarter Sales and Profit-4* from your sample files folder (if it isn't already open).

Notice that columns B, C, D and E are far too wide for their contents. It would be useful to make them narrower to keep the worksheet compact.

2 Re-size column B so that it is just wide enough to contain the January sales figures.

Hover over the line separating the letters B and C until you see the *re-size* cursor shape:

When you see this shape, keep the mouse still and then click and drag to the left. Column B will re-size as you drag. Make it narrower so that the values just fit in the column. Notice that the column width in points and pixels are displayed as you drag (one point = 1/72 inch).

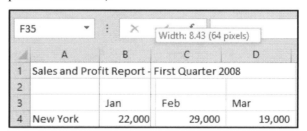

3 Re-size column B so that it is too narrow to contain the January sales figures.

Notice that when the column isn't wide enough to contain the contents, hash signs are shown instead of values (if you're used to hashes being called **pound signs** or **number signs** see the sidebar).

	A	B	C	D
1	Sales and Profit Report - First Quarter 2008			
2				
3		Jan	Feb	Mar
4	New York	#####	29,000	19,000

4 Automatically re-size column B so that it is a perfect fit for the widest cell in the column.

1. Hover over the line separating the letters B and C until you see the re-size cursor shape:

2. When you see this shape, double-click to automatically re-size column B.

5 Automatically re-size every column in the worksheet in one operation.

First Quarter Sales and Profit-4

note

Other ways to re-size rows and columns

You can also re-size rows and columns using the Ribbon.

Click: Home→Cells→Format.

A drop-down menu appears.

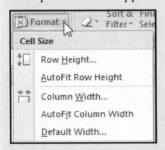

You can use the *Row Height* and *Column Width* options to set the row or column to a specific number of points (a point is 1/72 of an inch).

You can also use the *AutoFit Row Height* and *AutoFit Column Width* options to automatically size the row or column (you achieved this more efficiently with a double-click in the lesson).

Default Width... often confuses as it doesn't appear to work. This is because it re-sets all columns to default width *except those that have already been re-sized.*

note

Making several columns or rows the same size

Sometimes you will want to make several columns exactly the same width.

To do this, select the multiple columns and then click and drag the intersection of any of the selected columns.

When the mouse button is released, this will make each of the selected columns exactly the same width.

1. Select every cell in the worksheet by clicking the *select all* button in the top left corner of the worksheet (you can also do this by clicking in any blank cell and then pressing **<Ctrl>+<A>**).

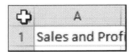

2. Hover over the intersection of any two columns until you see the re-size cursor shape and then double-click.

   Every column is now perfectly sized.

   Notice that Auto-resize has done its job rather too well. Column A is now wide enough to accommodate all of the text in cell A1.

	A	B
1	Sales and Profit Report - First Quarter 2008	

6 Automatically re-size column A so that it is only wide enough to contain the longest city name (Los Angeles).

1. Select cells A4:A9.

2. Click: Home→Cells→Format→AutoFit Column Width.

This time the column is automatically sized so that it is wide enough to contain all of the text in the selected cells.

	A	B	C	D	E
1	Sales and Profit Report - First Quarter 2008				
2					
3		Jan	Feb	Mar	Total
4	New York	22,000	29,000	19,000	70,000
5	Los Angeles	42,000	39,000	43,000	

Notice that the text has spilled over from cell A1 into the adjoining columns B, C, D and E. This always happens when a cell contains text and the adjacent cells are empty.

7 Manually size row 3 so that it is about twice as tall as the other rows.

Do this in exactly the same way you re-sized the column but, this time, hover between the intersection of rows 3 and 4 until you see the re-size cursor shape, and then click and drag downwards.

1	Sales and Profit Report - First Quarter 2008			
2	Height: 30.00 (40 pixels)			
		Jan	Feb	Mar
3	New York	22,000	29,000	19,000
4	Los Angeles	42,000	39,000	43,000

8 Auto-resize row 3 so that it is the same size as the other rows again.

1. Hover over the line separating the numbers 3 and 4 until you see the re-size cursor shape.

2. When you see this shape, double-click to automatically re-size row 3.

9 Close Excel without saving.

Lesson 2-10: Use AutoSum to sum a non-contiguous range

In: *Lesson 2-7: Select non-contiguous cell ranges and view summary information,* you learned how to view the sum of January and March sales using the status bar. But how can you put that value onto the worksheet?

Now that you have the hang of selecting non-contiguous ranges you can use this skill in conjunction with your AutoSum skills to create a formula that will calculate the total of a non-contiguous range.

1   Open *First Quarter Sales and Profit*-4 from your sample files folder (if it isn't already open).

2   Enter the text **Jan/Mar Sales** in cell A10 and press the <Tab> key.

The active cell moves to cell B10.

3   Re-size column A so that it is wide enough to contain the text.

1.   Hover over the line separating the letters A and B until you see the re-size cursor shape:

A	✛	B

2.   When you see this shape, keep the mouse still and then click and drag to the right. Column A will re-size as you drag. Make it wider so that the words *Jan/Mar Sales* comfortably fit in the column:

3		Jan	Feb	Mar
4	New York	22,000	29,000	19,000
5	Los Angeles	42,000	39,000	43,000
6	London	18,000	20,000	22,000
7	Paris	35,000	26,000	31,000
8	Munich	12,000	15,000	13,000
9	USA Sales	64,000		
10	Jan/Mar Sales			

4   Use AutoSum to calculate the total sales for January and March in cell B10.

1.   Click Home→Editing→ (the AutoSum button).

An AutoSum appears in cell B10 but it isn't anything like what we want yet. AutoSum guesses that we simply want to repeat the value in the USA Sales cell.

8	Munich	12,000	15,000	13,000
9	USA Sales	64,000		
10	Jan/Mar Sales	=SUM(B9)		
11		SUM(**number1**, [number2], ...)		

2.   Select the range B4:B8 with the mouse.

3.   Hold down the <Ctrl> key and select the range D4:D8 with the mouse.

First Quarter Sales and Profit-4

Notice that the non-contiguous range **B4:B8,D4:D8** is shown in the AutoSum's formula:

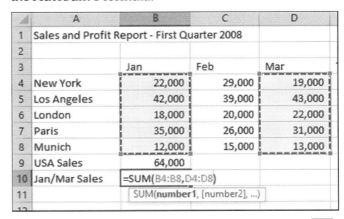

4. Press the **<Enter>** key or click the AutoSum button 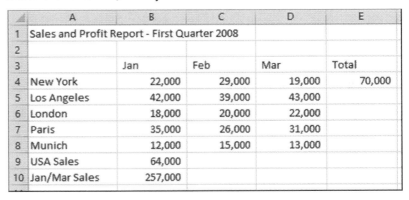 again to show the sales for January and March in cell B10.

	A	B	C	D	E
1	Sales and Profit Report - First Quarter 2008				
2					
3		Jan	Feb	Mar	Total
4	New York	22,000	29,000	19,000	70,000
5	Los Angeles	42,000	39,000	43,000	
6	London	18,000	20,000	22,000	
7	Paris	35,000	26,000	31,000	
8	Munich	12,000	15,000	13,000	
9	USA Sales	64,000			
10	Jan/Mar Sales	257,000			

5   Save your work as *First Quarter Sales and Profit-5*.

Lesson 2-11: Use AutoSum to quickly calculate averages

Excel's *AutoSum* feature isn't only restricted to addition. It is also able to compute averages and maximum/minimum values.

In this lesson we'll use AutoSum to calculate the average sales for each month.

1   Open *First Quarter Sales and Profit 5* from your sample files folder (If it isn't already open).

2   Delete cells E3:E4.

Select cells E3 and E4 and press the **<Delete>** key on your keyboard.

3   Type the word *Average* in cell E3 and press the **<Enter>** key.

The cursor moves to cell E4:

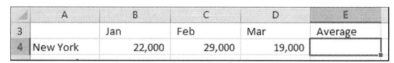

	A	B	C	D	E
3		Jan	Feb	Mar	Average
4	New York	22,000	29,000	19,000	

4   Use AutoSum to create a formula that will show the average New York sales in cell E4.

    1. Click: Home→Editing→AutoSum →Drop down arrow (see sidebar).

    A drop down menu is displayed showing all of the different ways in which AutoSum can operate upon a range of cells:

    2. Click *Average*.

    3. Excel generates an Average function and inserts the cell range B4:D4. This is exactly what we want:

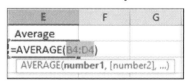

E	F	G
Average		
=AVERAGE(B4:D4)		
AVERAGE(**number1**, [number2], ...)		

    4. Press the **<Enter>** key or click the AutoSum button ∑ again to see the average sales for New York:

3		Jan	Feb	Mar	Average
4	New York	22,000	29,000	19,000	23,333

5   Type the word: **Maximum** into Cell F3 and then press the **<Enter>** key.

6   Use AutoSum to create a formula in cell F4 that will show the Maximum New York Sales for this period.

    1. Place an AutoSum in cell F4 but this time, choose *Max* from the drop-down menu.

Click Here

∑ ▾ A↓Z ▾ 🔍
⬇
    Sort & Find &
✎ ▾ Filter ▾ Select ▾
Editing

∑ ▾ A ▾ 🔍
∑ Sum
   Average
   Count Numbers
   Max
   Min
   More Functions...

First Quarter Sales and Profit-5

This time we have a small problem. AutoSum is including the average value (23,333) in the calculation.

B	C	D	E	F
Jan	Feb	Mar	Average	Maximum
22,000	29,000	19,000	23,333	=MAX(B4:E4)

2. Select cells B4:D4 with the mouse

The marquee corrects and the average value in cell E4 is no longer included.

3		Jan	Feb	Mar	Average	Maximum
4	New York	22,000	29,000	19,000	23,333	=MAX(B4:D4)

Notice that the MAX function is now working with the range B4:D4.

3. Press the **<Enter>** key or click the AutoSum button Σ once more to see the maximum sales the New York office managed during the first quarter of the year:

3		Jan	Feb	Mar	Average	Maximum
4	New York	22,000	29,000	19,000	23,333	29,000

7 Change the words *USA Sales* in cell A9 back to *Sales* and press the **<Tab>** key.

8 Press the **<F2>** key on the keyboard (or double-click cell B9) to bring back the marquee (shown as a blue box).

9 Adjust the marquee using click and drag so that all offices are included in the Sales total.

Notice that there is a small blue spot on each corner of the range. These are called *sizing handles*.

1. Hover the mouse cursor over the bottom right (or bottom left) sizing handle until the cursor shape changes to a double headed arrow. It is really important that you see the double headed arrow and not the four headed arrow or white cross.

4	New York	22,000
5	Los Angeles	42,000

2. When you see the double headed arrow click and drag with the mouse down to cell B8.

3. Release the mouse button.

4. Press the **<Enter>** key or click the AutoSum button again.

	A	B
3		Jan
4	New York	22,000
5	Los Angeles	42,000
6	London	18,000
7	Paris	35,000
8	Munich	12,000
9	Sales	129,000
10	Jan/Mar Sales	257,000

10 Save your work as *First Quarter Sales and Profit-6.*

tip

Another way to bring back the blue box showing a range is to click the range in the *Formula Bar.*

Lesson 2-12: Create your own formulas

The AutoSum tool is very useful for quickly inserting SUM(), AVERAGE(), COUNT(), MAX() and MIN() formulas into cells. Many Excel users never get any further with their formulas than this.

In this session you'll create your own formulas without the use of AutoSum. You'll be amazed at how easy it is.

1   Open *First Quarter Sales and Profit*-6 from your sample files folder (if it isn't already open).

2   Select cells A10:B10 and press the **<Delete>** key once.

The previous contents of cells A10:B10 are removed.

3   Type the word **Costs** into cell A11 and **Profit** into cell A12.

4   Type the value **83,000** into cell B11 and press the **<Enter>** key to move down to cell B12.

11	Costs	83,000
12	Profit	

5   Enter a formula into cell B12 to compute the profit made in January.

    1.   Type: **=B9-B11** into cell B12.

    2.   Press the **<Enter>** key.

The profit for January is displayed:

9	Sales	129,000
10		
11	Costs	83,000
12	Profit	46,000

6   Enter the formula again using the mouse to select cell references.

The method that you have just used to enter the formula works just fine but it isn't the best method. Sooner or later you will make a mistake. For example you could easily type **=B8-B11** resulting in an incorrect answer.

To eliminate such errors you should always select cell references visually rather than simply type them in. You can visually select cells using either the mouse or the keyboard. First we'll use the mouse method.

    1.   Click in cell B12 and press the **<Delete>** key on the keyboard to clear the old formula.

    2.   Press the equals <=> key on the keyboard.

    3.   Click once on the value 129,000 in cell B9.

    4.   Press the minus <-> key on the keyboard.

First Quarter Sales and Profit-6

5.   Click once on the value 83,000 in cell B11.

6.   Press the **<Enter>** key on the keyboard.

If you followed the above steps carefully you will see that you have created the same formula but with a much lower possibility of making a mistake.

7   Enter the formula again using the visual keyboard technique.

The very best Excel experts hardly use the mouse. You waste valuable seconds every time you reach for the mouse.

Here's the expert technique of visual selection via keyboard:

1.   Use the arrow keys to navigate to cell B12 and then press the **<Delete>** key on the keyboard to clear the old formula.

2.   Press the **<=>** key on the keyboard.

3.   Press the **<Up Arrow>** key three times to move to cell B9.

4.   Press the **<->** key on the keyboard.

5.   Press the **<Up Arrow>** key once to move to cell B11.

6.   Press the **<Enter>** key on the keyboard.

8   Enter a formula that uses the multiplication operator.

This employer is very generous and pays the staff ten percent of all profits as an incentive bonus.

In cell A13 type the words: **10% Bonus** and then press the **<Tab>** key on the keyboard to move to cell B13.

9   Enter a formula that uses the multiplication operator.

The multiplication operator is not an X as you might expect but an asterisk (*). The other Excel operators are shown in the sidebar.

You need to press **<Shift>+<8>** to enter an asterisk. If you are using a full size keyboard with a numeric keypad at the right-hand side you can also use the numeric keypad's **<*>** key.

Whichever key you use you'll still see an asterisk in the formula.

Use either the *mouse selection* technique or the *visual keyboard* technique to enter the formula shown below into cell B13 and then press the **<Enter>** key to see how much bonus was earned:

	A	B
11	Costs	83,000
12	Profit	46,000
13	10% Bonus	=B12*0.1

Note that multiplying a value by 0.1 calculates ten percent of the value. You'll learn more about calculating percentages later, in: *Lesson 4-3: Format numbers using built-in number formats.*

	A	B
11	Costs	83,000
12	Profit	46,000
13	10% Bonus	4,600

10   Save your work as *First Quarter Sales and Profit-7.*

The Excel Operators

	Name	Example
+	Addition	1+2
-	Subtraction	7-5
*	Multiplication	6*3
/	Division	15/5
%	Percent	25%
^	Exponentiation	4^2

note

Excel automatically adds closing brackets to functions

If you type:

=SUM(B4:B5

... and then press the **<Enter>** key, Excel will automatically add the closing bracket for you resulting in:

=SUM(B4:B5)

First Quarter Sales and Profit-7

Lesson 2-13: Create functions using Formula AutoComplete

1 Open *First Quarter Sales and Profit*-7 from your sample files folder (if it isn't already open).

2 Type the words **USA Sales** into cell A15 and **European Sales** into cell A16.

Notice that the text *European Sales* spills over into column B because column A isn't wide enough to contain it.

3 Re-size column A so that it is wide enough for the words *European Sales* to fit within the column.

You learned how to do this in: *Lesson 2-9: Re-size rows and columns.*

4 Click into cell B15 and type **=S** into the cell.

Something amazing happens:

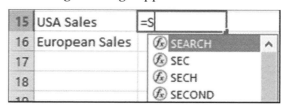

A list drops down showing every function in the Excel function library beginning with S. This feature is called *Formula AutoComplete* (if AutoComplete didn't display as expected see the facing-page sidebar).

You've already encountered the SUM(), AVERAGE() and MAX() functions courtesy of AutoSum.

You may be pleased (or dismayed) to know that there are over 300 functions in the Excel function library. The good news is that most untrained Excel users only ever get to understand SUM() and AVERAGE()!

When you typed =S Excel listed all functions beginning with S.

5 Continue typing: **=SU**.

Notice that the list now only shows functions beginning with SU and look... there's the *SUM()* function you need three down in the list.

You could simply click on it with the mouse but let's work like an Excel pro and do it with the keyboard.

6 Press the **<Down Arrow>** key twice to move the cursor over the SUM function.

The Sum function now has a tip telling you what the function does:

note

Enabling and disabling AutoComplete

As with so many other features, Microsoft allows you to turn this very useful feature off.

You'd never want to do this but you may work on a machine that has had Formula AutoComplete switched off and you need to turn it on again.

Click: File→Options→Formulas and make sure that the *Formula AutoComplete* box is checked.

note

The syntax box

The Syntax box tells you which arguments (sometimes called parameters) the function needs.

SUM(**number1**, [number2], ...)

The first argument has no square brackets meaning that you can't leave it out.

The second argument (shown in square brackets) is optional.

The third argument is an ellipsis (a row of three dots). This means that you could continue with more arguments such as [number3], [number4] etc.

For such a simple function as SUM() the syntax box is hardly needed but later you'll encounter functions that require several arguments and then the syntax box will be invaluable.

| 15 | USA Sales | 64,000 |
| 16 | European Sales | 65,000 |

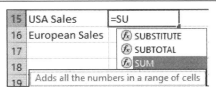

7 Display detailed information about the SUM() function.

The tip tells you a little about the SUM() function but to get the full story press the **<F1>** key while SUM is still highlighted in the dropdown list.

The Excel help system opens showing detailed help for the SUM() function.

Read the help text if you are interested and then close the help window.

Notice that Excel has now left you with only =SU in the cell. Complete the formula by typing **M(**

| 15 | USA Sales | =SUM(|
| 16 | European Sales | SUM(**number1**, [number2], ...) |

Notice that a little box has appeared beneath the function. This box displays the *Syntax* of the SUM function (see sidebar for more information).

8 Select the cells that you need to sum (cells B4:B5) with the mouse or keyboard.

If you want to be a real pro you should select them with the keyboard. To do this:

1. Press the **<Up Arrow>** key repeatedly until you reach cell B4.

2. Hold down the **<Shift>** key and press the **<Down Arrow>** key once to select cells B4:B5.

9 Type a closing bracket to complete the formula and then press the <Enter> key.

The total USA sales are displayed in cell B15.

10 Use the same technique to create a SUM() function in cell B16 to show the total European sales (cells B6:B8).

1. Click in cell B16.

2. Type = **SU.**

3. Press the **<Down Arrow>** key twice to move the cursor over the SUM function.

4. Press the **<Tab>** key to automatically enter the SUM function into cell B16.

5. Select the range B6:B8.

6. Type the closing bracket (this isn't actually necessary – see sidebar facing page).

7. Press the **<Enter>** key.

The formula should now be: **=SUM(B6:B8).**

11 Save your work as *First Quarter Sales and Profit 8.*

Lesson 2-14: Use AutoFill for text and numeric series

1   Open *First Quarter Sales and Profit-8* from your sample files folder (if it isn't already open).

2   Delete the text **Feb** and **Mar** from cells C3:D3.

Select cells C3:D3 and then press the **<Delete>** key on your keyboard.

3   Make B3 the active cell.

Notice that there is a green border around the cell and a spot on the bottom right-hand corner. This is the AutoFill handle. If you don't see it, refer to the sidebar.

note

If you don't see the AutoFill handle somebody has disabled AutoFill

It's almost certain that AutoFill will be enabled on any computer that you work on. It is such a useful feature that you wouldn't want to disable it.

If you don't see the AutoFill handle (the black spot on the bottom right hand corner of the active cell) it's because somebody has switched AutoFill off.

To bring it back click:

File→Options→Advanced

In the first section (*Editing Options*) check the box next to *Enable fill handle and cell drag and drop*.

4   Hover over the AutoFill handle with your mouse until the cursor shape changes to a black cross.

Many of my students have great difficulty with this when they try it for the first time.

- You don't want the four-headed arrow: – that would move the cell.

- You don't want the white cross: – that would select the cell.

- You want the black cross: – the AutoFill cursor.

5   When the black cross cursor is visible, hold down the mouse button and drag your mouse to the right to AutoFill the other months: **Feb** and **Mar**.

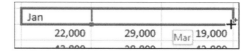

Notice the tip that appears as you drag, previewing the month that will appear in each cell.

When you release the mouse button, the name of each month appears in cells C3 and D3.

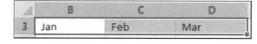

6   Type: **Monday** into cell A18 and AutoFill down to cell A24 to show the days of the week.

(If you are not using an English language version of Excel you will need to type **Monday** in your own language).

First Quarter Sales and Profit-8

7   In cell B18 type the number **1** and in cell B19 type the number **2**.

8   Select cells B18 and B19.

9   AutoFill down to B24 to create sequential numbers:

	A	B
18	Monday	1
19	Tuesday	2
20	Wednesday	3

10   In cell C18 type **9** and in cell C19 type **18**.

11   Select cells C18 and C19.

12   AutoFill down to B24 to create the nine times table.

	A	B	C
18	Monday	1	9
19	Tuesday	2	18
20	Wednesday	3	27

13   Use AutoFill to create sequential dates.

   1.   Type 01-Jan-08 into cell D18.

   2.   Type 02-Jan-08 into cell D19.

   3.   Select Cells D18:D19.

   4.   AutoFill down to D24 to create sequential dates.

14   Use AutoFill to quickly copy text.

Sometimes you will want to duplicate the value from one cell into many others to the right of, left of, beneath, or above the active cell.

When a cell containing text is the active cell and it isn't defined as a *fill series* (the built-in fill series are days of the week and months of the year), AutoFill will simply duplicate the contents of the cell.

Type the text **Adjusted** into cell E18 and then AutoFill it down as far as cell E24.

The same text is now shown in each of the cells:

	A	B	C	D	E
18	Monday	1	9	01-Jan-08	Adjusted
19	Tuesday	2	18	02-Jan-08	Adjusted
20	Wednesday	3	27	03-Jan-08	Adjusted
21	Thursday	4	36	04-Jan-08	Adjusted
22	Friday	5	45	05-Jan-08	Adjusted
23	Saturday	6	54	06-Jan-08	Adjusted
24	Sunday	7	63	07-Jan-08	Adjusted

15   Save your work as *First Quarter Sales and Profit-9*.

Lesson 2-15: Use AutoFill to adjust formulas

AutoFill can save you a lot of time when extending or copying text and number sequences. But the story's not over yet.

AutoFill's ability to copy and adjust formulas is one of the most powerful tools in Excel's impressive armory.

1 Open *First Quarter Sales and Profit 9* from your sample files folder (If it isn't already open).

2 Consider the formula in cell B9.

Click onto cell B9 and view the formula displayed in the formula bar (the formula bar is at the top right of the screen grab below).

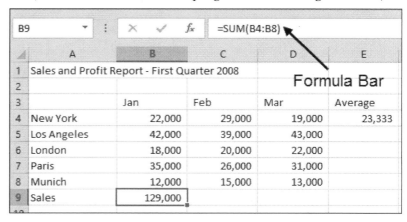

The formula is **=SUM(B4:B8).** AutoSum created it for us in: *Lesson 2-3: Use AutoSum to quickly calculate totals.* The formula uses the SUM() function to add together the values in the range B4:B8.

Think about the formula that would work in cell C9 (the total sales for February). It would be: **=SUM(C4:C8).** Similarly the formula that would work in cell D9 (the total sales for March) would be **=SUM(D4:D8).**

As we move to the right, all that is needed is to increment the letter for each cell reference in the formula and we'll get the right answer every time.

AutoFill is very clever and realizes this. When we AutoFill a cell containing a formula to the right, AutoFill increments the letters in each cell reference.

Most of the time that is exactly what we want.

Later, in *Lesson 3-12: Understand absolute and relative cell references,* and *Lesson 3-13: Understand mixed cell references* you'll learn how to fine-tune the way in which AutoFill adjusts cell references. This will allow you to implement some more advanced AutoFill techniques.

3 AutoFill cell B9 to the right as far as cell D9.

You learned how to do this in: *Lesson 2-14: Use AutoFill for text and numeric series.*

First Quarter Sales and Profit-9

You may see a row of hashes in Cell C9. This is because the value may be too wide to fit in the cell. If this is the case, AutoFit the column using the skills learned in: *Lesson 2-9: Re-size rows and columns.*

The correct answers for *Feb* and *Mar* sales are shown on the worksheet. Click on the *Feb* total cell (C9) and look at the formula in the formula bar.

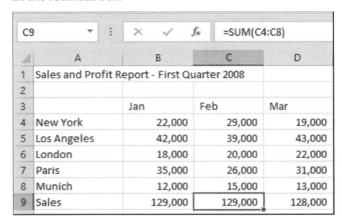

You can see that AutoFill has done its job perfectly, creating the sum of the values in cells C4:C8. Our five branches have sold exactly the same amount in both January and February, but a little less in March.

4   Consider the formula in cell E4.

Click onto cell E4 and view the formula displayed in the formula bar.

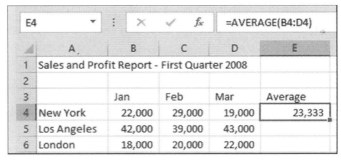

The formula is **=AVERAGE(B4:D4)**. AutoSum created it for us in: *Lesson 2-11: Use AutoSum to quickly calculate averages.*

Think about the formula that would work in cell E5 (the average sales for Los Angeles). It would be: **=AVERAGE(B5:D5)**. Similarly the formula that would work in cell E6 (the total sales for London) would be **=AVERAGE(B6:D6)**.

As we move downward, all that is needed is to increment the number for each cell reference in the formula. This is exactly what AutoFill will do.

E	F
Average	Maximum
23,333	29,000
41,333	43,000
20,000	22,000
30,667	35,000
13,333	15,000

5   AutoFill cell E4 down to E8 to see the Average sales for each branch.

6   AutoFill cell F4 down to F8 to view the maximum sales for each branch.

7   Save your work as *First Quarter Sales and Profit-10.*

Lesson 2-16: Use AutoFill options

Sometimes AutoFill begins to misbehave and actually gets in the way of efficient work by wrongly anticipating what you need.

1   Open *First Quarter Sales and Profit-10* from your sample files folder (If it isn't already open).

2   Populate cells F18 to F24 with sequential dates beginning with 1-Jan-09 using AutoFill.

     1.   In cell F18 type the date: **1-Jan-09**

     2.   AutoFill cell F18 down as far as cell F24.

     The cells are populated with sequential dates:

◢	A	B	C	D	E	F
18	Monday	1	9	01-Jan-08	Adjusted	01-Jan-09
19	Tuesday	2	18	02-Jan-08	Adjusted	02-Jan-09
20	Wednesday	3	27	03-Jan-08	Adjusted	03-Jan-09
21	Thursday	4	36	04-Jan-08	Adjusted	04-Jan-09
22	Friday	5	45	05-Jan-08	Adjusted	05-Jan-09
23	Saturday	6	54	06-Jan-08	Adjusted	06-Jan-09
24	Sunday	7	63	07-Jan-08	Adjusted	07-Jan-09

3   Populate cells G18 to G24 with the date *31-Mar-09* using the AutoFill Smart Tag.

     1.   In cell G18 type the date: **31-Mar-09.**

     2.   AutoFill down as far as cell G24.

     At some time you'll need to add transaction dates to a worksheet and will have four or five entries with the same date.

     AutoFill is perfect for eliminating the need to re-type the date for each transaction, but its insistence upon incrementing the date every time could be very frustrating.

     Fortunately we can change the default behavior.

     3.   Click the Auto Fill Options Smart Tag 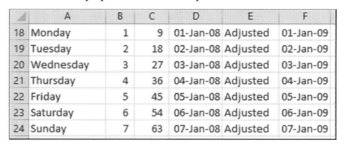 at the bottom right corner of the filled cells.

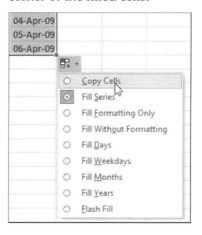

First Quarter Sales and Profit-10

4. Click *Copy Cells* to tell AutoFill not to increment the date.

4 Understand AutoFill options.

The *Fill Formatting* options will be covered later in: *Session Four: Making Your Worksheets Look Professional*.

Flash Fill will be introduced later in: *Lesson 2-18: Use automatic Flash Fill to split delimited text*. Here's what the other options will do:

Copy Cells	Fill Series	Fill Days	Fill Weekdays	Fill Months	Fill Years
This is what we just did. The first cell is copied to the other cells.	The default for dates that include the day. The date increments by one day at a time.	The date increments by one day at a time.	Because 3rd April 2009 is a Friday the weekend days are omitted and the series jumps from 3rd April to 6th April.	Normally this would show the same day number for each month. In this example, there are only 30 days in two of the months so 30th is shown instead of 31st.	The same calendar day is shown for each subsequent year.
31-Mar-09	31-Mar-09	31-Mar-09	31-Mar-09	31-Mar-09	31-Mar-09
31-Mar-09	01-Apr-09	01-Apr-09	01-Apr-09	30-Apr-09	31-Mar-10
31-Mar-09	02-Apr-09	02-Apr-09	02-Apr-09	31-May-09	31-Mar-11
31-Mar-09	03-Apr-09	03-Apr-09	03-Apr-09	30-Jun-09	31-Mar-12
31-Mar-09	04-Apr-09	04-Apr-09	06-Apr-09	31-Jul-09	31-Mar-13
31-Mar-09	05-Apr-09	05-Apr-09	07-Apr-09	31-Aug-09	31-Mar-14
31-Mar-09	06-Apr-09	06-Apr-09	08-Apr-09	30-Sep-09	31-Mar-15

5 Populate cells F18 to F24 with sequential dates using a right-click AutoFill.

1. Click on cell F18 to make it the active cell.

2. AutoFill down to cell F24, but this time hold down the right mouse button.

   When you release the mouse button you are instantly presented with the AutoFill options (see sidebar).

   This method is preferred to the Smart Tag method because it is faster (one click instead of two).

3. Click: *Fill Series* or *Fill Days*.

   In this example *Fill Series* and *Fill Days* produce exactly the same result.

6 Save your work as *First Quarter Sales and Profit-11*.

Copy Cells

Fill Series

Fill Formatting Only

Fill Without Formatting

Fill Days

Fill Weekdays

Fill Months

Fill Years

Linear Trend

Growth Trend

Flash Fill

Series...

Lesson 2-17: Speed up your AutoFills and create a custom fill series

In this lesson we're going to learn some advanced AutoFill techniques that will massively speed up your efficient use of the AutoFill feature.

1   Open *First Quarter Sales and Profit*-11 (if it isn't already open).

2   Use an AutoFill double-click to populate cells G19:G24 with sequential dates.

   1.   Delete the contents of cells G18:G24.

   2.   Type: **31-Mar-09** into cell G18.

	A	B	C	D	E	F	G
17							
18	Monday	1	9	01-Jan-08	Adjusted	01-Jan-09	31-Mar-09
19	Tuesday	2	18	02-Jan-08	Adjusted	02-Jan-09	
20	Wednesday	3	27	03-Jan-08	Adjusted	03-Jan-09	
21	Thursday	4	36	04-Jan-08	Adjusted	04-Jan-09	
22	Friday	5	45	05-Jan-08	Adjusted	05-Jan-09	
23	Saturday	6	54	06-Jan-08	Adjusted	06-Jan-09	
24	Sunday	7	63	07-Jan-08	Adjusted	07-Jan-09	

   3.   Double click the AutoFill handle to automatically fill cells G19:G24.

   Hover over the AutoFill handle (the black spot at the bottom right hand corner of cell G18). When you are sure that you have the correct black cross cursor shape, double click to automatically fill down.

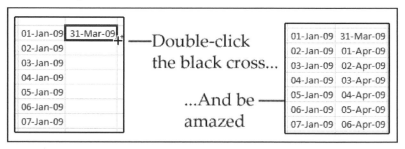

3   Use an *AutoFill <Ctrl>-Drag* to copy the value in cell G18 to cells G19:G24.

   1.   Delete all of the dates from cells G19:G24 leaving only the date *31-Mar-09* in cell G18.

   2.   Click in cell G18 to make it the active cell.

   3.   Hold down the **<Ctrl>** key and AutoFill cell G18 down as far as cell G24 by dragging the AutoFill handle down with the mouse.

   4.   Release the mouse button.

   Because you held the <Ctrl> key down, AutoFill simply copied the cell instead of creating a series of values.

First Quarter Sales and Profit-11

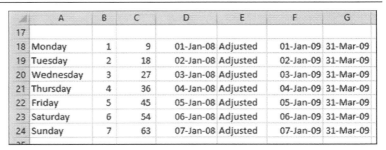

	A	B	C	D	E	F	G
17							
18	Monday	1	9	01-Jan-08	Adjusted	01-Jan-09	31-Mar-09
19	Tuesday	2	18	02-Jan-08	Adjusted	02-Jan-09	31-Mar-09
20	Wednesday	3	27	03-Jan-08	Adjusted	03-Jan-09	31-Mar-09
21	Thursday	4	36	04-Jan-08	Adjusted	04-Jan-09	31-Mar-09
22	Friday	5	45	05-Jan-08	Adjusted	05-Jan-09	31-Mar-09
23	Saturday	6	54	06-Jan-08	Adjusted	06-Jan-09	31-Mar-09
24	Sunday	7	63	07-Jan-08	Adjusted	07-Jan-09	31-Mar-09

This is even faster than using the right-click method when you want to prevent the date incrementing.

4 Create a custom list containing the values: *North, South, East* and *West.*

1. Click: File→Options→Advanced.

2. Scroll down to the *General* category and click the gray *Edit Custom Lists...* button.

Edit Custom Lists...

The *Custom Lists* dialog appears.

3. Click in the *List entries* window and add four custom list entries: **North, South, East** and **West.**

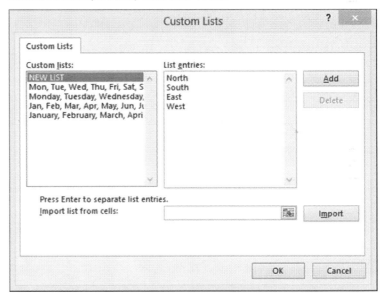

4. Click the OK button and OK again to close the dialogs.

5 Use the newly created custom list.

Type **North** in any cell and AutoFill down.

As you AutoFill, the custom list entries appear in the worksheet (see sidebar).

6 Delete the North, South, East, West... cells from the worksheet.

7 Save your work as *First Quarter Sales and Profit-12.*

note

If Flash Fill doesn't work for you, somebody has switched it off

It's almost certain that Flash Fill will be enabled on any computer that you work on. It is such a useful feature that you wouldn't want to disable it.

If Flash Fill doesn't work, there are two possible explanations:

1. You are using an earlier version of Excel than Excel 2013. Flash fill is a brand new feature for Excel 2013.

2. Somebody has switched Flash Fill off.

To switch it back on click:

File→Options→Advanced

In the first section (*Editing Options*) make sure that the *Automatically Flash Fill* check box is checked.

note

Help Flash Fill to work correctly by formatting header rows differently

You will notice that, in this lesson's sample file, I have bold-faced the header row:

	B	C
3	**First Name**	**Last Name**
4	Jessica	Sagan
5	Stephen	Bell
6	John	Jennings

When Flash Fill sees different formatting in the first row, it will treat this row (correctly) as a header row. Flash Fill then excludes the value in this row from its logic, providing more reliable results.

Employee Names-1

Lesson 2-18: Use automatic Flash Fill to split delimited text

When you place data in cells it is useful to observe an important rule:

"Keep data atomic"

If you strictly observe this rule you'll avoid an enormous number of potential problems.

The rule means that, in the same way that the atom is the smallest basic unit we can divide matter into, each worksheet cell should contain the smallest possible amount of data.

Here's a simple example to illustrate the concept:

	A	B
3	**Name**	
4	Jessica Sagan	
5	Stephen Bell	
6	John Jennings	

Imagine that you want to use the worksheet above to create a mail merge in Word. In this case you'd need the first names in a cell of their own. This would enable you to personalize the mail merge with an introduction such as: *Dear Jessica.*

If you had observed the *keep data atomic* rule, you would have split your data into multiple columns like this:

	B	C
3	**First Name**	**Last Name**
4	Jessica	Sagan
5	Stephen	Bell
6	John	Jennings

Excel 2013 has a wonderful new feature called *Flash Fill*. This feature enables you quickly and simply split delimited text (such as the above) into separate cells. The term *delimited text* means text that is split using a separator. In this case the separator is a space (see facing page sidebar).

Automatic Flash Fill will only work for very simple text splitting tasks such as the one described above. In the lessons that follow you'll learn more complex Flash Fill techniques that will enable you to perform some very advanced text splitting tasks.

1   Open *Employee Names-1* from your sample files folder.

2   Add column headings for *First Name* and *Last Name* in cells B3 and C3.

   1.   Click in cell B3.

   2.   Type: **First Name**

   3.   Press the **<Tab>** key to move to cell C3.

   4.   Type: **Last Name**

   5.   Press the **<Tab>** key to save the value into the cell and move to cell D3.

3   Bold face the text in cells B3 and C3.

note

Limitations of automatic Flash Fill

Automatic Flash Fill always works perfectly when the source data column has the same type of *separators*.

In this lesson's example, space separators are used. The following example (using comma separators) would also work perfectly:

Sting, Musician
Kingdom Brunel, Engineer
Billie Jean King, Tennis Player

You can see that, without the commas, Flash Fill wouldn't know where the name ended and the occupation began.

Sometimes you will need to extract data that does not have separators.

You'll discover how to solve this type of problem later, in: *Lesson 2-19: Use manual Flash Fill to split text.*

note

Use automatic Flash Fill to extract initials

You can often save a lot of space by showing initials instead of full names. Automatic Flash Fill is well suited to this task.

Try this (at the end of the lesson, after populating columns B and C with first and last names).

1. Type: **JS** (for Jessica Sagan) in cell D4.

2. Type **S** (Stephen Bell's first initial) into cell D5.

3. Press the **<Enter>** key to accept the Flash Fill.

	B	C	D
4	Jessica	Sagan	JS
5	Stephen	Bell	SB
6	John	Jennings	JJ

You learned how to do this in: *Lesson 1-15: Use the Mini Toolbar, Key Tips and keyboard shortcuts.*

	A	B	C
3	Name	First Name	Last Name

4 Use *Flash Fill* to extract the *First Name* values from column A into Column B.

1. Type: **Jessica** into cell B4. Be careful to type it exactly as it is spelled in cell A4. Be careful not to leave any leading or trailing spaces.

2. Press the **<Enter>** key to move to cell B5.

3. Type: **S** (the first letter of *Stephen*) into cell B5.

   Notice that something interesting has happened. *Flash Fill* has figured out that you possibly want to extract all of the first names from Column A and has shown them all as greyed out names in the cells below:

	A	B	C
3	Name	First Name	Last Name
4	Jessica Sagan	Jessica	
5	Stephen Bell	Stephen	
6	John Jennings	John	
7	Meryl Simpson	Meryl	
8	Alfred Hawking	Alfred	

4. Press the **<Enter>** key to instruct Flash Fill to enter all of the remaining *First Name* values.

   All of the first names appear in column B.

	A	B	C
3	Name	First Name	Last Name
4	Jessica Sagan	Jessica	
5	Stephen Bell	Stephen	
6	John Jennings	John	
7	Meryl Simpson	Meryl	
8	Alfred Hawking	Alfred	

The status bar (at the bottom left of the screen) also confirms how many cells were changed:

READY   FLASH FILL CHANGED CELLS: 23

5 Use *Flash Fill* to extract the *Last Name* values from column A into Column C.

Follow exactly the same procedure you used to extract the first names:

	A	B	C
3	Name	First Name	Last Name
4	Jessica Sagan	Jessica	Sagan
5	Stephen Bell	Stephen	Bell
6	John Jennings	John	Jennings
7	Meryl Simpson	Meryl	Simpson

6 Save your work as *Employee Names-2*.

note

You can also flash fill more quickly by using the AutoFill handle

The *AutoFill handle* is the small black dot on the bottom-right corner of the active cell (or range of cells).

In: *Lesson 2-16: Use AutoFill options,* you learned that if you right-click and drag the AutoFill handle you are presented with *AutoFill options:*

You can use the *Flash Fill* item on the *AutoFill options* list to request a Flash Fill.

This will do exactly the same as clicking:

Home→Editing→Fill→Flash Fill

You'll find that this method is faster than using the Ribbon.

This method is also the preferred way to provide Flash Fill with more than one example result for more complex problems (you'll do this in: *Lesson 2-20: Use multiple example Flash Fill to concatenate text*).

Phone Book-1

Lesson 2-19: Use manual Flash Fill to split text

Here are two examples of international telephone numbers.

+44 (0)113-4960227 (a UK telephone number)
+356 (0)2138-3393 (a Maltese telephone number)

The *country code* (or international dialling code) is shown as a + symbol followed by one or more numbers. The *NDD* (National Direct Dialling prefix) is shown in brackets. This is the access code used to make a call within the relevant country but is omitted when calling from outside the country. The *Area Code* consists of the numbers after the closing bracket but before the hyphen.

In this lesson we'll use manual Flash Fill to split telephone numbers into the *Country Code, Area Code* and *Phone Number* like this:

	A	B	C	D	E
3	Company	Telephone	Country Code	Area Code	Phone Number
4	Books A Million	+44 (0)113-4960227	+44	113	4960227
5	Maltese Books	+356 (0)2138-3393	+356	2138	3393
6	Bargain Bookstore	+44 (0)115-4960498	+44	115	4960498

In Excel versions prior to Excel 2013 you'd have had to use some very complex formulas in order to split this type of text. With the new *Flash Fill* feature you can achieve the same result in seconds.

1   Open *Phone Book-1* from your sample files folder.

2   Extract the *Country Code* from the telephone number in column B and place it into column C.

If you were to type **+44** into cell C4, Excel would interpret it as a positive number and display the result as 44 (without the plus sign).

In order to signal to Excel that you want the plus sign to be displayed, you will need to indicate that +44 should be regarded as text rather than as a number.

You discovered the technique for doing this in: *Lesson 2-1: Enter text and numbers into a worksheet.*

If an apostrophe is placed before a number, Excel will regard it as text.

1. Type: **'+44** into cell C4 (an apostrophe followed by **+44**).

2. Press: **<Enter>**

3. Making sure that the active cell is in one of the cells that will be Flash Filled (ie anywhere in the range C3:C18), click:

    Home→Editing→Fill→Flash Fill

    (Alternatively, you could also use the shortcut keys: **<Ctrl>+<E>** to flash fill).

    The country code is extracted into the remaining cells in column C.

note

The difference between Flash Fill and a formula-based solution

There are two ways to solve the problem posed in this lesson:

1. Use Flash Fill

This is the method used in this lesson. Flash Fill provides a fast and simple solution.

2. Use complex formulas

Only expert Excel users could construct the complex formulas required to split the telephone numbers contained in the sample file without the use of Flash Fill.

In the *Expert Skills* book in this series we solve exactly the same problem presented in this lesson without Flash Fill.

Complex formulas are used instead, to provide a formula-based solution.

Advantage of a formula-based solution

The results of a Flash Fill do not automatically update when the source data changes.

This means that if you change the telephone number in column B you will then need to Flash Fill three times to update columns C, D and E.

Formula results automatically update whenever the source cells change.

This means that if you change the telephone number in the formula-based solution, the *Country Code, Area Code* and *Phone Number* will automatically update.

	A	B	C
3	Company	Telephone	Country Code
4	Books A Million	+44 (0)113-4960227	+44
5	Maltese Books	+356 (0)2138-3393	+356
6	Bargain Bookstore	+44 (0)115-4960498	+44

Notice that Excel has placed a green triangle in the top-left corner of each cell. Excel thinks you may have made an error but, of course, the value is fine. If you want to remove the green triangles, use the method you learned in: *Lesson 2-4: Select a range of cells and understand Smart Tags.*

3 Extract the *Area Code* from the telephone number in column B and place it into column D.

Use exactly the same method as you did for the country code. The first area code you need to type is: '**113**

Even though there is no plus sign, it is still useful to include the apostrophe as it will prevent Excel from re-formatting numbers (see next step for more on this).

4 Extract the *Phone Number* from the telephone number in column B and place it into column E.

Use exactly the same method as you did for the country code. The first telephone number is: '**4960227**

In this case you must use a leading apostrophe to prevent Excel from re-formatting large numbers. For example, the telephone number: *20180948* would be displayed as *2E+07* if you didn't include the apostrophe.

The *Country Code, Area Code* and *Phone Number* are now extracted for every international telephone number:

	A	B	C	D	E
3	Company	Telephone	Country Code	Area Code	Phone Number
4	Books A Million	+44 (0)113-4960227	+44	113	4960227
5	Maltese Books	+356 (0)2138-3393	+356	2138	3393
6	Bargain Bookstore	+44 (0)115-4960498	+44	115	4960498

5 Save your work as *Phone Book-2*.

note

Flash Fill doesn't understand mathematics

You could be forgiven for thinking that Flash Fill could solve this problem:

	A	B
1	100	101
2	120	121
3	150	

It seems obvious that column B simply adds 1 to the value in column A. Unfortunately Flash Fill doesn't understand mathematical calculation so you are out of luck.

Flash Fill can, however, work with numbers in the same way that it works with text. Consider this example:

	A	B
1	123	23
2	777	77
3	727	27

Flash Fill is happy to strip off the first digit from column A. It can do this because no calculations are involved.

You need to be careful with the treatment of zeros when tackling this sort of problem. Consider this example:

	A	B
1	123	23
2	777	77
3	707	7

You may have thought that Flash Fill would have entered **07** in cell B3 rather than **7**.

In: *Session Four: Making Your Worksheets Look Professional*, you'll learn about number formatting. You'll then have the skills to apply a leading zero to the numbers in column B (if that was what you wanted to do).

Client Names-1

Lesson 2-20: Use multiple example Flash Fill to concatenate text

Understand concatenation

In: *Lesson 2-18: Use automatic Flash Fill to split delimited text*, you learned how to split text with this example:

	A	B	C
3	**Name**	**First Name**	**Last Name**
4	Jessica Sagan	Jessica	Sagan
5	Stephen Bell	Stephen	Bell

In the above example the text: *Jessica Sagan* was split into two separate words: *Jessica* and *Sagan.*

Concatenation is exactly the opposite of splitting. The two separate words *Jessica* and *Sagan* can be concatenated to produce the single word: *Jessica Sagan.* This is an example of very simple concatenation.

In this lesson we'll perform some very advanced concatenation using *Flash Fill*.

1   Open *Client Names-1* from your sample files folder.

This workbook contains a list of very inconsistently formatted client names:

	A	B	C	D
3	**Last**	**Middle**	**First**	
4	Sagan	Elizabeth	Jessica	
5	Bell	p	Stephen	
6	Jennings		John	

We want to clean up this data so that client names are consistently formatted like this:

	A	B	C	D
3	**Last**	**Middle**	**First**	**Formatted Name**
4	Sagan	Elizabeth	Jessica	Sagan, Jessica E.
5	Bell	p	Stephen	Bell, Stephen P.
6	jennings		John	Jennings, John
7	Simpson	Jane	Meryl	Simpson, Meryl J.
8	hawking		Alfred	Hawking, Alfred
9	Ashe	m	Lucille	Ashe, Lucille M.

In order for Flash Fill to automate this task you will need to tell Flash Fill what is needed by providing more than one example.

2   Type: **Formatted Name** into cell D3 and bold face the text.

(Excel will probably bold-face the text automatically).

It is important that the header text in row 3 is bold faced.

When Flash Fill sees different formatting in the first row the row is assumed to be a header row. Flash Fill excludes the value in the header row from its logic, providing more reliable results.

3   Provide a single example result in cell D4.

Type: **Sagan, Jessica E.** into cell D4.

4   Flash fill cells D5:D9 based upon the example result in cell D4.

You learned how to do this in: *Lesson 2-19: Use manual Flash Fill to split text.*

Excel completes the task but the results are not what we wanted (see sidebar).

With only one example, Flash Fill has completely misunderstood the requirement.

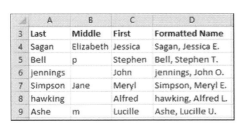

5   Provide two example results in cells D3 and D4.

1.   Delete the names in cells D5:D9.

2.   Provide another example of the correct result (in cell D4).

	A	B	C	D
3	Last	Middle	First	Formatted Name
4	Sagan	Elizabeth	Jessica	Sagan, Jessica E.
5	Bell	p	Stephen	Bell, Stephen P.
6	Jennings		John	

6   Flash fill cells D6:D9 based upon the example results in cells D4 and D5.

1.   Select cells D4:D9.

2.   Click: Home→Editing→Fill→Flash Fill.

This time Flash Fill has done a better job (see sidebar).

Notice the two blank results (for *John Jennings* and *Alfred Hawking*).

Flash Fill doesn't yet understand how to treat clients without a middle name. The blank spaces are Flash Fill's way of asking you for yet another example.

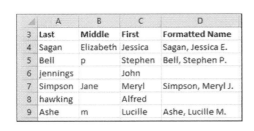

7   Provide another example result in cell D6.

1.   Type: **Jennings, John** into cell D6.

2.   Press the **<Enter>** key.

Usually Flash Fill will instantly replace the value in cell D8. If it doesn't, you'll have to manually flash fill the entire list based upon the three examples provided. Do this by completing the following steps:

3.   Select cells D4:D9.

4.   Click: Home→Editing→Fill→Flash Fill.

This time Flash Fill has completed the task successfully (see sidebar).

8   Save your work as *Client Names-2.*

Lesson 2-21: Use Flash Fill to solve common problems

Flash Fill is one of the Excel 2013's most useful new features. It isn't possible to over-state how useful this tool is. I find myself using Flash Fill almost every day to solve a huge number of different problems.

This lesson gives examples of many everyday tasks that I have found can be quickly and simply completed using Flash Fill. I've also included all of the examples in the sample file: *Flash Fill Examples.*

In the following examples, the shaded cells were filled by Flash Fill.

Split text

Full Name	First Name	Last Name
Jessica Elizabeth Sagan	Jessica	Sagan
Stephen Bell	Stephen	Bell
John Paul Jennings	John	Jennings

Extract initials from names

Name	Initials
Jessica Elizabeth Sagan	JES
Stephen Bell	SB
John Paul Jennings	JPJ

Remove title from names

Full Name	Short Name
Miss Jessica Elizabeth Sagan	Jessica Sagan
Mr Stephen Bell	Stephen Bell
Mr John Paul Jennings	John Jennings

Add commas (a useful name format for alphabetical sorting)

Name	Sort Name
Jessica Elizabeth Sagan	Sagan, Jessica
Stephen Bell	Bell, Stephen
John Paul Jennings	Jennings, John

Concatenate text

First Name	Middle Name	Last Name	Full Name
Jessica	Elizabeth	Sagan	Jessica Elizabeth Sagan
Stephen		Bell	Stephen Bell
John	Paul	Jennings	John Paul Jennings

Concatenate text and insert extra text

First Name	Middle Name	Last Name	Full Name
Jessica	Elizabeth	Sagan	First Name: Jessica, Last Name: Sagan
Stephen		Bell	First Name: Stephen, Last Name: Bell
John	Paul	Jennings	First Name: John, Last Name: Jennings

Flash Fill Examples

Change capitalization

Mixed Case	Title Case
jessica elizabeth sagan	Jessica Elizabeth Sagan
stephen Bell	Stephen Bell
john Paul jennings	John Paul Jennings

Extract the day, month or year from a date

In all of the date based examples note that the *Date* column is formatted as a date. You will learn how to format cells as dates later in: *Lesson 4-1: Format dates.*

Date	Day	Date	Month	Date	Year
19th January 2013	19	19th January 2013	January	19th January 2013	2013
5th August 1967	5	5th August 1967	August	5th August 1967	1967
20th September 1999	20	20th September 1999	September	20th September 1999	1999

Extract the day/month from a date

Date	Day/Month
19th January 2013	19th January
5th August 1967	5th August
20th September 1999	20th September

Extract domain names from e-mail addresses

E-mail address	Domain
Mary@QuiteContrary.com	QuiteContrary.com
Humpty@Dumpty.com	Dumpty.com
Jack@Nimble.com	Nimble.com

Format telephone numbers

Name	Tel (unformatted)	Tel (formatted)
Books A Million	1134960227	(113) 496-0227
Bargain Bookstore	1154960498	(115) 496-0498
Books for Less	1164960593	(116) 496-0593

Lesson 2-22: Use the zoom control

Zooming is used to magnify or reduce the worksheet. If you have a lot of rows in a worksheet and have good eyes, you might want to zoom out sometimes to see more of the worksheet on one screen.

1 Open *First Quarter Sales and Profit-12* from your sample files folder.

2 Zoom in and out of the worksheet using the mouse wheel.

The fastest way to zoom a worksheet is by using the mouse.

Most mice these days have a wheel in the middle of the buttons. To zoom using this wheel hold down the **<Ctrl>** key on the keyboard and roll the wheel to zoom in and out.

3 Zoom in and out of a worksheet using the zoom control.

The zoom control is at the bottom right of your screen,

Click and drag on the zoom control slider to zoom in and out of your worksheet. You can also zoom by clicking the plus and minus buttons on either side of the Zoom control.

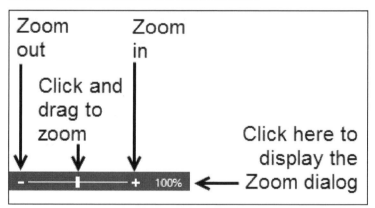

4 Use the Zoom dialog to make cells A3:D9 fill the screen.

1. Select cells A3:D9.

	A	B	C	D	E
2					
3		Jan	Feb	Mar	Average
4	New York	22,000	29,000	19,000	23,333
5	Los Angeles	42,000	39,000	43,000	41,333
6	London	18,000	20,000	22,000	20,000
7	Paris	35,000	26,000	31,000	30,667
8	Munich	12,000	15,000	13,000	13,333
9	Sales	129,000	129,000	128,000	

2. Click on the right hand side of the zoom bar.

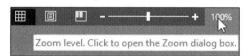

Zoom level. Click to open the Zoom dialog box.

The *Zoom* dialog is displayed.

First Quarter Sales and Profit-12

3.   Select the *Fit Selection* option button.

4.   Click the OK button.

The worksheet is zoomed so that the selected cells completely fill the screen.

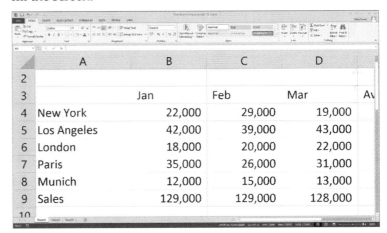

5   Zoom back to 100% using the Ribbon.

You'll probably find the zoom bar to be the quickest and most convenient way to zoom, but you can also zoom using the Ribbon.

Click: View→Zoom→100%.

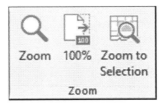

The screen is restored to normal size.

Lesson 2-23: Print out a worksheet

We aren't going to explore every option for preparing and printing a worksheet in this lesson. Printing is such a huge subject that we devote a whole session to it in: *Session Seven: Printing Your Work.*

This lesson only aims to teach you the bare minimum skills you need to put your work onto paper.

1   Open *First Quarter Sales and Profit-12* from your sample files folder (if it isn't already open).

	A	B	C	D	E	F	G
1	Sales and Profit Report - First Quarter 2008						
2							
3		Jan	Feb	Mar	Average	Maximum	
4	New York	22,000	29,000	19,000	23,333	29,000	
5	Los Angeles	42,000	39,000	43,000	41,333	43,000	
6	London	18,000	20,000	22,000	20,000	22,000	
7	Paris	35,000	26,000	31,000	30,667	35,000	
8	Munich	12,000	15,000	13,000	13,333	15,000	
9	Sales	129,000	129,000	128,000			
10							
11	Costs	83,000					
12	Profit	46,000					
13	10% Bonus	4,600					
14							
15	USA Sales	64,000					
16	European Sales	65,000					
17							
18	Monday	1	9	01-Jan-08	Adjusted	01-Jan-09	31-Mar-09
19	Tuesday	2	18	02-Jan-08	Adjusted	02-Jan-09	31-Mar-09
20	Wednesday	3	27	03-Jan-08	Adjusted	03-Jan-09	31-Mar-09
21	Thursday	4	36	04-Jan-08	Adjusted	04-Jan-09	31-Mar-09
22	Friday	5	45	05-Jan-08	Adjusted	05-Jan-09	31-Mar-09
23	Saturday	6	54	06-Jan-08	Adjusted	06-Jan-09	31-Mar-09
24	Sunday	7	63	07-Jan-08	Adjusted	07-Jan-09	31-Mar-09

2   Click File→Print.

Backstage View appears offering many preview and print options:

First Quarter Sales and Profit-12

Send the worksheet to the printer

Select printer

Preview of how the page will look when printed

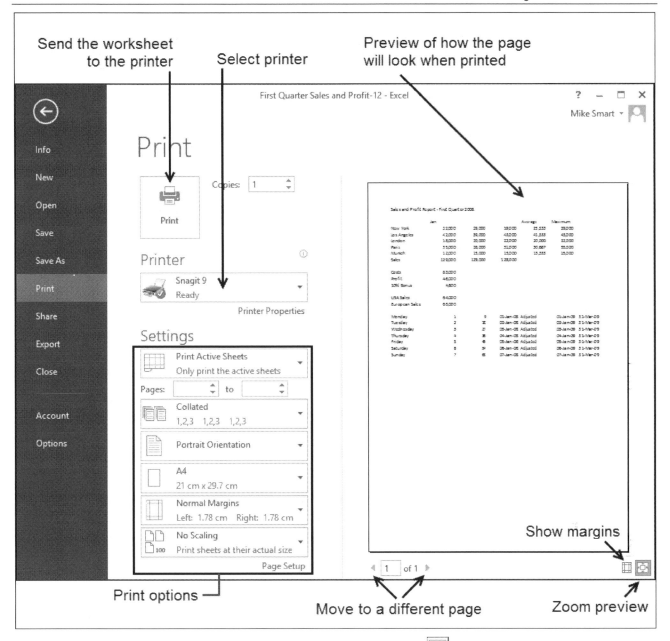

Print options

Move to a different page

Show margins

Zoom preview

3   Click on the zoom button to see the zoom feature working.

Each time you click on the button the page zooms in and out.

4   Print the worksheet.

Click the *Print* button:

The page is printed on the selected printer.

Session 2: Exercise

1 Open a new blank workbook.

2 Use AutoFill to put the three months Jan, Feb, and Mar into cells A4:A6.

3 Using only the keyboard add the following data:

	A	B	C	D	E
1	Profit Analysis				
2					
3		London	Paris	New York	Average
4	Jan	2,500	3,100	2,300	
5	Feb	2,200	2,700	2,600	
6	Mar	2,100	2,600	2,800	
7	Total				

4 Use AutoSum to compute London's total profit for Jan/Feb/Mar in cell B7.

5 Use AutoSum to compute the average January profit in cell E4.

6 Use AutoFill to extend the London total in cell B7, to the Paris and New York totals in cells C7 and D7.

7 Use AutoFill to extend the January average profit in cell E4, to the February and March average profits in cells E5 and E6.

8 Select all of Column A and all of Column E (at the same time) and bold face the values in them.

9 Select row 3 and row 7 (at the same time) and bold face the values in them.

	A	B	C	D	E
1	**Profit Analysis**				
2					
3		London	Paris	New York	**Average**
4	**Jan**	2,500	3,100	2,300	**2,633**
5	**Feb**	2,200	2,700	2,600	**2,500**
6	**Mar**	2,100	2,600	2,800	**2,500**
7		6,800	8,400	7,700	
8					

10 Select cells B4:B6 and cells D4:D6 at the same time and then read the total London and New York sales figure for Jan, Feb and March from the summary information displayed on the status bar.

11 Select cells B4:D6 and zoom the selection so that these cells fill the screen.

12 Save your work as *Exercise2-End*.

If you need help slide the page to the left

Session 2: Exercise answers

These are the four questions that students find the most difficult to remember:

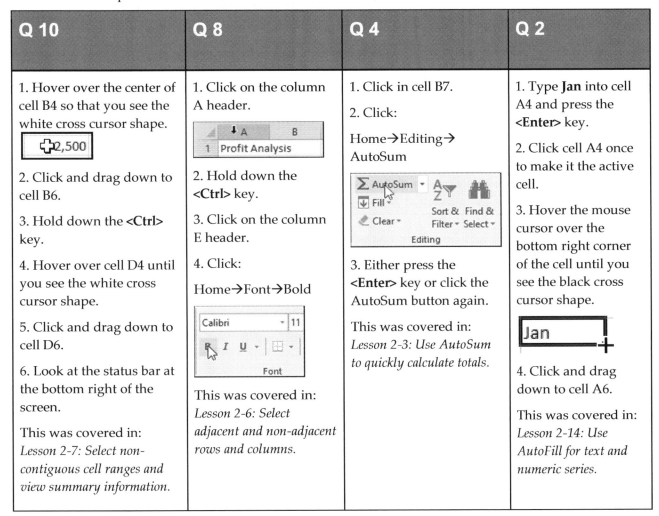

Q 10	Q 8	Q 4	Q 2
1. Hover over the center of cell B4 so that you see the white cross cursor shape. ⊹2,500 2. Click and drag down to cell B6. 3. Hold down the **<Ctrl>** key. 4. Hover over cell D4 until you see the white cross cursor shape. 5. Click and drag down to cell D6. 6. Look at the status bar at the bottom right of the screen. This was covered in: *Lesson 2-7: Select non-contiguous cell ranges and view summary information.*	1. Click on the column A header. ↓A | B 1 | Profit Analysis 2. Hold down the **<Ctrl>** key. 3. Click on the column E header. 4. Click: Home→Font→Bold Calibri ▾ 11 B *I* U ▾ Font This was covered in: *Lesson 2-6: Select adjacent and non-adjacent rows and columns.*	1. Click in cell B7. 2. Click: Home→Editing→ AutoSum Σ AutoSum ▾ ↓ Fill ▾ ◆ Clear ▾ Sort & Find & Filter ▾ Select ▾ Editing 3. Either press the **<Enter>** key or click the AutoSum button again. This was covered in: *Lesson 2-3: Use AutoSum to quickly calculate totals.*	1. Type **Jan** into cell A4 and press the **<Enter>** key. 2. Click cell A4 once to make it the active cell. 3. Hover the mouse cursor over the bottom right corner of the cell until you see the black cross cursor shape. Jan ┼ 4. Click and drag down to cell A6. This was covered in: *Lesson 2-14: Use AutoFill for text and numeric series.*

If you have difficulty with the other questions, here are the lessons that cover the relevant skills:

1   Refer to: Lesson 1-1: Start Excel and open a new blank workbook.

3   Refer to: Lesson 2-1: Enter text and numbers into a worksheet.

5   Refer to: Lesson 2-3: Use AutoSum to quickly calculate totals.

6   Refer to: Lesson 2-15: Use AutoFill to adjust formulas.

7   Refer to: Lesson 2-15: Use AutoFill to adjust formulas.

9   Refer to: Lesson 2-6: Select adjacent and non-adjacent rows and columns.

3

Session Three: Taking Your Skills to the Next Level

> One only gets to the top rung of the ladder by steadily climbing up one at a time, and suddenly all sorts of powers, all sorts of abilities which you thought never belonged to you – suddenly become within your own possibility.
>
> *Margaret Thatcher,*
> *Prime Minister of the United Kingdom from 1979-1990*

After mastering all of the techniques covered in session two, you're already able to do useful work with the world's most powerful business tool, but of course, you're only on the first rung of a very long ladder.

While you are now able to do the simple things well, there are a few more insights you need to really get Excel working.

Most of the skills covered in this session will take your powers beyond those of casual Excel users.

Session Objectives

By the end of this session you will be able to:

- Insert and delete rows and columns
- Use AutoComplete and fill data from adjacent cells
- Cut, copy and paste
- Cut, copy and paste using drag and drop
- Use Paste Values
- Increase/decrease decimal places displayed
- Transpose a range
- Use the multiple item clipboard
- Use Undo and Redo
- Insert, View and Print cell comments
- Understand absolute, relative and mixed cell references
- Understand templates and set the default custom template folder
- Create a template
- Use a template
- Add an App to a workbook
- Freeze columns and rows
- Split the window into multiple panes
- Check spelling

Lesson 3-1: Insert and delete rows and columns

1   Open *The World's Fastest Cars* from your sample files folder.

	A	B	C	D	E	F	G
1	The World's Fastest Cars						
2							
3	Make	Model	Top Speed (MPH)	0-60	BHP	Price (USD)	Country
4	Bugatti	Veyron	253	2.5	1001	1,444,000	Germany
5	Koenigsegg	CCX	250	3.2	806	695,000	Sweden
6	Saleen	S7	248	3.2	750	555,000	USA
7	McLaren	F1	240	3.2	627	970,000	UK
8	Ferrari	Enzo	217	3.4	660	670,000	Italy
9	Jaguar	XJ220	217	4	542	345,000	UK
10	Pagani	Zonda	215	3.5	650	741,000	Italy
11	Lamborghini	Murcielago LP640	213	3.3	640	430,000	Italy
12	Porsche	Carrera GT	209	3.9	612	440,000	Germany
13	Mercedes	SLR McLaren 722	209	3.6	650	480,000	Germany

A worksheet opens showing some of the fastest cars in the world.

Until September 2007 the Bugatti Veyron was the fastest car in the world. Shelby has now stolen the crown with their SSC Ultimate Aero. There will be an even faster car by the time you read this book. We need to insert a row above row 4 to add the new car to the list.

2   Insert a blank row above row 4.

Right-click the row header button [4] and click *Insert* from the shortcut menu.

3   Add the following data to the new row:

3	Make	Model	Top Speed (MPH)	0-60	BHP	Price (USD)	Country
4	Shelby	SSC Ultimate Aero	257	2.7	1183	654,400	USA

4   If the text is bold faced restore it to normal.

You learned how to do this in: *Lesson 1-15: Use the Mini Toolbar, Key Tips and keyboard shortcuts.*

5   Add a column to the left of column A.

Adding columns is just like adding rows. Right-click on the column header [A] and then click *Insert* from the short cut menu.

A blank column appears on the left hand side of the worksheet:

	A	B	C	D	E
1		The World's Fastest Cars			
2					
3		Make	Model	Top Speed (MPH)	0-60
4		Shelby	SSC Ultimate Aero	257	2.7
5		Bugatti	Veyron	253	2.5
6		Koenigsegg	CCX	250	3.2

The World's Fastest Cars

6   Delete the newly-inserted Column A.

Deleting is just like adding. Right-click on the column header

A
but, this time, select *Delete* from the shortcut menu.

7   Insert four rows above row 3.

Nearly every Excel user does this by inserting a single row four times until they learn the correct technique.

1. Select the four rows 3:6 by clicking and dragging across the row header buttons.

2. Right-click anywhere in the selected area.

3. Click *Insert* from the shortcut menu.

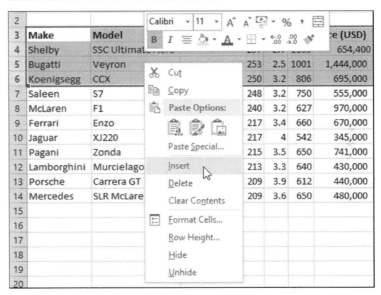

Four blank rows are inserted.

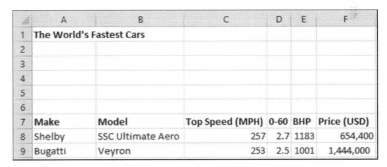

8   Delete the four newly-inserted rows.

1. Select the four rows you want to delete (by dragging the mouse over row headers 3,4,5 and 6).

2. Right-click anywhere in the selected area.

3. Click *Delete* from the shortcut menu.

9   Save your work as: *The World's Fastest Cars-2*.

Lesson 3-2: Use AutoComplete and fill data from adjacent cells

1   Open *The World's Fastest Cars-2* from your sample files folder (if it isn't already open).

	A	B	C	D	E	F	G
1	The World's Fastest Cars						
2							
3	Make	Model	Top Speed (MPH)	0-60	BHP	Price (USD)	Country
4	Shelby	SSC Ultimate Aero	257	2.7	1183	654,400	USA
5	Bugatti	Veyron	253	2.5	1001	1,444,000	Germany
6	Koenigsegg	CCX	250	3.2	806	695,000	Sweden
7	Saleen	S7	248	3.2	750	555,000	USA
8	McLaren	F1	240	3.2	627	970,000	UK
9	Ferrari	Enzo	217	3.4	660	670,000	Italy
10	Jaguar	XJ220	217	4	542	345,000	UK
11	Pagani	Zonda	215	3.5	650	741,000	Italy
12	Lamborghini	Murcielago LP640	213	3.3	640	430,000	Italy
13	Porsche	Carrera GT	209	3.9	612	440,000	Germany
14	Mercedes	SLR McLaren 722	209	3.6	650	480,000	Germany
15							

2   Type the letter **F** into cell A15.

Notice that Excel guesses that you want to type *Ferrari* into the cell. This is because the word Ferrari appears above it in the column.

If this doesn't happen, somebody has switched AutoComplete off. See the sidebar to find out how to switch it back on.

13	Porsche	Carrera GT	209	3.9	612
14	Mercedes	SLR McLaren 722	209	3.6	650
15	Ferrari				

3   Press the **<Tab>** key to accept the guess.

4   Enter **599 GTB** for the model and **205** for the top speed.

14	Mercedes	SLR McLaren 722	209	3.6	650
15	Ferrari	599GTB	205		

5   Use the *Fill* command to enter **3.6** into cell D15.

The Ferrari has the same 0-60 time as the McLaren SLR. Instead of typing **3.6** into the cell we can use the *Fill* command.

1. Click in cell D15.

2. Click: Home→Editing→Fill→Down.

The World's Fastest Cars-2

note

You can also Fill Down and Fill Right, using keyboard shortcuts

The following shortcut key combinations can be used for the *Fill Down* and *Fill Right* commands:

<Ctrl>+<D>   Fill Down

<Ctrl>+<R>   Fill Right

Unfortunately there is no simple shortcut key combination for *Fill Up* or *Fill Left*.

You can, as with all Ribbon commands, use *key tips* to reveal shortcut keys that can be used to directly activate *Fill Up* and *Fill Left*.

Key Tips were described in detail in: *Lesson 1-15: Use the Mini Toolbar, Key Tips and keyboard shortcuts.*

Key tips reveal the following shortcut keys:

Fill Left:

<Alt>+<H>+<FI>+<L>

Fill Up:

<Alt>+<H>+<FI>+<U>

Notice that there are also *Right, Up* and *Left* options. These can be used to copy values to adjacent cells in any direction.

6 Enter **620** for the BHP value and **264,034** for the price.

7 Right-click in G15 and choose *Pick from Drop down list...* from the shortcut menu.

All unique countries that currently exist in column G are displayed as a list.

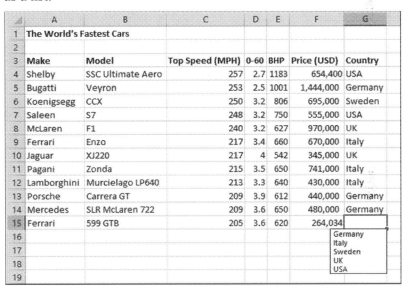

	A	B	C	D	E	F	G
1	The World's Fastest Cars						
2							
3	**Make**	**Model**	**Top Speed (MPH)**	**0-60**	**BHP**	**Price (USD)**	**Country**
4	Shelby	SSC Ultimate Aero	257	2.7	1183	654,400	USA
5	Bugatti	Veyron	253	2.5	1001	1,444,000	Germany
6	Koenigsegg	CCX	250	3.2	806	695,000	Sweden
7	Saleen	S7	248	3.2	750	555,000	USA
8	McLaren	F1	240	3.2	627	970,000	UK
9	Ferrari	Enzo	217	3.4	660	670,000	Italy
10	Jaguar	XJ220	217	4	542	345,000	UK
11	Pagani	Zonda	215	3.5	650	741,000	Italy
12	Lamborghini	Murcielago LP640	213	3.3	640	430,000	Italy
13	Porsche	Carrera GT	209	3.9	612	440,000	Germany
14	Mercedes	SLR McLaren 722	209	3.6	650	480,000	Germany
15	Ferrari	599 GTB	205	3.6	620	264,034	
16							Germany
17							Italy
18							Sweden
19							UK
							USA

8 Click *Italy* to automatically enter the country.

9 Save your work as *The World's Fastest Cars-3*.

trivia

The origins of cut and paste

The terms *Cut, Copy* and *Paste* remind us of the days when things weren't as easy as they are today.

Before the advent of computer technology, graphic artists would generate text for their work using a phototypesetting machine.

This machine used a photographic process to produce a strip of paper with high quality type printed upon it.

The layout artist would then cut the type into words or phrases and then paste it onto a sheet of paper.

When the work was finished it would be photographed to create a negative image ready to convert to a printing plate.

During the 1990's the layout business changed dramatically when graphic artists began to move to computer based desktop publishing.

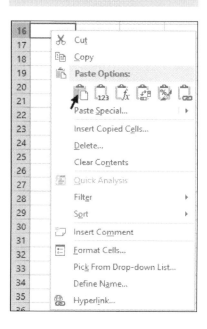

The World's Fastest Cars-3

Lesson 3-3: Cut, copy and paste

1   Open *The World's Fastest Cars-3* from your sample files folder (if it isn't already open).

2   Click cell A1 to make it the active cell.

3   Copy the text from cell A1 to the clipboard.

The clipboard is a container for copied text and is common to all of Microsoft Office. When you ask Excel to copy, Excel takes the value in cell A1 (in this case text) and places a copy of it onto the clipboard. The existing contents of cell A1 remain unaltered.

The clipboard is useful because we can later paste the clipboard's contents back into the worksheet (or into any other Office document such as a PowerPoint presentation, Word document or Outlook Email).

There are three ways to copy but these two are the quickest:

EITHER

Right click and select *Copy* from the shortcut menu.

OR

Press **<Ctrl>+<C>** on the keyboard.

The third (and slowest) method is to click:

Home→Clipboard→Copy

4   Click cell A17 to make it the active cell.

5   Paste the copied text into cell A17.

There are also three ways to paste but these two are the quickest:

EITHER

Right click cell A17 and then select: Paste Options→Paste from the shortcut menu (see sidebar). The other paste options will be covered later in this lesson.

OR

Click cell A17 and then Press **<Ctrl>+<V>** on the keyboard.

The third (and slowest) method is to click:

Home→Clipboard→Paste

The text appears in cell A17.

14	Mercedes	SLR McLaren 722		209
15	Ferrari	599GTB		205
16				
17	**The World's Fastest Cars**			

6   Edit the text in cell A17 to read: The World's Fastest Italian Cars.

You learned how to do this in: *Lesson 2-1: Enter text and numbers into a worksheet.*

7 Select all of row 9 and copy it to the clipboard.

Selecting an entire row was covered in: *Lesson 2-6: Select adjacent and non-adjacent rows and columns.*

8 Select all of row 19 and paste into it.

The contents of row 9 are copied to row 19.

17	The World's Fastest Italian Cars				
18					
19	Ferrari	Enzo		217	3.4

9 Select the range A11:G12.

These cells contain data for two more Italian cars.

10	Jaguar	XJ220	217	4	542	345,000	UK
11	Pagani	Zonda	215	3.5	650	741,000	Italy
12	Lamborghini	Murcielago LP640	213	3.3	640	430,000	Italy
13	Porsche	Carrera GT	209	3.9	612	440,000	Germany

10 Cut the text from A11:G12 to place it onto the clipboard.

When you cut text, the text is copied from the source cell(s) to the clipboard. If you then paste the text to a new location, the text is then automatically deleted from the source cells(s).

There are three ways to cut but these two are the quickest:

EITHER

Right click and select *Cut* from the shortcut menu.

OR

Press **<Ctrl>+<X>**.

The third (and slowest) method is to click:

Home→Clipboard→Cut.

11 Click in cell A20 to make it the active cell.

12 Paste the cut range into the range beginning in cell A20.

The cut text appears with the top left hand corner in cell A20.

10	Jaguar	XJ220	217	4	542	345,000	UK
11							
12							
13	Porsche	Carrera GT	209	3.9	612	440,000	Germany
14	Mercedes	SLR McLaren 722	209	3.6	650	480,000	Germany
15	Ferrari	599GTB	205				
16							
17	The World's Fastest Italian Cars						
18							
19	Ferrari	Enzo	217	3.4	660	670,000	Italy
20	Pagani	Zonda	215	3.5	650	741,000	Italy
21	Lamborghini	Murcielago LP640	213	3.3	640	430,000	Italy
22							

13 Save your work as *The World's Fastest Cars-4.*

Lesson 3-4: Cut, copy and paste using drag and drop

1   Open *The World's Fastest Cars-4* from your sample files folder (if it isn't already open).

2   Move cells A20:G21 to cells A11:G12 using drag and drop.

1.   Select cells A20:G21.

2.   Hover the mouse cursor over the black border surrounding the range until you see the four-headed arrow cursor shape.

19	Ferrari	Enzo		217	3.4	660	670,000	Italy
20	Pagani	Zonda		215	3.5	650	741,000	Italy
21	Lamborghini	Murcielago LP640		213	3.3	640	430,000	Italy
22								

It is very important that you see the four headed arrow and not the white cross or AutoFill cursor shape.

If you do not see a four headed arrow somebody may have switched the drag and drop facility off. See sidebar for how to bring it back.

3.   Click and drag the selected cells, dropping them to their previous location (beginning at cell A11).

You'll see a green outline showing where the cells will be dropped. Move them to the location shown in the screen grab below.

10	Jaguar	XJ220		217	4	542	345,000	UK
11								
12								
13	Porsche	Carrera GT	A11:G12	3.9	612		440,000	Germany

4.   Release the mouse button.

The contents of the cells are moved back to A11:G12.

10	Jaguar	XJ220		217	4	542	345,000	UK
11	Pagani	Zonda		215	3.5	650	741,000	Italy
12	Lamborghini	Murcielago LP640		213	3.3	640	430,000	Italy
13	Porsche	Carrera GT		209	3.9	612	440,000	Germany

3   Copy cells A11:G12 to cells A20:G21 using right-click drag and drop.

1.   Select cells A11:G12.

2.   Hover the mouse cursor over the green border surrounding the range until you see a four-headed arrow.

3.   Right-click and drag the rectangle to rows 20 and 21.

4.   Release the mouse button.

Several options are presented (see sidebar).

5.   Click *Copy Here* from the shortcut menu.

This time the contents of the cells are copied rather than moved.

Move Here

Copy Here

Copy Here as Values Only

Copy Here as Formats Only

Link Here

Create Hyperlink Here

Shift Down and Copy

Shift Right and Copy

Shift Down and Move

Shift Right and Move

Cancel

The World's Fastest Cars-4

17	The World's Fastest Italian Cars						
18							
19	Ferrari	Enzo		217	3.4	660	670,000	Italy
20	Pagani	Zonda		215	3.5	650	741,000	Italy
21	Lamborghini	Murcielago LP640		213	3.3	640	430,000	Italy
22							

note

Another way to copy cells via drag and drop

Hover over the border of the selected cells with the <Ctrl> key held down. You will see the mouse cursor shape change to a plus sign.

	215
LP640	213
	209

You can now drag and drop (holding the left mouse button down) to copy the cells to a new location.

4 Copy the contents of row 15 to row 22 using right-click drag and drop.

17	The World's Fastest Italian Cars						
18							
19	Ferrari	Enzo	217	3.4	660	670,000	Italy
20	Pagani	Zonda	215	3.5	650	741,000	Italy
21	Lamborghini	Murcielago LP640	213	3.3	640	430,000	Italy
22	Ferrari	599 GTB	205	3.6	620	264,034	Italy

5 Rename Sheet1 to *World Cars* and Sheet2 to *Italian Cars*.

You learned how to rename tabs in: *Lesson 1-9: View, move, add, rename, delete* and navigate worksheet tabs.

6 Move cells A17:G22 on the *World Cars* worksheet to cells A1:G6 on the *Italian Cars* worksheet.

1. Select cells A17:G22 on the *World Cars* worksheet.

2. Cut the cells and paste them into cell A1 of the *Italian Cars* worksheet.

	A	B	C	D	E	F	G
1	The World's Fastest Italian Cars						
2							
3	Ferrari	Enzo	217	3.4	660	670,000	Italy
4	Pagani	Zonda	215	3.5	650	741,000	Italy
5	Lamborgh	Murcielag	213	3.3	640	430,000	Italy
6	Ferrari	599 GTB	205	3.6	620	264,034	Italy
7							

World Cars | **Italian Cars** | ... ⊕ ⋮ ◀

7 Insert one blank row above row 3 on the *Italian Cars* worksheet.

You learned how to do this in: *Lesson 3-1: Insert and delete rows and columns.*

8 Copy the titles from row 3 of the *World Cars* worksheet to row 3 of the *Italian Cars* worksheet.

	A	B	C	D	E	F	G
1	The World's Fastest Italian Cars						
2							
3	Make	Model	Top Speed (MPH)	0-60	BHP	Price (USD)	Country
4	Ferrari	Enzo	217	3.4	660	670,000	Italy

9 Save your work as *The World's Fastest Cars-5*.

Lesson 3-5: Use Paste Values and increase/decrease decimal places displayed

1   Open *The World's Fastest Cars-5* from your sample files folder (if it isn't already open).

2   Select the *World Cars* worksheet and add a new column to the left of column D.

Right click on the column D header and click *Insert* from the shortcut menu.

3   Rename cell C3 from *Top Speed (MPH)* to *MPH*.

4   Type **KM/H** into cell D3.

5   Re-size column C so that it is just wide enough for the contents.

This skill was covered in: *Lesson 2-9: Re-size rows and columns.*

6   Given that one mile=1.609344 Km, enter a formula into cell D4 to convert MPH into KM/H.

This skill was covered in: *Lesson 2-12: Create your own formulas.*

The correct formula is: **=C4*1.609344.**

The Shelby's top speed is now displayed in Kilometers per hour.

	A	B	C	D	E	F
3	Make	Model	MPH	KM/H	0-60	BHP
4	Shelby	SSC Ultimate Aero	257	413.601408	2.7	1183

7   AutoFill the formula in Cell D4 down to the bottom of the list (cell D15).

This skill was covered in: *Lesson 2-15: Use AutoFill to adjust formulas.*

	A	B	C	D	E	F
3	Make	Model	MPH	KM/H	0-60	BHP
4	Shelby	SSC Ultimate Aero	257	413.601408	2.7	1183
5	Bugatti	Veyron	253	407.164032	2.5	1001

The worksheet is giving the right answers, but we're not really interested in seeing speeds to six decimal places. It would be nice to simply show whole numbers (also called integers) as we do for MPH.

8   Use the *Decrease Decimal* button to format the values in column D to display as whole numbers.

1. Select cells D4:D15.

2. Click the Home→Number→Decrease Decimal button ⊞ six times.

9   Make column D narrower to make things neater.

This skill was covered in: *Lesson 2-9: Re-size rows and columns.*

The World's Fastest Cars-5

	A	B	C	D	E	F
3	Make	Model	MPH	KM/H	0-60	BHP
4	Shelby	SSC Ultimate Aero	257	414	2.7	1183
5	Bugatti	Veyron	253	407	2.5	1001
6	Koenigsegg	CCX	250	402	3.2	806

note

Other ways to paste values

Using the Smart Tag

If you perform a regular *paste* and then suddenly realize that you really wanted to *paste values* you don't need to start again.

Notice that a Smart Tag is displayed at the bottom right corner of the pasted cells.

You can click the Smart Tag to change the paste to *Values*.

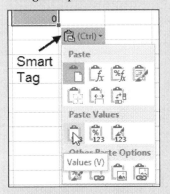

Smart Tag

Using the Ribbon

If you click:

Home→Clipboard→Paste

... you'll be presented with the same set of icons. You've only learned about the *Paste* and *Paste Values* options so far but you'll encounter some of the others later in this course:

10 Copy cells D4:D15 to cells D17:D28 using copy and paste.

1. Select cells D4:D15.

2. Right-click anywhere in the selected range and then click *Copy* from the shortcut menu.

3. Right-click cell D17 and click: Paste Options→Paste from the shortcut menu.

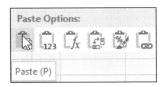

Unexpectedly, all of the values are pasted as zeros.

	A	B	C	D	E
17				0	
18				0	

11 Inspect the formula in cell D17.

Click cell D17 and look at the formula displayed in the Formula Bar at the top of the screen:

f_x =C17*1.609344

It is now clear why the value was correctly calculated as zero.

When you paste a formula, Excel will by default, adjust the formula in exactly the same way it does when you AutoFill.

12 Undo the previous paste.

Click the undo button on the quick access toolbar.

13 Paste again, this time using Paste Values.

Right-click in cell D17 and click: Paste Options→Values from the shortcut menu.

This time the values within the cells (rather than the formulas used to calculate the values) are pasted.

15	Ferrari	599 GTB	205	330	3.6	620
16					
17				414	
18				407	

14 Delete the values in cells D17:D28.

Select cells D17:D28 and press the **<Delete>** key.

15 Save your work as *The World's Fastest Cars-6*.

Lesson 3-6: Transpose a range

Paste Values is the most used special pasting option but there's another that is often very useful.

If a worksheet has many columns but few rows it may become impossible to print. In this case you may wish to reverse the arrangement so that the worksheet has many rows but few columns.

Transposing allows you to do this automatically.

1   Open *The World's Fastest Cars-6* from your sample files folder (if it isn't already open).

2   Rename Sheet3 to *Transposed*.

      This skill was covered in: *Lesson 1-9: View, move, add, rename, delete and navigate worksheet tabs.*

3   Select and copy the range A3:H15 on the *World Cars* worksheet.

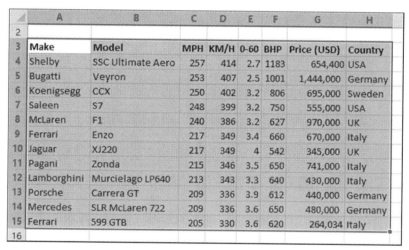

4   Select cell A3 on the *Transposed* worksheet.

5   Click: Home→Clipboard→Paste→Transpose.

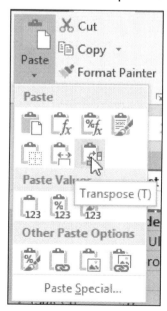

The World's Fastest Cars-6

The cells are copied in a rather interesting way. The columns have now become rows and the rows have become columns.

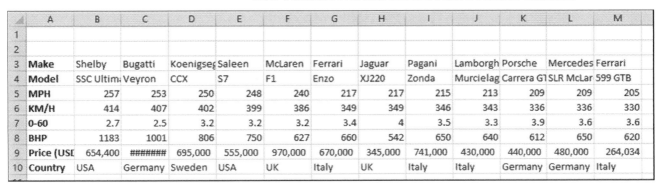

	A	B	C	D	E	F	G	H	I	J	K	L	M
1													
2													
3	Make	Shelby	Bugatti	Koenigseg	Saleen	McLaren	Ferrari	Jaguar	Pagani	Lamborgh	Porsche	Mercedes	Ferrari
4	Model	SSC Ultim:	Veyron	CCX	S7	F1	Enzo	XJ220	Zonda	Murcielag	Carrera G1	SLR McLar	599 GTB
5	MPH	257	253	250	248	240	217	217	215	213	209	209	205
6	KM/H	414	407	402	399	386	349	349	346	343	336	336	330
7	0-60	2.7	2.5	3.2	3.2	3.2	3.4	4	3.5	3.3	3.9	3.6	3.6
8	BHP	1183	1001	806	750	627	660	542	650	640	612	650	620
9	Price (USI	654,400	#######	695,000	555,000	970,000	670,000	345,000	741,000	430,000	440,000	480,000	264,034
10	Country	USA	Germany	Sweden	USA	UK	Italy	UK	Italy	Italy	Germany	Germany	Italy

Notice also that the width of the columns has not been maintained.

In the case of the (very expensive) Bugatti Veyron there isn't even enough space in the cell to display the price and a row of hashes is displayed instead.

(If you're used to calling the hash (#) a **pound sign** or **number sign** see the sidebar in: *Lesson 2-9: Re-size rows and columns* for an explanation).

6 Automatically size all columns in one operation.

1. Select every cell in the workbook by clicking the *select all* button in the top left corner of the worksheet:

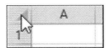

2. Hover the mouse cursor over the intersection of any two columns until you see the *re-size* cursor shape ⟷ and then double-click.

3. Every column is now perfectly sized.

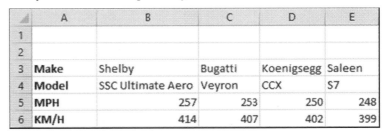

	A	B	C	D	E
1					
2					
3	Make	Shelby	Bugatti	Koenigsegg	Saleen
4	Model	SSC Ultimate Aero	Veyron	CCX	S7
5	MPH	257	253	250	248
6	KM/H	414	407	402	399

7 Save your work as *The World's Fastest Cars-7*.

note

About task panes

Task panes are similar to dialogs but there are several important differences.

1. Task panes are modeless.

Windows dialogs (with very few exceptions) are *modal*, while task panes are *modeless*.

Until you've dismissed a dialog (usually by clicking an *OK* or *Cancel* button) you can't do anything else.

If you click anywhere on the worksheet or Ribbon when a modal dialog is open, you'll just hear a "ding" noise!

Task panes are modeless.

This means that you can go on working and leave task panes happily sitting in the background.

2. Task panes can automatically update as you work.

Task panes can respond dynamically to any actions you take on the worksheet.

You can see this in action with the *Clipboard* task pane.

As you copy new items they automatically update in the task pane.

3. Task panes can be re-sized and either docked to the left or right of the screen or floated.

If you click and drag the title bar of a task pane, you can "dock" the pane to the right or left of the screen. This means that the task pane snaps into place and is then re-sized with the Excel window.

If you drag a task pane to the centre of the screen it becomes a "floating" task pane and can be positioned anywhere.

The World's Fastest Cars-7

Lesson 3-7: Use the Multiple Item Clipboard

When you copy items from any non-Office Windows application, the selected item is copied to the *Windows Clipboard*. You are then able to paste this item into any other Windows application.

While the *Windows Clipboard* can only contain one item, Office has its own clipboard that can contain up to 24 items.

Because all Office applications share the same *Office Clipboard*, it is possible to copy and paste up to 24 items between Excel, PowerPoint, Word, Access, Outlook… and all other Office applications.

In this lesson we'll use the *Office Clipboard* to add content to a new page in the workbook. The new page will contain details of the world's fastest *German* cars.

1   Open *The World's Fastest Cars-7* from your sample files folder (if it isn't already open).

2   Insert a new worksheet and name it *German Cars*.

This skill was covered in: *Lesson 1-9: View, move, add, rename, delete and navigate worksheet tabs.*

3   Click: Home→Clipboard→Dialog Launcher.

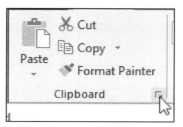

This is our first experience of using a *dialog launcher* button. The dialog launcher button is situated on the bottom right-hand corner of some Ribbon command groups.

The *Clipboard* task pane is displayed:

This is also your first use of a *Task Pane* (see sidebar for more on task panes).

4   If any items are shown on the Clipboard click the *Clear All* button
to remove them.

5   Copy row 3 on the World Cars worksheet to the clipboard.

Right-click the row 3 row header and click *Copy* on the shortcut menu.

6   Copy row 5 in the *World Cars* worksheet to the clipboard.

7   Copy row 13 in the *World Cars* worksheet to the clipboard.

8   Copy row 14 in the *World Cars* worksheet to the clipboard.

The header row, along with details for the three German cars, are now displayed on the clipboard (see sidebar).

9   Click the *German Cars* tab.

The blank *German Cars* worksheet is displayed.

10   Type **The World's Fastest German Cars** into cell A1 and bold face the text.

11   Click cell A3 to make it the Active Cell.

12   Complete the worksheet with a single click by clicking the *Paste All* button.

It would be possible to click once upon each of the four items on the Clipboard. Because we want the entire contents of the Clipboard four clicks are saved by using the *Paste All* button.

When you click the *Paste All* button, all of the items on the clipboard are pasted into adjacent rows:

13   Automatically Re-size all of the columns.

This skill was covered in: *Lesson 2-9: Re-size rows and columns.*

14   Close the clipboard task pane.

Click the *Close* button at the top right-hand corner of the clipboard task pane.

15   Save your work as *The World's Fastest Cars-8.*

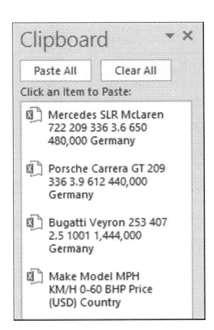

Lesson 3-8: Use Undo and Redo

Excel's (fantastically useful) *Undo* feature enables you to reverse an action when you have made a mistake.

It is only possible to undo the previous 100 actions.

Sometimes you may undo an action and then change your mind. Redo will step through the operations in reverse, in effect "undoing the undo"!

1   Close any workbooks that are open and then re-open Excel.

Excel keeps tabs on the last 100 actions taken. By closing and re-opening Excel you'll clear the existing list of actions available for undo.

2   Open *The World's Fastest Cars-8* from your sample files folder and select the *World Cars* worksheet.

3   Type **USA Cars** into cell A17 and bold face the text.

4   Copy row 3 into row 19.

5   Copy row 4 into row 20.

6   Copy row 7 into row 21.

The worksheet should now look like this:

	A	B	C	D	E	F	G	H
1	The World's Fastest Cars							
2								
3	**Make**	**Model**	**MPH**	**KM/H**	**0-60**	**BHP**	**Price (USD)**	**Country**
4	Shelby	SSC Ultimate Aero	257	414	2.7	1183	654,400	USA
5	Bugatti	Veyron	253	407	2.5	1001	1,444,000	Germany
6	Koenigsegg	CCX	250	402	3.2	806	695,000	Sweden
7	Saleen	S7	248	399	3.2	750	555,000	USA
8	McLaren	F1	240	386	3.2	627	970,000	UK
9	Ferrari	Enzo	217	349	3.4	660	670,000	Italy
10	Jaguar	XJ220	217	349	4	542	345,000	UK
11	Pagani	Zonda	215	346	3.5	650	741,000	Italy
12	Lamborghini	Murcielago LP640	213	343	3.3	640	430,000	Italy
13	Porsche	Carrera GT	209	336	3.9	612	440,000	Germany
14	Mercedes	SLR McLaren 722	209	336	3.6	650	480,000	Germany
15	Ferrari	599 GTB	205	330	3.6	620	264,034	Italy
16								
17	**USA Cars**							
18								
19	**Make**	**Model**	**MPH**	**KM/H**	**0-60**	**BHP**	**Price (USD)**	**Country**
20	Shelby	SSC Ultimate Aero	257	414	2.7	1183	654,400	USA
21	Saleen	S7	248	399	3.2	750	555,000	USA

7   Click the undo button on the quick access toolbar.

The Saleen details disappear from row 21.

8   Click the redo button on the quick access toolbar.

The Saleen details re-appear in row 21.

---

note

Using the keyboard to undo and redo

It is well worth remembering the undo keyboard shortcut:

<Ctrl>+<Z>

I use it all of the time. It is also the undo shortcut for the other Office applications.

You'll use the Redo action far less, but for completeness it is:

<Ctrl>+<Y>

If you forget them, you'll see the keyboard shortcuts in the tooltip when you hover over the undo and redo buttons.

Undo Paste (Ctrl+Z)

The World's Fastest Cars-8

---

9 Click the drop-down arrow to the right of the undo button on the quick access toolbar.

A drop-down menu appears showing all of the actions that have taken place (or the previous 100 actions if more than 100 actions have taken place) since the workbook was opened.

10 Click the Bold action to *Undo 4 Actions*.

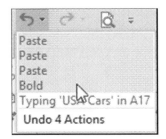

Only the text *USA Cars* remains on the worksheet and it is no longer bold faced.

14	Mercedes	SLR McLaren 722	209	336
15	Ferrari	599 GTB	205	330
16				
17	USA Cars			

11 Click the drop-down arrow to the right of the redo button on the quick access toolbar.

A drop-down menu appears showing all of the actions that have been undone and can be potentially re-done.

12 Click the last *Paste* action to redo four actions.

The worksheet reverts to its former state.

17	USA Cars								
18									
19	Make	Model	MPH	KM/H	0-60	BHP		Price (USD)	Country
20	Shelby	SSC Ultimate Aero	257	414	2.7	1183		654,400	USA
21	Saleen	S7	248	399	3.2	750		555,000	USA

13 Delete rows 17 to 21.

14 Save your work as *The World's Fastest Cars-9*.

Lesson 3-9: Insert cell comments

1　Open *The World's Fastest Cars-9* from your sample files folder (if it isn't already open) and select the *World Cars* worksheet.

2　Using Microsoft Word (not Excel), open *Car Descriptions* from your sample files folder.

　　1.　Open Microsoft Word.

　　2.　Click: Office→Open and open *Car Descriptions* from your sample files folder.

3　Return to Excel without closing Word.

　　You will notice two buttons on the Windows status bar at the bottom of the screen:

　　Click the button with the Excel logo to return to Excel.

4　Set up the name that will appear in the comment box.

　　Whenever you enter a comment, your name is added to the top.

　　This allows other users to identify the source of each comment if you later distribute the workbook.

　　1.　Click: File→Options→General.

　　2.　In the category *Personalize your copy of Microsoft Office* type your name into the *User Name* box.

　　3.　Click the OK button.

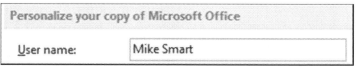

5　Copy the text for the Shelby SSC Ultimate Aero from the Word document.

　　1.　Return to Word.

　　2.　Drag across the Shelby text with the mouse cursor.

　　3.　Right-click within the selected text and click *Copy* from the shortcut menu.

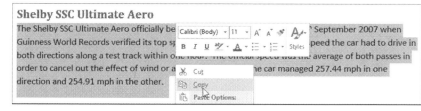

Car Descriptions

The World's Fastest Cars-9

6　Add the comment text to the Shelby model cell (cell B4).

　　1.　Return to Excel.

2. Right-click cell B4 and click *Insert Comment* on the shortcut menu.

A comment box with your name at the top is shown next to cell B4.

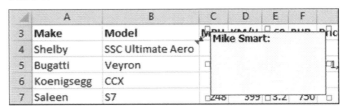

3. Paste into the comment box.

The text that you copied from the Word document appears in the box.

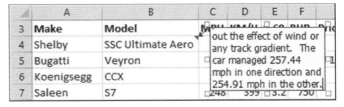

7   Enlarge the comment box, using the sizing handles, so that all text is visible.

The sizing handles are the small white dots that appear on the corners and edges of the comment box. When you hover over a sizing handle the cursor shape changes to a double headed arrow.

1. Hover carefully over the bottom-right sizing handle until you see the double-headed arrow cursor shape.

2. Click and drag to re-size the comment box.

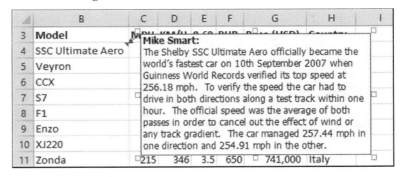

8   Click anywhere in the worksheet.

The comment disappears but a small red triangle has appeared in the top right corner of the cell.

9   Add two more comments for the Saleen S7 and Pagani Zonda.

10 Save your work as *The World's Fastest Cars-10.*

Lesson 3-10: View cell comments

1   Open *The World's Fastest Cars-10* from your sample files folder (if it isn't already open) and select the *World Cars* worksheet.

Cells with comments show a small red triangle in their top right-hand corner.

2   View the comment behind a single cell.

Hover the mouse cursor over any of the cells with a red triangle. The cell comment is displayed.

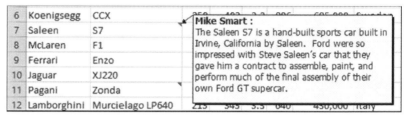

3   View all of the comments in a worksheet at the same time.

Click: Review➔Comments➔Show All Comments.

Every comment on the worksheet is displayed.

Unfortunately, the comments overlap so you are unable to read them all at the same time. It is possible to view each comment by clicking it, as this brings the window to the front, but it isn't very elegant.

4   Move the comments so that they do not overlap.

Click a comment and then hover anywhere on the border *but not on a sizing handle* until you see a four headed arrow. When you see the four-headed arrow click and drag to move the comment.

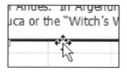

The World's Fastest Cars-10

	A	B	C	D	E	F	G	H	I	J
1	**The World's Fastest Cars**									
2										
3	**Make**	**Model**	**MPH**	**K**						
4	Shelby	SSC Ultimate Aero	257							
5	Bugatti	Veyron	253							
6	Koenigsegg	CCX	250							
7	Saleen	S7	248							
8	McLaren	F1	240							
9	Ferrari	Enzo	217							
10	Jaguar	XJ220	217							
11	Pagani	Zonda	215							
12	Lamborghini	Murcielago LP640	213							
13	Porsche	Carrera GT	209							
14	Mercedes	SLR McLaren 722	209							
15	Ferrari	599 GTB	205							
16										
17										
18										
19										
20										
21										
22										

Mike Smart :
The Shelby SSC Ultimate Aero officially became the world's fastest car on 10th September 2007 when Guinness World Records verified its top speed at 256.18 mph. To verify the speed the car had to drive in both directions along a test track within one hour. The official speed was the average of both passes in order to cancel out the effect of wind or any track gradient. The car managed 257.44 mph in one direction and 254.91 mph in the other.

Mike Smart :
The Saleen S7 is a hand-built sports car built in Irvine, California by Saleen. Ford were so impressed with Steve Saleen's car that they gave him a contract to assemble, paint, and perform much of the final assembly of their own Ford GT supercar.

Mike Smart :
The Zonda is one of the world's most exclusive supercars as the Italian manufacturer, Pagani, only build around 25 cars per year. By April 2008 only 91 Zondas had ever been built. Horacio Pagani named the car after a powerful warm wind that blows over the Argentinean Andes. In Argentina the wind is also known as Huayrapuca or the "Witch's Wind".

note

Other ways to show/hide comments

The right-click method is definitely the fastest but you can also show and hide comments using the Ribbon.

To show or hide a comment:

1. Click the cell containing the comment to make it the active cell.

2. Click:

   Review→Comments→ Show/Hide Comment

5 Hide all of the comments.

Click: Review→Comments→Show All Comments.

The comments disappear.

6 Make the Zonda comment display all of the time.

Sometimes you will want to send somebody a worksheet and make sure that an important comment is on view when they open it.

Right click cell B11 and choose *Show/Hide Comments* from the shortcut menu.

The comment remains on display all of the time (even if you are not hovering over the comment cell).

7 Hide the Zonda comment.

Right click cell B11 and choose *Hide Comment* from the shortcut menu.

8 Save your work as *The World's Fastest Cars-11*.

Lesson 3-11: Print cell comments

One of the most common comment-related questions asked in my Excel classroom courses is: "how can I print a list of comments at the end of a worksheet"? Excel can do this but the feature is hidden away in the *Page Setup* dialog and missed by most users.

1 Open *The World's Fastest Cars-11* from your sample files folder (if it isn't already open) and select the *World Cars* worksheet.

2 Tell Excel to print comments at the end of the worksheet.

1. Click: Page Layout→Page Setup→Dialog Launcher.

The *Dialog Launcher* is the small button on the bottom-right corner of the *Page Setup* group.

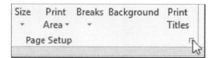

The *Page Setup* dialog is displayed.

2. Click the *Sheet* tab.

3. Click the *Comments* drop-down and select: *At end of sheet.*

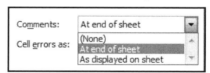

3 Click the *Print Preview* button to view the comments as they would print.

You can either click the *Print Preview* button on the *Page Setup* dialog or close the dialog and click: File→Print.

Whichever way you choose, the *Backstage* view opens and displays a print preview of the worksheet in the right-hand pane.

Click the *Next Page* button ◁ [1] of 2 ▷ to view Page 2 of the preview. The comments are displayed exactly as they would print.

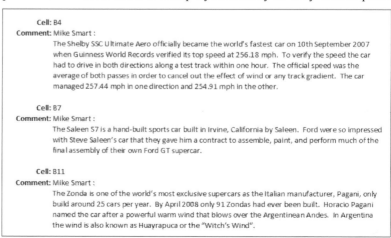

The World's Fastest Cars-11

4   Click the *Back Button*  to return to the worksheet.

5   Make the Zonda comment display all of the time.

Right click cell B11 and click: *Show/Hide Comments* from the shortcut menu.

6   Move the Zonda comment so that it doesn't obscure the data in the worksheet.

This was covered in: *Lesson 3-10: View cell comments.*

7   Tell Excel to print comments exactly as they are displayed on the worksheet.

1.   Click: Page Layout→Page Setup→Dialog Launcher.

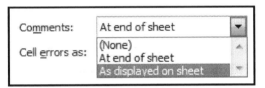

The *Page Setup* dialog is displayed.

2.   Click the *Sheet* tab.

3.   Click the *Comments* drop-down and select: *As displayed on sheet.*

Comments:	At end of sheet ▼
Cell errors as:	(None)
	At end of sheet
	As displayed on sheet

8   Click the *Print Preview* button to view the comment as it would print.

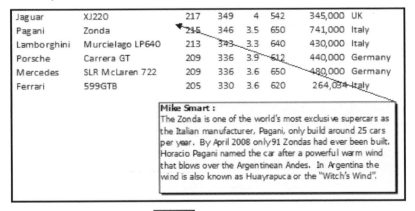

9   Click the *Back Button*  on the ribbon to return to the worksheet.

10   Hide the comment.

Right click cell B11 and click: *Hide Comment* from the shortcut menu.

11   Save your work as: *The World's Fastest Cars-12.*

Lesson 3-12: Understand absolute and relative cell references

You've seen how useful Excel's AutoFill is when copying formulas. Most of the time things work perfectly, as you normally want to increment row and column references when you AutoFill down and across.

Sometimes AutoFill can be a little too helpful when it adjusts cell references that you would like to be left alone. This lesson will illustrate the type of worksheet that requires *absolute cell references* as we convert USD (US Dollar) prices to GBP (Great Britain Pounds).

1   Open *The World's Fastest Cars-12* from your sample files folder (if it isn't already open) and select the *World Cars* worksheet.

2   Insert a column to the left of column H.

   This skill was covered in: *Lesson 3-1: Insert and delete rows and columns.*

3   Type **Price (GBP)** into cell H3.

4   Type **USD/GBP** into cell G1.

5   Type **0.51195** into cell H1.

   If you want more realism you can get the current exchange rate from www.oanda.com. If you are not in England or America it might be fun to change the exchange rate to match your own currency.

6   Place a formula in cell H4 that will calculate the price of a Shelby SSC Ultimate Aero in GBP (Great Britain Pounds).

   Formulas were covered in: *Lesson 2-12: Create your own formulas.*

   The correct formula is:

   =G4*H1

   We can now see that the Shelby costs £335,020 in Great Britain Pounds.

	G	H	I
1	USD/GBP	0.51195	
2			
3	Price (USD)	Price (GBP)	Country
4	654,400	335,020	USA

7   Consider what will happen if we AutoFill this formula.

   AutoFill was covered in: *Lesson 2-15: Use AutoFill to adjust formulas.*

   As the formula is AutoFilled downward the number part of each formula will be incremented like this:

The World's Fastest Cars-12

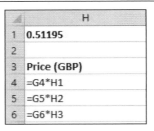

Consider cell H5 (the price of the Bugatti Veyron). The formula in this cell is **=G5*H2**.

AutoFill has done a wonderful job with G5. It has changed the reference from the Shelby's price to the Bugatti, and that's exactly what we wanted.

But AutoFill has seriously messed up with the H2 reference. The exchange rate is always in cell H1. It never moves.

To express this in Excel terminology: G4 is a **relative reference** (ie we want AutoFill to adjust it) while H1 is an **absolute reference** (ie we want AutoFill to leave it alone).

8   Change the formula in cell H4 to make H1 into an absolute reference.

To make a reference absolute you simply add a dollar sign in front of both the letter and number.

So: H1 becomes $H$1.

Click cell H4 and then edit the formula (shown in the formula bar) so that it now reads:

=G4*$H$1

9   AutoFill the formula in cell H4 to the end of the list.

(AutoFill was covered in: *Lesson 2-15: Use AutoFill to adjust formulas*).

The price of each car is now displayed in both US Dollars and Great Britain Pounds.

	G	H	I
3	Price (USD)	Price (GBP)	Country
4	654,400	335,020	USA
5	1,444,000	739,256	Germany
6	695,000	355,805	Sweden

Click on each of the GBP prices and observe the formula shown in the formula bar at the top of the screen.

In each cell Excel has adjusted the G4 part of the formula but left the H1 part of the formula alone.

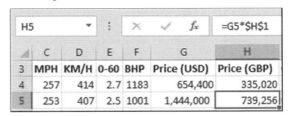

10   Save your work as *The World's Fastest Cars-13*.

note

Don't worry if you're unable to understand this concept at first

In my "Essential Skills" classroom courses I've found that many students find mixed cell references a very difficult concept to understand.

I never waste a lot of time on this lesson if it is clear that some students are unable to easily follow the logic.

I'd advise that you take the same approach and don't waste a lot of time on this lesson if you find it difficult to follow.

You won't need to use mixed cell references anywhere else in the *Essential Skills* course and it's a skill that most office workers don't have.

If you do skip this lesson it's well worthwhile returning to it later, when you've completed the course and have been using Excel for a few months.

By then you will probably have encountered some of the real-world business problems that are more efficiently solved using mixed cell references.

Lesson 3-13: Understand mixed cell references

Before we tackle mixed cell references I must warn you that this subject is a bit of a brain teaser (see sidebar). The skill is well worth mastering as you'll find it extremely useful in many types of real-world worksheets.

1   Open *International Price List* from your sample files folder.

This worksheet will calculate the price of each car in five different currencies. The exchange rates are shown in row 4.

2   Add a formula to cell D6 that will calculate the UK price of a Shelby SSC Ultimate Aero.

Formulas were covered in: *Lesson 2-12: Create your own formulas.*

The correct formula is:

=C6*D4

We can see that the Shelby costs £335,020.

	C	D	E	F	G	H
3		GBP	EUR	JPY	CAD	CHF
4		0.51195	0.64682	198.687	1.04422	1.05489
5	USA $	UK £	Euros €	Japan ¥	Canada $	Switzerland fr.
6	654,400	335,020				

3   Consider what will happen if we AutoFill this formula.

AutoFill was covered in: *Lesson 2-15: Use AutoFill to adjust formulas.*

As the formula is AutoFilled downward, the number part of each formula is incremented like this:

	C	D
6	654400	=C6*D4
7	1444000	=C7*D5
8	695000	=C8*D6

The reference to cell C6 is being correctly adjusted to point to the price of each car in the list. There is a problem with the reference to cell D4 as it should not be adjusted.

You may be thinking that this problem is exactly the same as the one solved in: *Lesson 3-12: Understand absolute and relative cell references.*

Why not simply make D4 into an absolute reference? Like this:

	C	D
3		GBP
4		0.51195
5	USA $	UK £
6	654400	=C6*$D$4

International Price List

This will work just fine for the GBP prices, but think carefully about what will then happen when you AutoFill to the right.

AutoFill knows that when you fill right you *usually* want the letter part of each formula incremented like this:

	C	D	E
3		GBP	EUR
4		0.51195	0.64682
5	**USA $**	**UK £**	**Euros €**
6	654400	=C6*$D$4	=D6*$D$4
7	1444000	=C7*$D$4	
8	695000	=C8*$D$4	

This will not correctly calculate the Euro price. AutoFill has made two errors.

1. It is still using the GBP exchange rate for the EUR prices because we made D4 an absolute reference.

2. It is referencing the UK price of the Shelby instead of the US dollar price because C6 is a relative reference.

Let's tackle each problem one at a time

1. We want the GBP exchange rate to adjust to the EUR exchange rate as the formula is filled to the right. In this case the D part of D4 should be relative but the 4 part should be absolute. This can be denoted by D$4 instead of $D$4.

2. We want the US Dollar price to always be used against the US Dollar Exchange rates in Row 4. Therefore we want the C part of C6 to be absolute. As AutoFill fills downward we need the price to be adjusted to the relevant car so the 6 part of C6 needs to be relative. This can be denoted by $C6 instead of $C$6.

4   Correct the formula so that it will AutoFill correctly.

Enter the formula =$C6*D$4 into cell D6.

This will AutoFill correctly like this:

	C	D	E
3		GBP	EUR
4		0.51195	0.64682
5	**USA $**	**UK £**	**Euros €**
6	654400	=$C6*D$4	=$C6*E$4
7	1444000	=$C7*D$4	=$C7*E$4
8	695000	=$C8*D$4	=$C8*E$4

5   AutoFill across to cell H6.

The correct Shelby prices are shown in five currencies.

6   AutoFill down to cell H17.

The correct prices are shown for all cars and all currencies.

7   Make the columns wide enough to display the prices.

8   Save your work as *International Price List-1*.

© 2013 The Smart Method® Ltd

tip

A faster way to add dollar signs to create mixed references

1. Click on the formula bar so that the cursor is touching the cell reference you want to convert to mixed:

    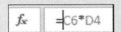
    fx =C6*D4

2. Press the <F4> key repeatedly on the keyboard.

    Each time you press <F4> Excel cycles through all possible absolute and mixed references:

    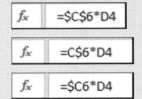
    fx =$C$6*D4

    fx =C$6*D4

    fx =$C6*D4

note

Templates and cloud computing

Until you've completed: *Session Eight: Cloud Computing,* you may not completely understand this sidebar as we're getting a little ahead of ourselves.

In: *Session Eight: Cloud Computing,* you'll learn how you can store your files on a OneDrive so that you can work on the same files from any device (computer, smartphone or pad), at any location.

This way of working is called *Cloud Computing.*

If you do decide to move your files to the cloud you'll also want your custom templates to reside in the cloud so that they are available on all of your devices.

In this case you'd set the default custom template folder to a location in your local synchronized OneDrive folder.

Lesson 3-14: Understand templates and set the default custom template folder

A template is simply a partially completed, normal workbook that contains the starting point for a task that you often need to do. You can put anything into a template that you can put into a regular workbook.

What are sample templates?

A sample template is a template that was created by Microsoft or another third-party. Sample templates aim to give you a starting point to solve common problems with Excel.

Several sample templates are shown on the *New* dialog (the dialog you see when you first start Excel), such as a *Wedding Budget* and *Weekly Chore Schedule.*

There are many thousands more sample templates available online.

It may seem, at first, as if sample templates are a replacement for having to learn Excel but they are not quite as useful as they first promise to be.

There are three potential problems in using them:

1. Sample templates often appear to provide a solution that is *almost* what you need. You may find that the work involved in converting them to *exactly* what you need takes longer than starting from scratch.

2. Some templates include very advanced Excel features that non-expert users will find difficult to understand.

3. Some templates include VBA (Visual Basic for Applications) code to extend Excel's normal capability. While VBA code can be used to implement some very impressive features, it can be impossible to maintain or customize this type of workbook unless you have access to a competent VBA programmer.

What is a custom template?

A custom template is a template that you have created yourself. Because you competely understand how custom templates work, you may find them far more useful than sample templates.

note

How do I create a subfolder?

The concept of folders, subfolders and files is a very fundamental Windows skill rather than an Excel skill.

If you do not have basic Windows skills (an understanding of how Windows organizes files) you would get good value from a Windows book to give you the foundation skills you need to use any Windows program.

Here's how you create a new subfolder:

1. Right-click on the *Custom Office Templates* folder.

2. Click *New Folder* in the shortcut menu.

A new folder will appear called *New Folder*.

3. You will now be able to type: **Excel** in order to name the folder.

If this doesn't work for you, right-click the new folder and select *Rename* from the shortcut menu. You'll then be able to type: **Excel** to rename the folder.

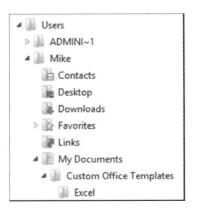

You'll often find yourself making copies of older workbooks that are nearly the same as the one you need. You'll then delete the bits you don't need and add the bits that you do.

If you find this happening, it's time to make a custom template.

You'll learn how to make your first custom template later, in: *Lesson 3-15: Create a template.*

What is the custom template folder?

The custom template folder is where custom templates are stored on your computer.

By default, all templates, for all Office applications (such as Excel, Word and PowerPoint), are stored in the same folder. This isn't a great idea as you may create a large number of templates and they will be easier to work with if you organize them.

A new feature for Office 2013 is the ability to set a different default custom template location for each Office application.

We're going to organize our templates properly, so we need a folder that will contain only *Excel* custom templates. If you work with Word and PowerPoint you can use the same technique to create different folders for Word and PowerPoint custom templates.

1 Create an *Excel* folder beneath the *Custom Office Templates* folder.

  1. Use *Windows File Explorer* to navigate to the folder:

     C:\Users\[Your Windows Log-in Name]\My Documents\ Custom Office Templates

  2. Create a sub-folder beneath the *Custom Office Templates* folder named *Excel*.

     Your folder will look different to the one shown in the sidebar, but you should see your own Windows log-in name instead of *Mike*.

2 Open a new blank workbook.

  When you open a blank workbook you are actually creating a workbook using the *Blank workbook* standard template.

3 Set the default *Custom Office Templates* folder so that it points to the new Excel folder you have just created.

  Click: File→Options→Save.

  In the *Save Workbooks* section, assuming that you are logged into Windows, you'll see that the current *Default personal templates folder* is set to:

  | Default personal templates location: | C:\Users\Mike\Documents\Custom Office Templates\ |

  Click at the end of the location path and type: **Excel**

  | Default personal templates location: | C:\Users\Mike\Documents\Custom Office Templates\Excel |

4 Close Excel.

Lesson 3-15: Create a template

1 Open *First Quarter Sales and Bonus* from your sample files folder.

note

This worksheet looks flashy!

If you are wondering how to make your own worksheets look as flashy as this one you'll only need a little more patience.

You'll learn every skill you need to make your worksheets look as good, and even a lot better than this one in the next session: *Session Four: Making Your Worksheets Look Professional.*

	A	B	C	D	E
1	First quarter sales and bonus				
2					
3	Sales				
4					
5	First Name	Last Name	Sales	Target	Over Target Sales
6	Andrew	Fuller	7,639.30	5,000	2,639.30
7	Anne	Dodsworth	2,979.30	5,000	- 2,020.70
8	Janet	Leverling	29,658.60	5,000	24,658.60
9	Laura	Callahan	19,271.60	5,000	14,271.60
10	Margaret	Peacock	44,795.20	5,000	39,795.20
11	Michael	Suyama	4,109.80	5,000	- 890.20
12	Nancy	Davolio	15,330.10	5,000	10,330.10
13	Robert	King	21,461.60	5,000	16,461.60
14	Steven	Buchanan	2,634.40	5,000	- 2,365.60
15		Total:	147,879.90		
16					
17	Bonus				
18					
19	First Name	Last Name	Salary	Bonus	Total
20	Andrew	Fuller	2,500	131.97	2,631.97
21	Anne	Dodsworth	2,000	-	2,000.00
22	Janet	Leverling	2,600	1,232.93	3,832.93
23	Laura	Callahan	2,800	713.58	3,513.58
24	Margaret	Peacock	3,000	1,989.76	4,989.76
25	Michael	Suyama	1,800	-	1,800.00
26	Nancy	Davolio	4,500	516.51	5,016.51
27	Robert	King	2,000	823.08	2,823.08
28	Steven	Buchanan	3,000	-	3,000.00
29		Total:	24,200	5,407.82	29,607.82

This is exactly the type of workbook you'd probably want to convert into a template. Only the data in cells C6:D14 will change each quarter.

Every quarter you could simply open last quarter's workbook, save it with a new name and then delete the old values in cells C6:D14. But you'd have to do that every quarter and then, one day, you might forget the *save it with a new name* step and end up overwriting the old file.

A much more efficient solution would be to save a copy of the workbook, with blank values in cells C6:D14, as a template.

2 Delete the contents of cells *C6:D14*.

This is the data that changes every quarter. Deleting it will provide an empty template, ready to be populated with each quarter's figures.

First Quarter Sales and Bonus

3 Replace the text in cell A1 with the words: *Bonus Calculator*.

This is a more generic title that can be used for any quarter.

4 Save your work as: *Bonus Calculator*.

5 Save the workbook again, this time as a template.

   1. Click: File→Save As→Computer→Browse.

   2. Click the drop down list arrow labeled *Save as Type* at the bottom of the *Save As* dialog.

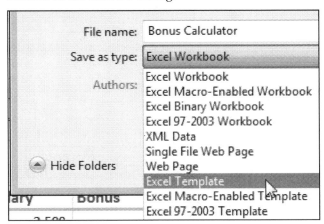

   3. The best choice for this workbook is: *Excel Template*.

      If this template needed to be used by users with very old versions of Excel you'd choose *Excel 97-2003* template.

      If the workbook contained macros (working with macros is an Expert level skill covered fully in the *Expert Skills* book in this series) you'd need to choose *Excel Macro-Enabled Template*.

   4. Click the *Save* button to save the template to the default template folder that you created in: *Lesson 3-14: Understand templates and set the default custom template folder*.

      The existing name: *Bonus Calculator* is fine.

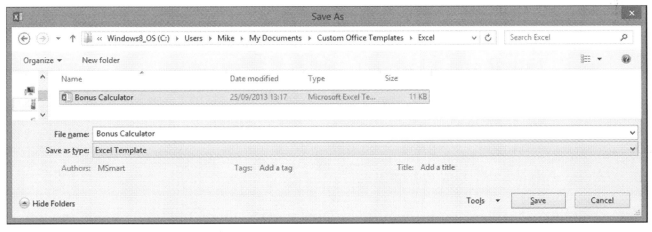

6 Close Excel.

note

How to make your custom template appear at the top of the Featured Templates list

Sometimes you may have a template that you use very often.

You may find it tedious to have to click:

File→New→Personal

... every time that you need to use it.

To save time you can *pin* the template. This means that it will appear at the top of the *Featured Templates* list.

The template will then be easy to find, and you'll also save a click every time you create a new worksheet based upon it.

To pin a template click the pin icon at the bottom-right of the template icon:

The unpinned icon: ⊀ will then change to a pinned icon: 📌.

The template will then appear at the top of the *Featured Templates* list.

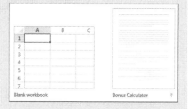

Lesson 3-16: Use a template

1   Open Excel.

2   Display your own custom templates.

Notice that there are two links above the templates labelled *Featured* and *Personal*. The Personal templates are your own custom templates.

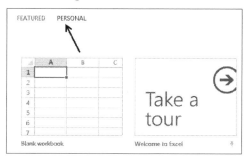

Click the *Personal* link

A dialog appears showing all of the templates in your custom templates folder:

At the moment the only custom template is the *Bonus Calculator* template you saved in: *Lesson 3-15: Create a template*.

3   Click the *Bonus Calculator* template.

A new workbook is created from the template.

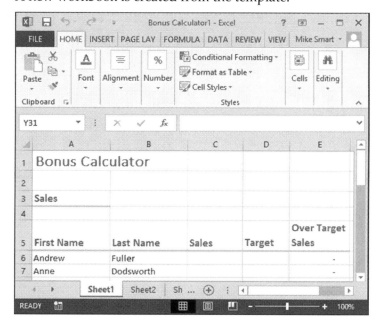

Notice that the workbook has been named *Bonus Calculator1*. You are not looking at the template but a new workbook created from the template.

4   Use a sample template.

A set of Microsoft sample templates are included with every copy of Excel.

1.   Click: File→New.

The start-up screen is displayed showing a number of standard Excel templates and apps. Apps are a brand new feature for Excel 2013 that you will learn about in: *Lesson 3-17: Add an App to a workbook.*

You can tell which are templates, and which are apps, because apps always have a postfix of *app.*

2.   Click one of Microsoft's sample templates.

Create

3.   Click the *Create* button.

A workbook is created from the template.

Some of Microsoft's sample templates may seem a little overwhelming at the moment but they'll seem far less intimidating by the time you reach the end of this book.

5   Create a workbook from Microsoft's library of online templates.

You'll need to be connected to the Internet to use an online template.

Microsoft have a huge library containing thousands of templates that they add to all of the time and make available to you for free.

1.   Click: File→New.

2.   Type: **Calendar** in the *Search for online templates* box at the top of the screen.

3.   Press the **<Enter>** key.

After a few moments a huge scrolling list of calendars appears on the screen.

4.   Click on any of the calendar templates.

5.   Click the *Create* button.

A workbook (containing a nicely formatted calendar) is created from the template.

note

Don't worry if you can't understand how some of the templates have been constructed

Don't worry if you can't understand how some of the calendar templates work yet.

Many have been constructed using very advanced techniques and some have even had features added using VBA (Visual Basic for Applications) programming code to extend Excel's normal feature set.

For the above reasons you may find that sample templates are not useful for real-world projects when you need to thoroughly understand how they have been constructed.

note

What are Excel apps useful for?

Excel apps are a brand new feature for Excel 2013 and it is likely that thousands of new apps will become available over the coming years.

Of the apps that have been developed so far, three types seem to be the most useful:

New Chart types

As you'll discover in: *Session Five: Charts and Graphics,* Excel already has a huge range of chart types. If the built-in chart types do not address a specific business need, it is now possible to pay a programmer to create any chart type that can be described as an *Excel content app.*

The *Gauge* content app shown in the lesson is a good example of this.

Interfacing with real-time data

Many users will need to interface with current real-time data (data that is constantly changing). Examples would include exchange rates or share and commodity prices.

There are many apps available to provide current currency exchange rates and stock prices.

Interfacing with databases

One of my favourite free content apps is the *Bing Maps app.*

This allows you to reference place names (for example *London* or *New York*) and associated data (for example the population of each city) in a worksheet range.

The location is then found in the Bing maps database and displayed as a map embedded within the worksheet. Hotspots on the map can then be clicked to display the associated data.

Lesson 3-17: Add an App to a workbook

Apps are a new feature for Excel 2013. Apps allow programmers to create new components that you can add to a workbook. These components can add functionality that isn't present in the Excel product.

Apps can take two forms:

Task Pane apps

You are already familiar with the *Clipboard* task pane that you used in: *Lesson 3-7: Use the Multiple Item Clipboard.*

A good example of a task pane app is the *Unit Converter* app. It is a handy calculator that allows you to quickly convert units from one category to another.

For example, it can convert *pounds* into *kilograms* or *miles per hour* into *kilometers per hour.*

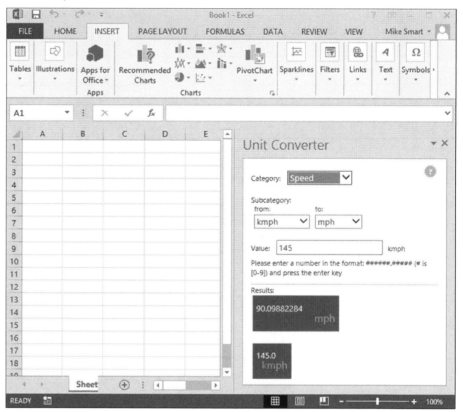

Content Apps

Content apps float within the grid (in a similar way to charts, which you will learn about later, in: *Session Five: Charts and Graphics*).

Content apps are useful for adding components to a worksheet. A good example of a content app is the *Gauge* app. This allows a value to be graphically represented on a dial gauge:

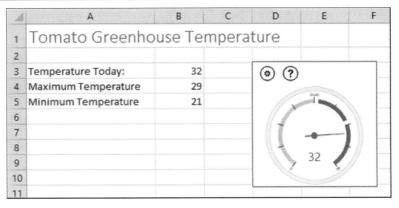

Excel does not support dial gauges. The above worksheet was created by adding a *Gauge* content app to a worksheet.

You will need to be connected to the Internet and logged in to a *Microsoft Account* in order to follow-through with this lesson (You'll learn more about Microsoft Accounts in: *Session Eight: Cloud Computing*).

1   Open a new blank workbook.

2   Add the *Merriam Webster dictionary* to the workbook.

(If the Merriam Webster dictionary is no longer available free of charge, see sidebar).

1.   Click: Insert→Apps→Store.

The *Apps for Office* dialog appears.

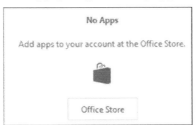

2.   Click the *Office Store* button.

Your web browser opens and displays a list of apps available at the Office Store.

3.   Click the *Merriam-Webster Dictionary* app.

4.   Click the *Add* button.

5.   Click the *Continue* button to download the app and make it available to Excel.

6.   Close the browser window.

7.   Click: Insert→Apps for Office→My Apps.

You should see the *Merriam-Webster dictionary* listed. If not click the *Refresh* button.

8.   Click the *Merriam Webster dictionary* icon.

9.   Click the *Insert* button.

The dictionary is added to your workbook as a task pane.

Lesson 3-18: Freeze columns and rows

1   Open *Sales First Quarter 2008* from your sample files folder.

Notice that it is easy to see which data is in each column when you are at the top of the worksheet and can see the top row:

	A	B	C	D
1	Date	First Name	Last Name	Company Name
2	01-Jan-08	Nancy	Davolio	Eastern Connection
3	01-Jan-08	Nancy	Davolio	Eastern Connection

But things get confusing when you scroll further down the list:

	A	B	C	D
128	17-Feb-08	Margaret	Peacock	Rancho grande
129	17-Feb-08	Margaret	Peacock	Rancho grande
130	18-Feb-08	Janet	Leverling	Blondel père et fils

It is no longer clear what information is contained in each column because the top row has disappeared.

2   Press **<Ctrl>+<Home>** to quickly move to Cell A1.

3   Click: View→Window→Freeze Panes.

A rich menu is displayed:

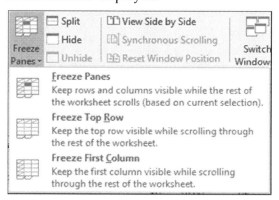

With Excel's rich menus, the meaning of each option is quite clear.

4   Click the *Freeze Top Row* menu item.

A small black line appears beneath the first row.

5   Scroll down the list.

Notice that as you scroll down, the top row now remains in place.

	A	B	C	D
1	Date	First Name	Last Name	Company Name
47	16-Jan-08	Margaret	Peacock	Simons bistro
48	16-Jan-08	Margaret	Peacock	Simons bistro
49	16-Jan-08	Margaret	Peacock	Simons bistro
50	17-Jan-08	Margaret	Peacock	QUICK-Stop

6   Unfreeze the top row.

note

Another way to freeze the top row would be to convert the range into a table.

Excel automatically freezes column headers in tables.

Working with tables is an Expert level skill covered fully in the *Expert Skills* book in this series.

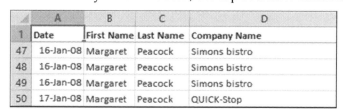

Sales First Quarter 2008

Click: View→Window→Freeze Panes once more.

The first choice has now changed to *Unfreeze Panes*. Click this menu item to put things back to normal.

7   Freeze the first column.

Do exactly as you did before but, this time, select *Freeze First Column* from the rich menu.

Notice that the date column is now locked into place. As you scroll to the right, the date remains in the first column.

	A	F	G	H
1	Date	Country	Product Name	Quantity
2	01-Jan-08	UK	Thüringer Rostbratwurst	21
3	01-Jan-08	UK	Steeleye Stout	35

8   Unfreeze the panes.

9   Freeze the first two rows and the left most three columns.

Whilst a simple freezing of the top row or first column may sometimes be what you need, you'll often want to freeze both columns *and* rows.

You'll sometimes also want to freeze more than one column and/or row.

1. Click in cell D3 to make it the active cell.

    This is your way of telling Excel that you want to freeze all cells above, and to the left of, cell D3.

2. Click: View→Window→Freeze Panes again but, this time, select the first option from the rich menu: *Freeze Panes*.

    The first two rows and first three columns are frozen.

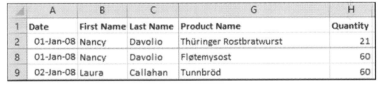

	A	B	C	G	H
1	Date	First Name	Last Name	Product Name	Quantity
2	01-Jan-08	Nancy	Davolio	Thüringer Rostbratwurst	21
8	01-Jan-08	Nancy	Davolio	Fløtemysost	60
9	02-Jan-08	Laura	Callahan	Tunnbröd	60

10   Unfreeze the panes.

Lesson 3-19: Split the window into multiple panes

1   Open *Sales First Quarter 2008* from your sample files folder (if it isn't already open).

2   Press **<Ctrl>+<End>** to quickly move to the end of the worksheet (cell J242).

This is quite a long list. Imagine that you need to compare sales for 3rd February 2008 to sales for 3rd March 2008.

This could involve a lot of scrolling unless you split the window into two panes.

3   Split the window into two horizontal panes.

1. Click in a cell in Column A that is positioned around half way down the screen.

As you'll see later in this lesson, the active cell determines whether the window will be split horizontally, vertically, or both horizontally and vertically.

For a horizontal split, the active cell needs to be a cell within column A.

The position of the active cell also determines where the screen will be split. By positioning it half way down the screen we will split the screen into two equally sized panes.

2. Click: View→Window→Split.

The screen is split into two independently scrolling horizontal panes.

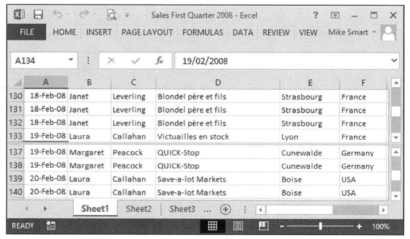

4   Scroll the lower pane so that the first sale on 3rd March 2008 is shown on the first line.

5   Scroll the upper pane so that the first sale on 3rd February 2008 is shown on the first line.

Sales First Quarter 2008

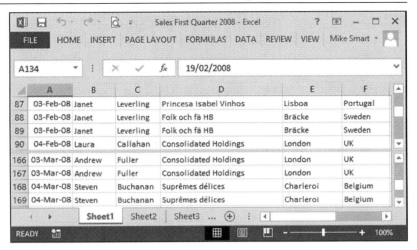

6   Remove the split window view.

Click: View→Window→Split.

<u>OR</u>

Double click the split bar with the mouse.

7   Split the window into two vertical panes.

1.   Click in cell D1.

If the active cell is in row 1, the screen will be split into two vertical panes.

2.   Click: View→Window→Split.

The window is split into two vertical panes

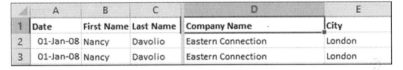

8   Move the split bar so that the left pane shows columns A to E.

Click and drag the split bar to its new location:

9   Remove the split window view.

10   Split the window into four panes.

If the active cell is not in row 1 or column A, the screen will split into four panes at the cursor position.

1.   Click in a cell towards the center of the screen

2.   Click: View→Window→Split.

The screen is split into four windows.

11   Remove the split window view.

155

Lesson 3-20: Check spelling

Excel shares the same powerful spell checker that is included with Word and other Office applications.

Most European companies have a corporate standard for their spelling, often American English or British English. Excel also includes standard support for eighteen different dialects of English as well as other languages.

While most words are included in Excel's dictionary, you will often be warned that a correct spelling is misspelled. When this is the case you can add the word to the dictionary so that Excel doesn't keep bothering you about it in the future.

1   Open *Empire Car Sales Stock List* from your sample files folder.

	F	G
5	Colour	Selling points
6	Black	Can accelarate faster than most sports cars.
7	Topaz Blue	One concientous owner from new.
8	Yellow	Acheives nearly 50 miles to the gallon.
9	Silver	Particulaly clean example of this executive coupe.
10	Blue	Reconised as one of the safest cars on the road.
11	Brown	A collector's car strictly for connisseurs.

We'll have to hope that Empire's cars are better than their spelling!

You may find it fun to try to identify their spelling errors before we set the Spell Checker loose on the job. The *Selling points* column contains many frequently incorrectly spelled words.

2   Check the spelling for the words in the range F5:G7.

If you select a range of cells before invoking the spell checker, only the selected range will be checked.

1.   Select the range F5:G7

2.   Click: Review→Proofing→Spelling to start the spell checker.

If all of the words are spelled correctly the spell checker does not display. In this case there are errors, so the *Spell Check* dialog is displayed.

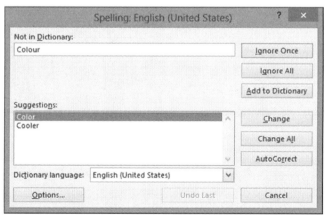

In the example above note that the *Dictionary language* was set to English (United States). The British spelling of the word *colour* does

note

Setting the default language

Click: File→Options→Proofing.

You are then able to set the Excel default dictionary language.

note

Dictionaries for other languages

The English version of Excel includes support for English, French and Spanish.

Microsoft also offer language packs for 35 other languages ranging from Chinese to Ukrainian.

not appear in the American English dictionary because, in America, it is spelled: *color*.

If your dictionary is set to English (United Kingdom) you will not see this error because *colour* is the correct UK English spelling.

See the sidebar if you want to change your dictionary to a different language.

3   Click *Change* to accept Excel's suggested correction.

4   Click *Change* twice more to accept Excel's suggestions for *accelerate* and *conscientious*.

The Spell checker exits and advises that the spell check is complete.

5   Click the OK button to dismiss the dialog.

6   Spell check the single word *Particulaly* in cell G9.

Sometimes you'll type a single word and be unsure that it is correctly spelled. You will want to be able to quickly check the single word.

1.   Click cell G9 and then select the word: *Particulaly* in the formula bar at the top of the window.

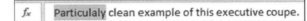

2.   Click: Review→Proofing→Spelling to start the Spell Checker.

3.   Click the *Change* button to accept the correct spelling.

4.   Click the OK button to dismiss the dialog.

7   Spell check the entire worksheet.

1.   Click in any cell on the worksheet. When you don't select a range, or a single word, the spell checker checks the entire worksheet.

If you didn't click cell A1, cells to the right and beneath the selected cell are checked first and then Excel asks: *Do you want to continue checking at the beginning of the sheet*?

2.   Click: Review→Proofing→Spelling to start the Spell Checker.

8   Click: *Change* to accept each change until you are prompted for Alfasud.

Alfasud is a real word for a car (a model produced by Alfa Romeo between 1976 and 1989) but it isn't in the Excel dictionary. Perhaps Empire sells a lot of Alfasuds and don't want to be pulled up by the spell checker every time the word is used.

To prevent this from happening, click the *Add to Dictionary* button so that Excel will recognize the word in the future.

When the spell check has ended, a dialog will display advising that the spell check is complete. Click the OK button to dismiss the dialog.

9   Save your work as *Empire Car Sales Stock List-1*.

Session 3: Exercise

1   Open *The Best Selling Albums of All Time* from your sample files folder.

2   Insert one row above row 7, type *AC/DC* for the Artist and *Back in Black* for the Album.

3   Use AutoComplete to put the text *Rock* into cell C7 and type *42* for copies sold (millions).

4   Delete rows 10 and 11 to remove the *Bee Gees* and *Pink Floyd* from the list.

5   Insert a formula in cell E6 to calculate how much revenue the album sales would have generated if sold at the Average Album Price shown in cell E3.

      Don't forget that the reference to cell E3 will have to be an absolute reference.

6   AutoFill the formula to the end of the list to see the estimated revenue for the top four selling albums.

7   Use AutoSum to add a value for total copies sold and total revenue to cells D10 and E10.

8   Remove decimal places displayed in cells E6:E10 so that the revenue is rounded to the nearest million.

9   Add a comment to cell B6 saying "Thriller was Michael Jackson's sixth studio album and was produced with a budget of $750,000."

10   Save your work as *The Best Selling Albums of All Time-1*.

	A	B	C	D	E
1	Best Selling Albums of All Time				
2					US$
3				Average Album Price	14.99
4					
5	Artist	Album	Genre	Copies Sold (millions)	Revenue (Million USD)
6	Michael Jackson	Thriller	Pop/R&B	108	1619
7	AC/DC	Back in Black	Rock	42	630
8	Whitney Houston	The Bodyguard	Pop/R&B	42	630
9	Eagles	Their Greates Hits (1971-1975)	Rock	41	615
10		Total:		233	3493
11					
12					
13					
14					

Mike Smart:
Thriller was Michal Jackson's sixth studio album and was produced with a budget of $750,000.

The Best Selling Albums of All Time

If you need help slide the page to the left

Session 3 Exercise answers

These are the four questions that most students find the most difficult to remember:

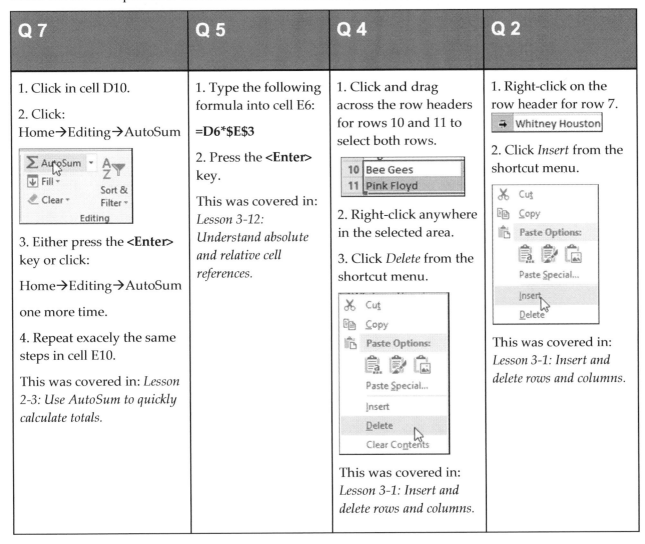

Q 7	Q 5	Q 4	Q 2
1. Click in cell D10. 2. Click: Home→Editing→AutoSum 3. Either press the **<Enter>** key or click: Home→Editing→AutoSum one more time. 4. Repeat exacely the same steps in cell E10. This was covered in: *Lesson 2-3: Use AutoSum to quickly calculate totals.*	1. Type the following formula into cell E6: **=D6*$E$3** 2. Press the **<Enter>** key. This was covered in: *Lesson 3-12: Understand absolute and relative cell references.*	1. Click and drag across the row headers for rows 10 and 11 to select both rows. 2. Right-click anywhere in the selected area. 3. Click *Delete* from the shortcut menu. This was covered in: *Lesson 3-1: Insert and delete rows and columns.*	1. Right-click on the row header for row 7. 2. Click *Insert* from the shortcut menu. This was covered in: *Lesson 3-1: Insert and delete rows and columns.*

If you have difficulty with the other questions, here are the lessons that cover the relevant skill:

1   Refer to: **Lesson 1-5: Download the sample files and open/navigate a workbook.**

3   Refer to: **Lesson 3-2: Use AutoComplete and fill data from adjacent cells.**

6   Refer to: **Lesson 2-15: Use AutoFill to adjust formulas.**

8   Refer to: **Lesson 3-5: Use Paste Values and increase/decrease decimal places displayed.**

9   Refer to: **Lesson 3-9: Insert cell comments.**

10   Refer to: **Lesson 1-6: Save a workbook.**

4

Session Four: Making Your Worksheets Look Professional

> It is only shallow people who do not judge by appearances.
>
> *Oscar Wilde (1854 - 1900)*

Never under-estimate the importance of presentation. In many areas of life it is valued more than content.

This session will enable you to make your worksheets get noticed.

By the end of this session everybody will be convinced that you are an Excel genius because your worksheets will be visually excellent.

Session Objectives

By the end of this session you will be able to:

- Format dates
- Understand date serial numbers
- Format numbers using built-in number formats
- Create custom number formats
- Horizontally and Vertically align the contents of cells
- Merge cells, wrap text and expand/collapse the formula bar
- Understand themes
- Use cell styles and change themes
- Add color and gradient effects to cells
- Add borders and lines
- Create your own custom theme
- Create your own custom cell styles
- Use a master style book to merge styles
- Use simple conditional formatting
- Manage multiple conditional formats using the Rules Manager
- Bring data alive with visualizations
- Create a formula driven conditional format
- Insert a Sparkline into a range of cells
- Apply a common vertical axis and formatting to a Sparkline group
- Apply a date axis to a Sparkline group and format a single Sparkline
- Use the Format Painter
- Rotate text

Lesson 4-1: Format dates

You may notice that I've been very careful to use internationally safe date formats throughout this book.

A classic cause of errors when dealing with international worksheets is the use of a date such as the following:

10/03/2008

This means *10ᵗʰ March 2008* in some countries (such as the UK) and *3ʳᵈ October 2008* in others (such as the USA).

If your work may be viewed by an international audience, it is far better to use a date format that cannot possibly cause confusion.

In this lesson we'll re-format a date into the compact and universally readable format of: *10-Mar-08*.

1   Open *Sales Week Ended 14ᵗʰ March 2008* from your sample files folder.

Notice the hashes in the date column. This tells you that the column isn't wide enough to display the date.

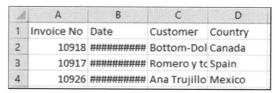

	A	B	C	D
1	Invoice No	Date	Customer	Country
2	10918	##########	Bottom-Dol	Canada
3	10917	##########	Romero y tc	Spain
4	10926	##########	Ana Trujillo	Mexico

If you're used to calling the hash (#) a **pound sign** or **number sign** see the sidebar in: *Lesson 2-9: Re-size rows and columns* for an explanation.

2   Auto-resize cells A1:G17 so that their contents are fully visible.

This was covered in: *Lesson 2-9: Re-size rows and columns.*

3   Format the dates in column B so that they display in the format: *10-Mar-08*

At present the dates are formatted with the month spelled out in full:

	A	B	C
1	Invoice No	Date	Customer
2	10918	10 March 2008	Bottom-Dollar Markets
3	10917	10 March 2008	Romero y tomillo
4	10926	10 March 2008	Ana Trujillo Emparedados y helados

We're going to re-format them to the shorter form: *10 Mar 08*.

4   Select cells B2:B17.

   1.   Select cells B2:B17.

   2.   Right-click anywhere in the selected range and choose *Format Cells…* from the shortcut menu.

   You can also do this from the Ribbon (see sidebar).

   The *Format Cells* dialog appears.

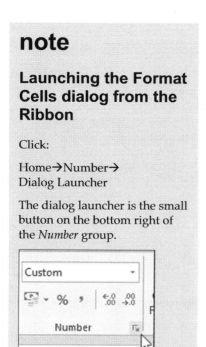
Sales Week Ended
14ᵗʰ March 2008

3.	Click the *Number* tab (if it isn't already selected) and then choose *Date* from the *Category* list box.

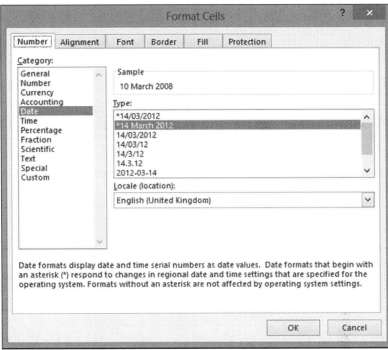

The dates you see may be different from those shown above (see sidebar).

I wanted the format *14-Mar-2008* but that isn't in the list. When you need a special format it is worth checking the *Custom* category to see whether there is a pre-defined format available.

4.	Click *Custom* in the category list box.

5.	Click on each of the entries in the *Type* list box, keeping your eye on the preview in the *Sample* frame.

If you reach the format *dd-mmm-yy* you will see *10-Mar-08* in the sample box. If the format *dd-mmm-yy* isn't shown for your locale (see sidebar) you'll need to manually type it into the *Type* box.

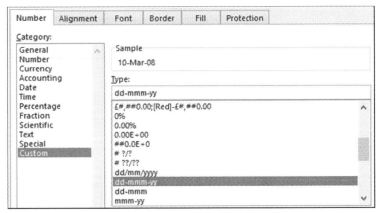

6.	Click the OK button.

5	Save your work as *Sales Week Ended 14th March 2008-1.*

© 2013 The Smart Method® Ltd

note

Why do I see different date formats in the Format Cells dialog?

The date formats shown in the *Format Cells* dialog may change based upon your default *Locale.*

You may have notice the *Locale* drop-down list at the bottom of the *Format Cells* dialog (shown when the *Date* category is selected):

This defaults to the Locale (location) set in your Windows *Regional and Language Options.*

You can change your default locale from the Windows control panel.

Lesson 4-2: Understand date serial numbers

Excel stores dates in a very clever way. Understanding Excel's date storage system empowers you to use date arithmetic. You can use date arithmetic to compute the difference between two dates (in days) or to shift date ranges by a given time interval.

How Excel stores dates

Dates are stored as simple numbers called *date serial numbers*. The serial number contains the number of days that have elapsed since 1st January 1900 (where 1st January 1900 is 1).

The world began in 1900

An interesting shortcoming of Excel is its inability to easily work with dates before 1900. Excel simply doesn't acknowledge that there were any dates before this time. If you work with older dates you will have to work-around this limitation.

In Excel every time is a date, and every date is a time

This one is an eye opener! We've already realized that 5th January 1900 is stored as the number 5. What would the number 5.5 mean? It would mean midday on 5th January 1900.

It is possible to format a date to show only the date, only the time, or both a time and a date.

When you enter a time into a cell without a date, the time is stored as a number less than one. Excel regards this as having the non-existent date of 00 January 1900!

When you enter a date into a cell without a time, the time is stored as midnight at the beginning of that day.

1   Create a new blank workbook and put the numbers 1 to 5 in cells A1:A5.

2   Type the formula **=A1** into cell B1 followed by the **<Enter>** key, and then AutoFill the formula to the end of the list.

AutoFill was covered in: *Lesson 2-14: Use AutoFill for text and numeric series.*

	A	B
1	1	1
2	2	2
3	3	3
4	4	4
5	5	5

3   Apply a date format to column A that will show a four digit year.

This was covered in: *Lesson 4-1: Format dates.*

	A	B
1	01 January 1900	1
2	02 January 1900	2

This reveals that the numbers 1 to 5 represent the dates 1-Jan-1900 to 05-Jan-1900.

4   Change the date format in column A so that it shows both dates and times.

Setting a custom format was covered in: *Lesson 4-1: Format dates.*

Choose the custom format: **dd mmm yyyy hh:mm.** (If it isn't shown in the list you will need to type it into the *Type* box).

Notice that when you enter a date without a time, the time is set to midnight at the beginning of that day.

	A	B
1	01 Jan 1900 00:00	1
2	02 Jan 1900 00:00	2

5   Change the time in cell A2 to 12:00.

Notice that the number in cell B2 has changed to 2.5 showing that times are stored by Excel as the decimal part of a number.

	A	B
1	01 Jan 1900 00:00	1
2	02 Jan 1900 12:00	2.5

6   Compute the number of days that occurred between 01/01/1900 and 01/01/2000.

Now that you have a good grasp of Excel's serial numbers, this task is easy.

1.   Enter the two dates in cells D1 and D2, one beneath the other.

2.   Click in cell D3 to make it the active cell.

3.   Click: Home→Number→Comma Style.

You'll be learning more about the comma style in: *Lesson 4-3: Format numbers using built-in number formats.*

4.   Subtract one date from the other by entering the formula: **=D2-D1** into cell D3.

	D
1	01/01/1900
2	01/01/2000
3	36,525.00

You now know that 36,525 days occurred during the twentieth century (actually 36,524 due to the Lotus 1-2-3 bug – see sidebar).

7   Close the workbook without saving.

Lesson 4-3: Format numbers using built-in number formats

Formatting fundamentals

When you format a number you never change its value. For example if you format the number:

> 483.45495

... so that it only displays two decimal places. The number displays like this:

> 483.45

It is important to realize that the actual value in the cell remains at the old value of 483.45495. All we have done is to change the way in which the value is presented to the user.

1   Open *Sales Week Ended 14th March 2008-1* from your sample files folder.

2   Apply the comma style to column E.

There is an extremely useful quick format button called the *comma style*. This is perfect for formatting monetary values with a single click. The comma style places a comma after thousands and displays exactly two decimal places.

1. Select all of Column E.

2. Click: Home→Number→Comma Style.

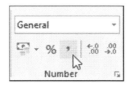

3. Widen column E if necessary so that it is wide enough to display the contents.

All of the values in Column E now display correctly.

	D	E	F	G
1	Country	Amount	Tax	Total
2	Canada	1,447.50	0.175	1700.8125
3	Spain	365.89	0.175	429.92075

Note that you can also use the *Accounting Number Format* style.

note

The Comma[0] and Currency[0] Styles

With pre-2007 versions of Excel, I was forever applying the comma style and then removing the decimal places as a quick way to add the thousand separators to whole numbers. This used to take three clicks (comma style | decrease decimal | decrease decimal).

Excel 2013 saves a click with the Comma[0] and Currency[0] styles.

To apply these styles click:

Home→Styles→Cell Styles→ Comma[0] or Currency[0]

You'll be learning a lot more about cell styles later in this session.

Sales Week Ended
14th March 2008-1

note

Solutions to the "penny rounding" problem

Formatting a floating point number to two decimal places often results in the *penny rounding problem* when you sum a column of numbers.

There are two solutions to the problem. One is a very good solution, the other can cause problems.

Best practice

The best solution to the problem is to address it when the column is first calculated.

In this lesson's example worksheet the formula used to calculate the value in cell G2 is:

$=E2*(F2+1)$

Excel has a Round() function that can be used to round the result to two decimal places at the point of calculation.

The new formula would become:

$=ROUND(E2*(F2+1),2)$

Changing precision

Click:

File→Options→Advanced

In the *When Calculating This Workbook* group click the *Set precision as displayed* check box.

This alters the default behaviour of Excel so that each value in the worksheet is regarded as being precisely the same as its display value when performing calculations.

Using this option can cause data to become inaccurate as it is a global setting, affecting the entire worksheet (and any other worksheets you may open before turning it off).

Use this feature with extreme caution, or better still, don't use it at all!

This is very similar to the comma style but adds a leading currency symbol and an appropriate number of decimal places. The *More Accounting Formats…* option supports a vast number of international currency styles.

Try the *Accounting Number Format* style out to see how it works. I've found that the comma style is more appropriate for most of my work, as I'm usually working in one country and one currency, making the currency type obvious.

3   Apply the comma style to column G.

Column G has many decimal places in some cases, as the sales tax calculation results in as many as six decimal places.

Apply the comma style to column G and notice how all of the values are displayed rounded to the nearest two decimal places.

It is a key concept (as discussed in the introduction to this lesson) to realize that the values in the cells have not changed. For example, if you add two cells containing the value 1.4, the result will be 1.4+1.4=2.8. If you then format the cells as whole numbers you'll see that 1+1=3 as each number is rounded up or down.

See the sidebar for potential solutions to this problem.

4   Apply the percentage style to column F.

The example sales tax rate is 17.5%. When working with percentages, it is useful to enter them so that you can calculate a percentage simply by multiplying by the cell.

Instead of 17.5 (more readable) the values are entered as 0.175 (easier to use in formulas). In order to make percentages both readable and easy to use, Microsoft has created the percentage style. If you type 17.5% into a cell, the actual value within the cell will be 0.175.

1.   Select column F.

2.   Click: Home→Number→Percentage Style.

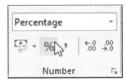

3.   Click: Home→Number→Increase Decimal ⌷ once, to make the values in column F display one decimal place.

	D	E	F	G
1	Country	Amount	Tax	Total
2	Canada	1,447.50	17.5%	1,700.81
3	Spain	365.89	17.5%	429.92

5   Save your work as *Sales Week Ended 14th March 2008-2.*

Lesson 4-4: Create custom number formats

The built-in number formats are very quick and convenient but are also quite limited. For example, there was a credit note on 11-Mar-08 for 637.49 plus tax. You could easily miss the little minus sign to the left of the amount.

	D	E	F	G
6	Germany	500.00	17.5%	587.50
7	Italy	637.49	17.5%	749.05
8	Italy	- 637.49	17.5% -	749.05

Old-school accountants like to show brackets around negative values. You just can't miss those brackets! Here's what we want to see:

	D	E	F	G
6	Germany	500.00	17.5%	587.50
7	Italy	637.49	17.5%	749.05
8	Italy	(637.49)	17.5%	(749.05)

There's one little problem with this requirement. For many locales, Excel 2013 doesn't support brackets in any of the built-in or pre-defined custom formats. Fortunately it is possible to create your own custom format when none of the built-in styles fit your requirement.

Overview of custom formats

There's plenty of documentation in the help system and on the Internet about the rather cryptic formatting codes provided with Excel 2013. Just about everything is possible once you've got to grips with the basic concepts.

To communicate the custom format to Excel, you must construct a custom format string.

Zeros mean "Display significant zeros". You tell Excel how many you want within the format string. For example, 0.00 means *display at least one leading zero and two decimal places*. The following examples should make things clear:

Custom Format String	Value	Display
0	1234.56	1235
0.0	1234.56 1234.5 .5	1234.6 1234.5 0.5
0.00	1234.56 1234.5 .5	1234.56 1234.50 0.50
00.000	4.56	04.560
0.000	1234.56	1234.560

Sales Week Ended 14th March 2008-2

note

More about custom number formats

It is only possible to give you a broad overview of custom number formats in a single lesson. This should be all that you need to discover more using Excel's help system or the Internet.

Here are a couple of other insights that may help if you want to explore them further:

- You can embed colors into number formats. For example, to make every negative value red you could use:

  0.00;[Red]0.00

- There are four possible parts to a number format:

  Positive format; Negative format; Zero format; Text format. Applying the custom format string:

  0.00;-0.00;"Zero";[Blue]

  To these cells:

  | Mike | 0 | 120.119 | -345.5744 |

  Would result in:

  | Mike | Zero | 120.12 | -345.57 |

  (Text in first cell is colored blue).

note

Hiding values with the three semicolon trick

You will often want to hide the values in specific cells, even though you want other values in the same column to display.

A common way of doing this is to format the cell as a white foreground color upon a white background.

A better solution is to create a custom format consisting of three semicolons:

;;;

The hash symbol (#) is mainly used to add comma separators to thousands and millions.

Custom Format String	Value	Display
#	123.4500	123
#.##	123.45 123.50	123.45 123.5
#,#	1234.56	1,236
#,#.##	1234.56 1234.50 12341234.56	1,234.56 1,234.5 12,341,234.56

Because the hash symbol can be used in conjunction with zeroes it is also possible to indicate that you want both thousand separators *and* a specific number of leading or trailing zeroes.

Custom Format String	Value	Display
#,#0.00	12341234.5	12,341,234.50

You can also specify two different format strings separated by a semi colon. The first provides formatting for positive values and the second for negative values. This information enables us to construct the custom format string required.

Custom format string	Value	Display
#,#0.00;(#,#0.00)	12341234.5 -12341234.5	12,341,234.50 (12,341,234.50)

1   Open *Sales Week Ended 14th March 2008-2* from your sample files folder (if it isn't already open).

2   Select columns E and G.

This was covered in: *Lesson 2-6: Select adjacent and non-adjacent rows and columns.*

3   Right-click anywhere in column E or G and then select *Format Cells…* from the shortcut menu.

4   Select *Custom* from the *Category* list on the left of the dialog.

5   Type the custom format: **#,#0.00;(#,#0.00)** into the box labeled *Type* and click the OK button.

Type:
#,#0.00;(#,#0.00)

The negative values on the worksheet are now surrounded by brackets.

| Italy | 637.49 | 17.5% | 749.05 |
| Italy | (637.49) | 17.5% | (749.05) |

6   Save your work as *Sales Week Ended 14th March 2008-3.*

Lesson 4-5: Horizontally align the contents of cells

Icon	Description	What it does	Example
General ▾	General (the default)	Aligns numbers and dates to the right and text to the left.	Canada 1,447.50 / Spain 365.89
	Align Left	Aligns cell contents left. If the cell contains text and the adjacent cell is empty, text spills to the right. If the cell contains text and the adjacent text isn't empty, text is truncated.	Bottom-Dollar Markets / Bottom-Dollar Markets / Bottom-Dollar M Canada
	Align Center	Aligns cell contents to the center. If the cell contains text and the adjacent cells are empty, text spills to the left and right. If the cell contains text and the adjacent cells are not empty, text is truncated.	Bottom-Dollar Markets / Bottom-Dollar Markets / 10-Mar-08 om-Dollar Mar Canada
	Align Right	Aligns cell contents to the right. If the cell contains text and the adjacent cell is empty, text spills to the left. If the cell contains text and the adjacent cell isn't empty, text is truncated.	Bottom-Dollar Markets / Bottom-Dollar Markets / 10-Mar-08 om-Dollar Markets C
	Justify	Text lines up to the left and right of the cell (like a newspaper)	to be or not to be, that is the question.
	Distributed	Words are distributed evenly across the cell.	City of London

Sales Week Ended 14th March 2008-3

note

The fill format

Fill repeats text until the cell is filled.

For example, if a cell contained the word *Cat*, here's how it would look after the fill format was applied:

I have seen the fill format used in very old Excel versions to create separator lines by adding a row of characters (such as a dash) to a cell:

Because Excel 2013 has very sophisticated underline and drawing features, it is unlikely that you will ever find a use for the fill format.

note

How to access the justified, distribute, and fill options

The *Justify*, *Distributed* and *Fill* options are not on the Ribbon as most users wouldn't find a use for them.

If you find them useful you can add buttons to the Quick Access Toolbar. Refer to: *Lesson 1-14: Customize the Quick Access Toolbar and preview the printout.*

The *Fill* option doesn't even have a toolbar button available. This needs to be accessed from the *Format Cells* dialog.

To access the *Format Cells* dialog, right-click any cell and choose *Format Cells...* from the shortcut menu.

You'll then find a *Horizontal Alignment* drop-down list on the *Alignment* tab.

The table on the facing page summarizes Excel's different horizontal alignment options.

1 Open *Sales Week Ended 14th March 2008-3* from your sample files folder (if it isn't already open).

2 Notice that the text in row 1 doesn't align with the column contents.

Numerical and date values are, by default, right aligned.

Columns E, F and G contain numerical data but the text headings of their columns are left aligned.

You can see the problem more clearly if the columns are widened:

E	F	G
Amount	Tax	Total
1,447.50	17.5%	1,700.81
365.89	17.5%	429.92

3 Right-align the column headers for columns E, F and G.

1. Select cells E1:G1.

2. Click: Home→Alignment→Align Right

The column headers now look much better.

E	F	G
Amount	Tax	Total
1,447.50	17.5%	1,700.81
365.89	17.5%	429.92

4 Right-align cell B1.

Column B also has a problem as the dates and column header do not align.

1. Select cell B1.

2. Click: Home→Alignment→Align Text Right.

	B	C
1	Date	Customer
2	10-Mar-08	Bottom-Dollar Markets
3	10-Mar-08	Romero y tomillo

You will normally align column headers to the right for numeric/date columns, and to the left for text columns.

5 Bold-face row 1.

1. Select row 1.

2. Click: Home→Font→Bold.

	A	B	C
1	**Invoice No**	**Date**	**Customer**
2	10918	10-Mar-08	Bottom-Dollar Markets

6 Save your work as *Sales Week Ended 14th March 2008-4.*

Lesson 4-6: Merge cells, wrap text and expand/collapse the formula bar

1   Open *Sales Week Ended 14th March 2008-4* from your sample files folder (if it isn't already open).

2   Insert three blank rows above row 1.

This was covered in: *Lesson 3-1: Insert and delete rows and columns.*

3   In cell A1 type: **Sales Week Ended 14th March 2008**

4   Center the title across columns A to G.

The title cell (A1) doesn't look bad, but wouldn't it be nice to center it above the transactions listed beneath? You could simply copy and paste the title text into cell D1 but that wouldn't be perfectly central.

The solution is to merge cells A1:G1 so that they turn into one big cell. It will then be possible to center the text inside the merged cell. Excel provides a handy *Merge and Center* button to do this in one click.

1.   Select cells A1:G1.

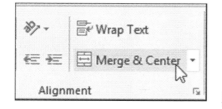

2.   Click: Home→Alignment→Merge & Center.

The title appears at the center of the merged cell.

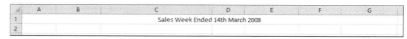

5   View the text in cell A22.

There is a long description in cell A22. You probably can't see all of it on your screen.

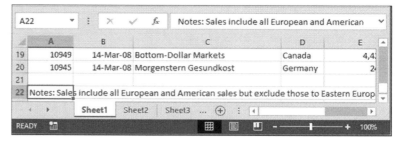

Re-sizing the formula bar allows all of the text to be read.

Click cell A22 and then click the *Expand Formula Bar* button.

The text becomes visible in the enlarged formula bar:

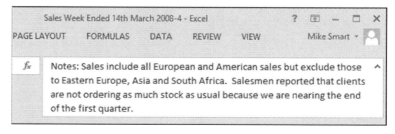

Sales Week Ended 14th March 2008-4

6 Resize the formula bar.

Sometimes there isn't enough space in the expanded formula bar to view all of the text.

If this is the case hover the mouse over the bottom border of the formula bar until you see the double-headed arrow cursor shape.

When the double-headed arrow is visible, click and drag downward or upward to resize the formula bar as required.

7 Collapse the formula bar.

After you have read the text there is no need to keep the formula bar expanded. Click the same button used to expand the formula bar ⌃ and the bar will collapse.

8 Merge cells A22:G22.

Expanding the formula bar isn't a great solution. We will create a box at the bottom of the report to display all of the text.

1. Select cells A22:G22.

2. Click: Home→Alignment→Merge & Center Drop Down.

    A drop-down menu is displayed.

    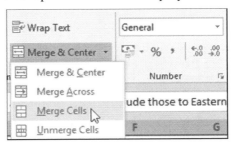

3. Click *Merge Cells* to make all of the selected cells into one large cell. (This is just like *Merge & Center* but without centering).

9 Make row 22 deep enough to display all of the text.

This was covered in: *Lesson 2-9: Re-size rows and columns.*

The cell is now deep enough to display the text, but you can still only see one line. This is because the text isn't *wrapping*.

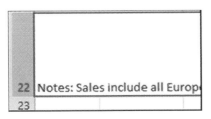

10 Wrap the text within the merged cells.

Click: Home→Alignment→Wrap Text.

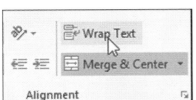

The text now displays well, except that it appears at the bottom of the cell. We'll discover how to fix this later, in: *Lesson 4-7: Vertically align the contents of cells.*

11 Save your work as *Sales Week Ended 14th March 2008-5.*

Lesson 4-7: Vertically align the contents of cells

This table summarizes Excel's different vertical alignment options.

Icon	Description	What it does	Example
General ▾	General (the default)	Aligns cell contents to the bottom of the cell.	Bottom-Dollar Markets
	Top Align	Aligns cell contents to the top of the cell	Bottom-Dollar Markets
	Middle Align	Aligns cell contents to the middle of the cell.	Bottom-Dollar Markets
	Bottom Align	Aligns cell contents to the bottom of the cell	Bottom-Dollar Markets
No icon	Justify	Lines of text are spread out so that the space between each is equal, the first line is at the top and the last line is at the bottom.	to be or not to be, that is the question.
No Icon	Distributed	The same as Justify!	to be or not to be, that is the question.

1   Open *Sales Week Ended 14th March 2008-5 from* your sample files folder (if it isn't already open).

2   Top align the contents of cell A22.

The contents of cell A22 are currently bottom aligned (the default).

Note: Sales include all European and American sales but exclude those to Eastern Europe, Asia and South Africa. Salesmen reported that clients are not ordering as much stock as usual because we are nearing the end of the first quarter.

22

When you place a block of text into a cell in this way, you will typically want it to be top-aligned.

1.   Select cell A22.

Sales Week Ended 14th March 2008-5

2. Click: Home→Alignment→Top Align  to align the text to the top of the cell.

Note: Sales include all European and American sales but exclude those to Eastern Europe, Asia and South Africa. Salesmen reported that clients are not ordering as much stock as usual because we are nearing the end of the first quarter.

3 Increase the height of row 4 so that it is about twice its present height.

This was covered in: *Lesson 2-9: Re-size rows and columns.*

Invoice No	Date	Customer
10918	10-Mar-08	Bottom-Dollar Markets

You can see why the default vertical alignment is *bottom align*. This alignment works really well for title rows.

4 Wrap the text in cell A4.

This was covered in: *Lesson 4-6: Merge cells, wrap text and expand/collapse the formula bar.*

5 Split the words *Invoice* and *No* so that they appear on separate lines.

1. Double-click cell A4 to enter Edit mode and then position the cursor to the left of the word *No*.

2. Press **<Alt>+<Enter>**.

3. Press the **<Enter>** key again to exit Edit mode.

The two words now appear on separate lines.

6 Horizontally right-align the text in cell A4.

This was covered in: *Lesson 4-5: Horizontally align the contents of cells.*

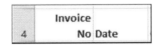

7 Automatically resize columns A to G so that each column is just wide enough for the cell contents.

This was covered in: *Lesson 2-9: Re-size rows and columns.*

8 Save your work as *Sales Week Ended 14th March 2008-6.*

note

What are serifs?

They are the little lines at the edges of text that allow the eye to more easily scan words.

Serifs

Sans Serif

note

Can I change the default theme?

The default theme is simply the theme applied to the *Blank Workbook* template.

If you want to use a different default theme (or change any of the standard Excel options) you will need to create an empty workbook, apply the new theme to it, and then save it as a template (for example: *My Blank Workbook*). You learned how to do this in: *Lesson 3-14: Understand templates and set the default custom template folder*.

If you pin the *My Blank Workbook* template, it will then appear at the top of the list when you open Excel.

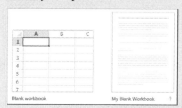

When you create new blank workbooks in future, you can then use your own customized *My Blank Workbook* custom template in place of Microsoft's *Blank Workbook* template.

Lesson 4-8: Understand themes

A theme is simply a set of fonts, colors and effects that go very nicely together.

Font sets

A font set consists of two complementary fonts that work well as a pair.

A golden rule of typesetting is to never have more than two fonts in a document. Old school typesetters would always use a serif font for the body text (also called the *Normal* text) and a sans-serif font for the titles (just as this book does). See sidebar for the difference between serif and sans-serif fonts.

There's a modern school of thought that suggests that breaking this rule is cool and Microsoft have done just that with their default set for Excel 2013 (called the *Office* set) by choosing a sans-serif font (Calibri Light) for titles and also a sans-serif font (Calibri) for normal text.

You can see all 25 pre-defined font sets by clicking:

Page Layout→Themes→Fonts

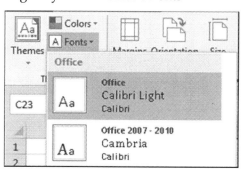

You can also create your own font sets if you don't like any of the pre-defined ones. You'll learn how to do this in: *Lesson 4-12: Create your own custom theme.*

Color sets

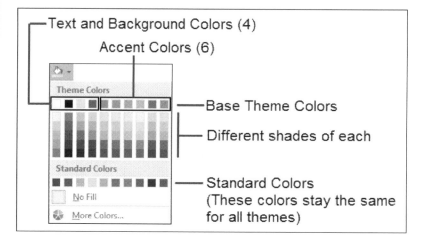

Color sets are a little more involved than font sets

The ten colors along the top row are the *Theme colors*. The leftmost four are used for *Text and Background colors* and the other six are *Accent colors*. This set of colors has been selected by design professionals to work well together. There are actually twelve theme colors but you can only see ten of them. The two hidden theme colors are used for hyperlinks.

The *Standard colors* are best avoided. They are colors that will remain the same no matter what theme is in use. If you use standard colors (or the *More Colors…* option) the worksheet may look odd if the theme needs to be changed in the future. You can see all 15 pre-defined color sets by clicking:

Page Layout→Themes→Colors

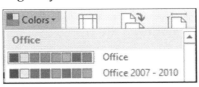

Effects

You'll only notice a change in theme effects if you have graphic elements on your worksheet, such as drawing shapes or chart objects. We'll see this working later in: *Lesson 5-8: Format 3-D elements and add drop shadows.*

Theme effects are applied to the outline and fill of shapes. You can see all 21 pre-defined effects by clicking:

Page Layout→Themes→Effects

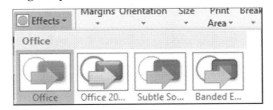

Themes

Themes are simply a group of one *color* set, one *font* set and one *effects* set.

Because Microsoft have consistently named their Colors, Fonts, Effects and Themes, the *Office* theme consists of the *Office* color set, the *Office* font set and the *Office* effects set.

Themes aren't just for Excel

The Themes feature is also included in Word, PowerPoint and Outlook.

Choosing the same theme for your documents, spreadsheets, presentations and Emails can give all of your communications a consistent and professional appearance.

Lesson 4-9: Use cell styles and change themes

In order for themes to work their magic, you must get into the habit of using cell styles to format cells based only upon the options available in the current theme.

For many years expert Word users have used styles to quickly produce professional documents. Their mortal sin would be to apply a font size or color directly to a document.

Now that Excel also supports styles (they were introduced in Excel 2007), professional Excel users should adopt the same discipline.

1   Open *Sales Week Ended 14th March 2008-6* from your sample files folder (if it isn't already open).

2   Apply the *Title* style to cell A1.

Even though cell A1 now encompasses cells A1:G1 it retains the cell reference A1.

A novice user might apply a font and color directly to cell A1 but we're going to do things the professional way and use the *Title* style.

1. Select cell A1.

2. Click: Home→Styles→Cell Styles.

The styles gallery appears.

3. Click *Title* to apply the Title style to cell A1.

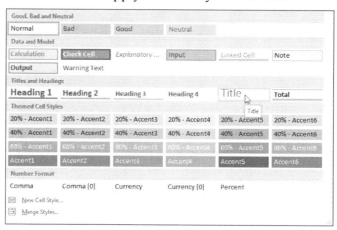

Cell A1 is formatted with the Title style.

3   Apply the *Heading 3* style to cells A4:G4.

1. Select cells A4:G4.

2. Click: Home→Styles→Cell Styles→Heading 3.

4   Apply the *Note* style to cell A22.

1. Select cell A22.

2. Click: Home→Styles→Cell Styles→Note.

5   Apply the *20% - Accent 1* style to cells A5:D20.

note

Removing a style from a cell

All cells have the *Normal* style by default. Select a cell or range of cells and click:

Home→Styles→
Cell Styles→Normal

You will then remove the cell style, and all other cell formatting such as bold face or underline, from the cell or range.

Sales Week Ended
14th March 2008-6

1. Select cells A5:D20

2. Click: Home→Styles→Cell Styles→20% - Accent 1.

6 Apply the *20% - Accent 2* style to cells E5:G20.

1. Select cells E5:G20.

2. Click: Home→Styles→Cell Styles→ 20% - Accent 2

The worksheet now looks very different

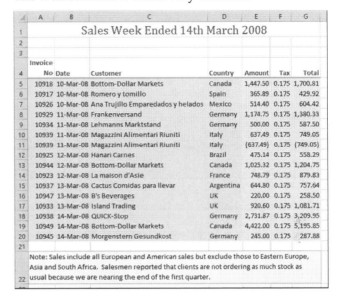

7 Insert a row above row 21.

This was covered in: *Lesson 3-1: Insert and delete rows and columns.*

8 Use AutoSum to place a total in cell G21.

This was covered in: *Lesson 2-3: Use AutoSum to quickly calculate totals.*

9 Apply the *Total* style to cell G21.

1. Select cell G21.

2. Click: Home→Styles→Cell Styles→Total.

The total cell is neatly formatted.

Canada	4,422.00	17.5%	5,195.85
Germany	245.00	17.5%	287.88
			18,137.37

10 Preview your finished work under different themes.

Because you did things the professional way, using styles instead of directly formatting cells, it is now possible to cycle through the themes. You may find one of the other themes more attractive.

1. Click: Page Layout→Themes→Themes.

The *Themes* gallery appears.

2. Hover over each theme in turn. You'll be amazed at how your work completely changes as each theme's style set is applied.

11 Save your work as *Sales Week Ended 14th March 2008-7.*

note

Why it is a good idea to restrict custom style colors to theme colors

If you restrict your color choice to the 60 *Theme Colors* you will make your worksheets design-compatible with documents that use other themes.

If you use non-theme colors your worksheets will not seamlessly integrate (from a design point of view) with PowerPoint presentations, Word documents, and other Office documents that use a different theme.

Example

John creates a worksheet using the default *Office* theme.

Mary wants to use this in her PowerPoint presentation that uses the *Circuit* theme. John emails the worksheet to her and then she simply pastes the required cells into her presentation and changes the theme to *Circuit*.

Joe sees the presentation and wants to use the same worksheet in his Word report that uses the *Berlin* theme. Mary emails the presentation to him and then he simply pastes the required slides into his Word document and changes the theme to *Berlin*.

The same worksheet has been used without modification and it blends perfectly into both Joe and Mary's work, because John followed best practice and restricted his color choices to theme colors.

Lesson 4-10: Add color and gradient effects to cells

Most of the time solid colors are all you need, but you may want to make data look more interesting for a PowerPoint presentation, or for publication in a newsletter or a web page.

When you add colors it is usually best to stay within those of the current theme. This enables you to quickly change the appearance of the worksheet to match that of a PowerPoint presentation or Word document that uses a different theme (see sidebar for an example of this in action).

In this lesson we'll add a gradient to the sharp transition between the orange totals section and the blue transaction details section of the worksheet.

1   Open *Sales Week Ended 14th March 2008-7* from your sample files folder (if it isn't already open).

2   Check the colors that are currently being used for the transaction and totals section in your worksheet.

   1. Click anywhere in the blue area of your worksheet (cells A5:C21).

   2. Click the drop-down arrow next to: Home→Font→Fill Color.

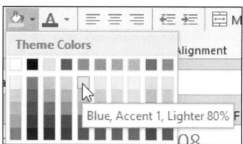

   Notice that one color has a small square around it. When you hover over this button you will see that the fill color for the left-hand side of the worksheet is *Blue, Accent 1, Lighter 80%*.

   3. Do the same for the orange colored cells (cells D5:G21). You'll find that they are *Orange, Accent 2, Lighter 80%*.

3   Set a gradient fill in column D.

   1. Select cells D5:D21.

   2. Right-click inside the selected range and click *Format Cells…* from the shortcut menu.

   3. Click the *Fill* Tab.

Sales Week Ended 14th March 2008-7

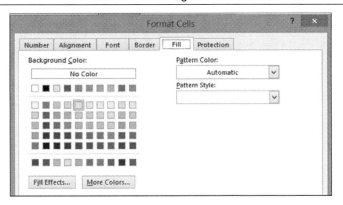

4. Click the *Fill Effects...* button.

5. In the *Colors* frame, choose *Blue, Accent 1, Lighter 80%* for *Color 1*.

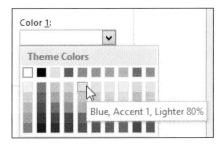

6. In the *Colors* frame, choose *Orange, Accent 2, Lighter 80%* for *Color 2*.

7. Select the *Vertical* shading style.

8. Select the top left variant.

Country	Amount
Canada	1,447.50
Spain	365.89
Mexico	514.40
Germany	1,174.75
Germany	500.00
Italy	637.49
Italy	(637.49)
Brazil	475.14
Canada	1,025.32
France	748.79
Argentina	644.80
UK	220.00

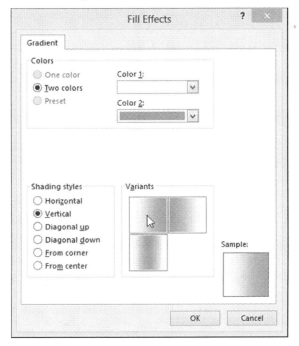

9. Click OK and then OK again.

A smooth gradient fill has been added to column D.

4 Save your work as *Sales Week Ended 14th March 2008-8*.

Lesson 4-11: Add borders and lines

1   Open *Sales Analysis* from your sample files folder.

We're going to use the powerful *borders and lines* feature to make this worksheet more readable.

Before

	A	B	C	D	E
1					
2			Total		
3		Analysis Type	Cash	Percent	
4		By Category			
5		Beverages	25,326	20%	
6		Meat/Poultry	65,780	52%	
7		Vegetables	35,679	28%	
8		Total	126,785		
9		By Month			
10		Oct	45,300	36%	
11		Nov	36,800	29%	
12		Dec	44,685	35%	
13		Total	126,785		
14		By Country			
15		UK	56,175	44%	
16		USA	42,368	33%	
17		Canada	28,242	22%	
18		Total	126,785		
19					

After

	A	B	C	D	E
1					
2			Total		
3		Analysis Type	Cash	Percent	
4		By Category			
5		Beverages	25,326	20%	
6		Meat/Poultry	65,780	52%	
7		Vegetables	35,679	28%	
8		Total	126,785		
9		By Month			
10		Oct	45,300	36%	
11		Nov	36,800	29%	
12		Dec	44,685	35%	
13		Total	126,785		
14		By Country			
15		UK	56,175	44%	
16		USA	42,368	33%	
17		Canada	28,242	22%	
18		Total	126,785		
19					

2   Add cell styles to rows 2,3,4,9 and 14.

    1.   Select cells B2:D3.

    2.   Click: Home→Styles→Cell Styles→40% Accent 6.

    3.   Select Cells B4:D4, B9:D9 and B14:D14.

       This was covered in: *Lesson 2-7: Select non-contiguous cell ranges and view summary information.*

    4.   Click: Home→Styles→Cell Styles→20% Accent 6.

    5.   Select cells B2:D3.

    6.   Click: Home→Styles→Cell Styles→Heading 4.

3   Switch off the worksheet gridlines.

When you are working with borders it is always a good idea to switch off the gridlines so that you can have a better idea of how the worksheet will print.

This feature appears in two different places on the Ribbon. Uncheck either of the following check boxes:

View→Show→Gridlines

OR

Page Layout→Sheet Options→Gridlines→View

4   Add a solid border around the entire range.

Sales Analysis

Font

tip

Use the draw border line tool to quickly add complex borders

The fastest way to quickly add borders is to simply draw them into place using the *Draw Border* tool.

Click:

Home→Font→
Borders drop-down arrow→
Draw Border

You can then simply draw borders straight onto the grid. There's also an *Erase Border* tool available on the same menu.

note

Changing the border line style or color from the drop-down menu

The *Format Cells* dialog method of adding borders is more powerful than the menu method.

The ability to change line style and color from the menu means you'll rarely have to resort to using the *Format Cells* dialog for borders.

To change line style or color from the *Borders* drop-down menu, select *Line Color or Line Style*.

The selected color and/or style will remain active until you close Excel. Next time you open Excel it will have returned to the default.

1. Select cells B2:D18.

2. Click: Home→Font→Borders drop-down arrow→ Outside Borders.

5 Add solid borders inside cells C2:D3.

   1. Select cells C2:D3.

   2. Click: Home→Font→Borders drop-down arrow→All Borders.

6 Add top and bottom borders to *By Category*, *By Month* and *By Country*.

   1. Select Cells B4:D4, B9:D9 and B14:D14.

   2. Click: Home→Font→Borders drop-down arrow→ Top and Bottom Border.

   Top and Bottom Border

7 Add dotted outlines to the borders of cells B5:D8, B10:D13 and B15:D18.

   1. Select cells B5:D8, B10:D13 and B15:D18.

   2. Right-click any of the selected cells and click *Format Cells...* from the shortcut menu.

      The *Format Cells* dialog appears.

   3. Click the *Border* tab of the *Format Cells* dialog.

   4. Click the *Dotted Line* style.

   5. Click the *Inside* button.

   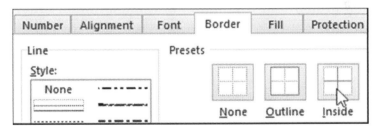

   6. Click the OK button.

      The dotted lines are displayed within the cells.

8 Add left and right borders to cells C5:C8, C10:C13 and C15:C18.

   1. Select cells C5:C8, C10:C13 and C15:C18.

   2. Click: Home→Font→Borders→Left Border.

   3. Click: Home→Font→Borders→Right Border.

9 Save your work as *Sales Analysis-1*.

Lesson 4-12: Create your own custom theme

If none of the 29 built-in themes suffice, you can create your own.

Some clients have a defined corporate style and are extremely particular that colors, fonts and other layout items reinforce their corporate identity.

When individuality is important, you need your own custom theme.

1 Open *Sales Week Ended 14ᵗʰ March 2008-8* from your sample files folder (if it isn't already open).

2 Select a different set of theme colors.

1. Click: Page Layout→Themes→Colors.

   All of the pre-defined sets of colors are displayed (see sidebar). Try hovering your mouse over them one at a time, to see how your worksheet would look if you changed the theme colors.

2. Choose a different set that you think look attractive.

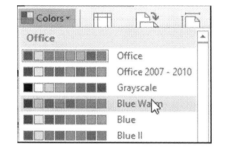

3 Create a custom set of theme colors.

1. Click: Page Layout→Themes→Colors→Customize Colors.

   The *Create New Theme Colors* dialog appears.

2. Click any of the colors on the left of the dialog and select a different color. Notice that, as you do, the *Sample* frame shows a preview of how your theme looks. Let your imagination run wild and create your own custom color theme.

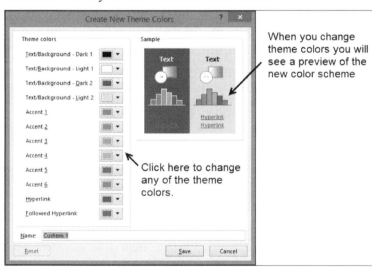

3. Type: **TSM Corporate** into the *Name* box.

4. Click the *Save* button to create your own personalized set of custom colors.

4 Select a different set of fonts.

As discussed in: *Lesson 4-8: Understand themes,* a theme consists of a color set, a font set and an effects set.

A font set consists of two fonts: a heading font and a body font.

Sales Week Ended 14ᵗʰ March 2008-8

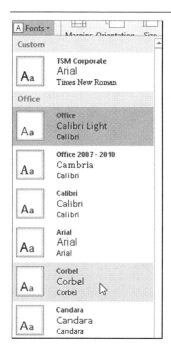

Click: Page Layout→Themes→Fonts.

All of the pre-defined sets of fonts are displayed (see sidebar). Try hovering your mouse over them one at a time, to see how your worksheet would look if you changed the theme fonts.

1. Choose a different set that you think look attractive.

5 Create a custom set of theme fonts.

1. Click: Page Layout→Themes→Fonts→Customize Fonts.

The *Create New Theme Fonts* dialog appears.

2. Select two complimentary fonts. Ideally the body font should be a serif font and the heading font should be a sans-serif font (this issue is discussed in: *Lesson 4-8: Understand themes*).

3. Type: **TSM Corporate** into the *Name* box.

4. Click the *Save* button to create your own personalized set of custom fonts.

6 Select a different set of effects.

Unlike colors and fonts, you can't create a custom set of effects. You have to choose from the pre-defined ones.

Effects change the appearance of drawing objects and you haven't yet covered these (they will make an appearance in: *Lesson 5-8: Format 3-D elements and add drop shadows*).

1. Click: Page Layout→Themes→Effects.

2. Choose a different set of effects.

7 Save the corporate theme.

1. Click: Page Layout→Themes→Themes→Save Current Theme.

2. Enter the name *TSM Corporate* in the *File Name* text box.

3. Click: the *Save* button.

8 Revert to the standard *Office* theme.

1. Click: Page Layout→Themes→Themes.

Notice that your custom theme is listed at the top in the *Custom* group.

2. Click the *Office* theme to put things back the way they were.

Lesson 4-13: Create your own custom cell styles

Excel 2013 has a large number of pre-defined cell styles grouped into:

- Good, Bad and Neutral – to mark particularly good or bad results.

- Data and Model – usually used in a worksheet containing formulas to mark cells that require user input or contain formula results.

- Titles and Headings – for section titles and column headers.

- Themed Cell Styles – to color cells based upon the theme colors.

- Number Format – to quickly apply number formats.

Custom styles are only available in the workbook in which they were originally created. In order to use them in another workbook, you need to use Excel's *merge styles* feature that will be covered in: *Lesson 4-14: Use a master style book to merge styles.*

1   Open *Sales Week Ended 14th March 2008-8* from your sample files folder (if it isn't already open).

2   Modify an existing cell style.

Click cell A23 to make it the active cell. This is the cell containing the *Note* text.

23	Note: Sales include all European and American Asia and South Africa. Salesmen reported that because we are nearing the end of the first qua

1. Click: Home→Styles→Cell Styles.

2. Right-click the *Note* style and click *Modify* from the shortcut menu.

   The *Style* dialog appears (see sidebar).

3. Click the *Format...* button. The *Format Cells* dialog appears.

4. Click the *Fill* tab and select a light green background color:

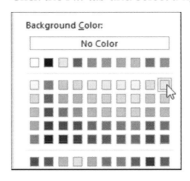

5. Click the OK button and then the OK button once more.

6. If cell A23 isn't green, click: Home→Styles→Cell Styles and click once on the *Note* style.

   Notice that the background color of cell A23 (which has the *Note* style applied to it) has now turned light green.

tip

Change the default font (of this workbook) by modifying the normal style

When you modify a cell style, the change affects every cell that depends upon that style.

For example, suppose you wanted to change the default font of a worksheet to *Times New Roman, 12 point.*

You'd simply modify the *Normal* style's font and then every un-formatted cell in the entire workbook would change to the new default font.

Sales Week Ended 14th March 2008-8

You haven't permanently changed the *Office* theme's *Note* style. You've simply changed it for this workbook only. When you open another workbook that uses the *Office* theme, the *Note* style will be light yellow once again.

3   Duplicate the *Note* built-in cell style.

1. Click: Home→Styles→Cell Styles to display the *Cell Styles* gallery.

2. Right-click the *Note* cell style and then click *Duplicate* from the shortcut menu.

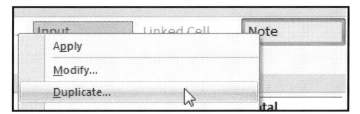

The *Style* dialog appears, suggesting the name *Note 2* for your new cell style. Change this to *Blue Note* (we're going to change the color in a moment) and click the OK button.

3. Click: Home→Styles→Cell Styles to display the *Cell Styles* gallery once more. Notice that the *Blue Note* style is at the top of the gallery in the *Custom* section.

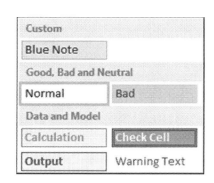

4. Change the background color of the new *Blue Note* style to light blue using the technique learned in: *Step 2 - Modify an existing cell style*.

4   Create a custom cell style *By Example*.

This is the easiest way to create custom cell styles.

1. Select Cell A23.

2. Click: Home→Font→Fill Color Drop-down and choose the *Gold, Accent 4, Lighter 80%* theme color.

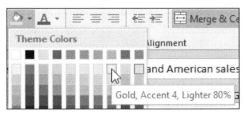

3. Click: Home→Styles→Cell Styles→New Cell Style.

The *Style* dialog appears but notice the words: *By Example*. This means that the style already contains all of the formatting information for cell A23.

4. Change the style name to **Gold Note** and click the OK button.

5   Save your work as *Sales Week Ended 14th March 2008-9*.

Lesson 4-14: Use a master style book to merge styles

When you create custom styles, they are only available within the workbook in which they were created. Sometimes it is useful to have the same set of custom styles available across multiple workbooks.

In this lesson we'll cater for the following scenario at Empire Car Sales:

Syd Slater, the owner of Empire Car Sales, knows that you have to keep your stock turning over.

His salesmen are allowed to discount 10% of the sticker price on all cars.

If the car has been on the forecourt for more than two weeks they are allowed to discount 15%, after three weeks 20%, and after four weeks the car goes back to auction.

Syd's salesmen need to know the maximum discount they can offer, but Syd doesn't want the customers to find this out, so they use a cunning system of color coding on the stock list:

10% Max Discount: Blue

15% Max Discount: Green

20% Max Discount: Orange

The stock list is produced each week in Excel with three custom cell styles, one for each discount.

To avoid having to constantly re-create custom cell styles, they are stored in a master style book called *Empire Styles* which Syd merges with his worksheets so that the three styles are always available.

1   Open a new blank workbook.

2   Create a custom style called *10% Max Discount* with a background color of *Light Blue*.

   This was covered in: *Lesson 4-13: Create your own custom cell styles.*

3   Create a custom style called *15% Max* Discount with a background color of *Light Green*.

4   Create a custom style called *20% Max* Discount with a background color of *Light Orange*.

Because you have used theme colors for the custom styles, their color will change if the theme is changed.

For example, if you change the theme to *Slate*, the *10% Max Discount* becomes red, *15%* becomes brown and *20%* becomes tan.

For this reason, you could argue that it would be better to set the colors using the *More Colors* option so that the colors remained the same even if the theme is changed.

Empire Car Sales
Stock List-1

For the purposes of this lesson we will assume that Syd will not change from the *Office* theme and will follow the normal rule of restricting color choice to theme colors. (See the sidebar in: *Lesson 4-10: Add color and gradient effects to cells,* for an explanation of why this is best practice).

5   Save the workbook as *Empire Styles* but don't close it.

6   Open *Empire Car Sales Stock List-1* from your sample files folder.

7   Merge the styles from the *Empire Styles* master style book.

    1.   Click: Home→Styles→Cell Styles→Merge Styles…

    2.   The *Merge Styles* dialog appears.

    3.   Select *Empires Styles.xlsx* and then click the OK button.

The three custom styles are now available within the current workbook.

8   Apply the 20% style to the Volkswagen and Mercedes.

9   Apply the 15% style to the BMW and Alfa Romeo.

10   Apply the 10% style to the Volvo and Ford.

Syd's salesmen are now ready to start selling!

11   Save your work as *Empire Car Sales Stock List-2*.

note

You can also apply simple conditional formats using the Quick Analysis button

Whenever you select a range of cells, a *Quick Analysis* button appears just outside the bottom-right corner of the selected range.

24	USA	49,190.99	
25	Venezuela	13,189.98	
26	Grand Total	266,644.33	

When you click the *Quick Analysis* button, the *Quick Analysis* dialog appears.

One of the menu options on this dialog is *Formatting*.

When you click the *Formatting* menu option, one of the options is *Greater Than*:

Greater Than

When you click the *Greater Than* icon you will see the same *Greater Than* dialog that you display using the Ribbon in this lesson.

Unfortunately, the *Quick Analysis* button is not as powerful as the Ribbon method used in this lesson.

There is no *Less Than* option, meaning that it would not be possible add the conditional format described in this lesson using only the *Quick Analysis* feature.

Lesson 4-15: Use simple conditional formatting

Simple conditional formatting applies a format to a cell based upon the value of the cell. In this lesson we'll change the cell background color to red if the cell has a value of less than 5,000 and to green if the value is over 30,000.

The same technique learned in this lesson can be used to apply conditional formats based upon text that begins with, ends with, or contains specific characters.

You can also apply conditional formats to cells containing dates. For example, you can highlight dates such as today, tomorrow, in the last seven days, last week and this week. Conditional formatting will then cause the worksheet to change every time that you open it based upon the current date.

1   Open *Sales Report* from your sample files folder.

2   AutoFit cells A4:A26.

   1. Select cells A4:A26.

   2. Click: Home→Cells→Format→AutoFit Column Width.

3   AutoFit cells D4:D13.

4   Apply the *Comma* style to column B and Column E.

This was covered in: *Lesson 4-3: Format numbers using built-in number formats.*

5   Merge cells A3:B3, D3:E3 and D18:E18.

This was covered in: *Lesson 4-6: Merge cells, wrap text and expand/collapse the formula bar.*

6   Apply the *Title* style to cell A1.

This was covered in: *Lesson 4-9: Use cell styles.*

7   Apply the *Heading 2* style to cells A3, D3 and D18.

8   Apply the *Heading 3* style to cells A4:B4, D4:E4 and D19:E19.

9   Apply the *Total* style to cells A26:B26, D13:E13 and D26:E26.

The worksheet is now well formatted and has a professional appearance:

	A	B	C	D	E
1	Sales Report - 6 Months ended March 2008				
2					
3	Sales By Country			Sales by Category	
4	Country	Total Sales		Category	Total Sales
5	Argentina	762.60		Beverages	70,168.10
6	Austria	33,462.58		Condiments	24,938.06

10   Select cells B5:B25.

note

You can have as many conditional formats as you need

Excel versions prior to Excel 2007 were limited to three conditional formats per cell.

In Excel 2013 you can define an infinite number of conditional formats.

3	Sales By Country	
4	Country	Total Sales
5	Argentina	762.60
6	Austria	33,462.58
7	Belgium	6,109.48
8	Brazil	20,524.42
9	Canada	21,306.29
10	Denmark	16,658.80
11	Finland	5,525.00
12	France	26,155.54
13	Germany	28,361.38
14	Ireland	6,157.76
15	Italy	2,585.69
16	Mexico	3,524.30
17	Norway	1,058.40
18	Poland	459.00
19	Portugal	5,584.13

3	Sales By Country	
4	Country	Total Sales
5	Argentina	762.60
6	Austria	33,462.58
7	Belgium	6,109.48
8	Brazil	20,524.42
9	Canada	21,306.29
10	Denmark	16,658.80
11	Finland	5,525.00
12	France	26,155.54
13	Germany	28,361.38
14	Ireland	6,157.76
15	Italy	2,585.69

11 Conditionally format the selected range so that any country with sales below 5,000 has a light red fill with dark red text.

1. Click: Home→Styles→Conditional Formatting→ Highlight Cell Rules→Less Than...

   The *Less Than* dialog appears.

2. Type 5,000 in the left-hand text box and choose *Light Red Fill with Dark Red Text* for the font and fill color.

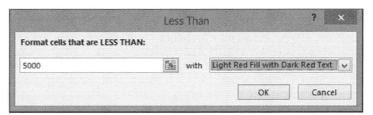

   Notice that when you change the value in the text box, the worksheet adjusts in the background to preview what will happen with this conditional format.

   Note also that there's a *Custom Format...* option (in the drop-down list) which enables you to choose effects such as underlines as well as any color.

3. Click the OK button.

   Cells that have a value of less than 5,000 are now highlighted in red (see sidebar).

12 Add another conditional format to the same range, so that any country with sales above 30,000 has a green fill with dark green text.

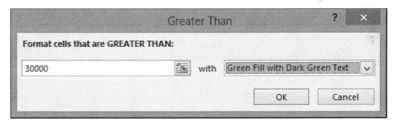

Both conditional formats now display with the two sales values over 30,000 displayed in green (see sidebar).

13 Remove both conditional formats.

1. Select cells B5:B25.

2. Click: Home→Styles→Conditional Formatting→ Clear Rules→Clear Rules from Selected Cells.

   The conditional formats are removed.

14 Save your work as *Sales Report-1*.

Lesson 4-16: Manage multiple conditional formats using the Rules Manager

The conditional formats applied in the previous lesson depended upon the value of a single cell.

Often you will want a cell to be formatted based upon its relationship to other cells in a range.

In this lesson we'll color the top 25% of sales green, the middle 50% yellow and the bottom 25% red.

This lesson also introduces the *Rules Manager* that allows you to edit conditional format rules and to specify the order in which conditional formats are applied.

1 Open *Sales Report-1 from* your sample files folder (if it isn't already open).

2 Select cells B5:B25.

3 Conditionally format the selected range so that any country whose sales are in the top 25% has a green fill with dark green text.

    1. Click: Home→Styles→Conditional Formatting→ Top/Bottom Rules→Top 10%.

        The *Top 10%* dialog appears.

    2. Change the value to 25% and choose *Green fill with Dark Green Text* for the fill.

    3. Click the OK button.

4 Conditionally format the selected range so that any country whose sales are in the bottom 25% has a light red fill with dark red text.

The top and bottom 25% of sales are now highlighted as specified in the two conditional formats (see sidebar).

3	Sales By Country	
4	Country	Total Sales
5	Argentina	762.60
6	Austria	33,462.58
7	Belgium	6,109.48
8	Brazil	20,524.42
9	Canada	21,306.29
10	Denmark	16,658.80
11	Finland	5,525.00
12	France	26,155.54
13	Germany	28,361.38
14	Ireland	6,157.76
15	Italy	2,585.69

Sales Report-1

5   Add another conditional format so that any country with sales greater than zero has a yellow fill with dark yellow text.

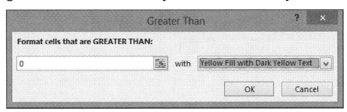

Remember that the specification was to color the middle 50% of sales yellow.

Unfortunately all sales are now yellow because the yellow cells are over-writing the red and green cells.

6   Use the *Rules Manager* to control the order in which conditional formats are applied.

1.   Select cells B5:B25.

2.   Click: Home→Styles→Conditional Formatting→Manage Rules.

The *Conditional Formatting Rules Manager* dialog is displayed.

3.   Click the first rule (the *Cell Value > 0* rule).

4.   Use the *Move Down* button ![down arrow] to move the *Cell Value > 0* rule to the bottom of the list (if you don't see the *Move Down* button it is because you haven't selected the rule).

5.   Click the OK button.

The red, green and yellow formatting rules are now applied as required. This works because of the conflict resolution rules (see sidebar).

7   Use the *Rules Manager* to edit the rules so that the top and bottom 30% values are now highlighted.

1.   Select cells B5:B25.

2.   Click: Home→Styles→Conditional Formatting→Manage Rules.

3.   Select the *Bottom 25%* rule.

4.   Click the *Edit Rule…* button ![Edit Rule... button] and change the criteria to: *30%*.

5.   Edit the *Top 25%* rule in the same way so that it will show the top 30% values.

8   Remove all three conditional formats.

This was covered in: *Lesson 4-15: Use simple conditional formatting.*

---

note

Conflict resolution rules

In this lesson we applied three different conditional formats to the selected range.

Sometimes there will be a conflict between different conditional formatting rules.

Consider this specification:

- Format every value over 50 as blue underlined and bold.

- Format every value over 75 as red and italic.

The rules manager has a dilemma with a value of 80. Should it be blue or red, bold, italic, underlined or all three?

To resolve the conflict, rules are applied in the order listed in the rules manager. Attributes are applied only if an earlier conditional format has not set a conflicting condition.

1.   The value is over 50 so apply blue, underlined, bold-face.

2.   The value is over 75. Can't format red because the earlier condition has made the cell blue.

3.   The value is over 75. Apply italics.

Lesson 4-17: Bring data alive with visualizations

Visualizations are a half-way house between raw data and charts. With a few clicks of the mouse they allow you to express numbers in a visual manner.

1 Open *Sales Report-1* from your sample files folder (if it isn't already open).

2 Add a data bar visualization to the *Sales by Country* figures.

1. Select cells B5:B25.

2. Click: Home→Styles→Conditional Formatting→ Data Bars→Gradient Fill→Red Data Bar.

The visualization is applied (see sidebar).

3 Add a color scale visualization to the *Sales by Category* figures.

1. Select cells E5:E12.

2. Click: Home→Styles→Conditional Formatting→ Color Scales→Green-Yellow Color Scale.

The visualization is applied (see sidebar).

4 Add an icon set visualization to the *Sales by Month* figures.

1. Select cells E20:E25.

2. Click: Home→Styles→Conditional Formatting→Icon Sets→ Indicators→3 Flags.

3. Re-size column E so that it is wide enough to display the values.

The visualization is applied (see sidebar).

When the icon set contains three icons, Excel assigns the relative icons to the top third, middle third, and bottom third of the value range.

You will often need to change these arbitrary values.

5 Use the *Rules Manager* to modify the *Sales by Month* visualization so that three green flags are shown.

The *Sales by Month* visualization may discourage our salesmen because only one month is flagged as green, with four months flagged red. We'll adjust the criteria for flag allocation so that three months are shown as green.

1. Select cells E20:E25.

2. Click: Home→Styles→Conditional Formatting→ Manage Rules…

The *Conditional Formatting Rules Manager* dialog is displayed.

Sales Report-1

3. Click the *Edit Rule* button. Edit Rule...

4. Change the criteria so that values over 45,000 are green, values over 38,000 are yellow and values under 38,000 are red.

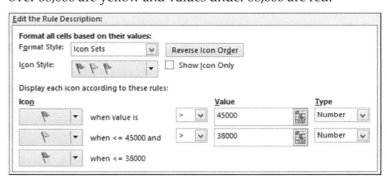

5. Click OK and OK again.

The flags are displayed as required, with three green flags (see sidebar).

6   Use the *Rules Manager* to show the visualizations for *Sales by Country* without the underlying data.

1. Select cells B5:B25.

2. Click: Home→Styles→Conditional Formatting→Manage Rules.

The *Conditional Formatting Rules Manager* dialog is displayed.

3. Click the *Edit Rule* button. ![Edit Rule...]

4. Check the *Show Bar Only* check box.

5. Click the OK button on each dialog to close them.

The bars are shown without the values (see sidebar).

7   Use the *Rules Manager* to bring back the values for *Sales by Country*.

Follow the same procedure as in the previous step to uncheck the *Show Bar Only* check box.

8   Save your work as *Sales Report-2*.

tip

Use the Show Bar Only feature to create quick charts

To create a "quick chart" for cells E5:E12:

1. Type the formula =E5 into cell F5.

2. AutoFill cell F5 down to F12.

3. Create a bar visualization for cells F5:F12 with the *Show Bar Only* option checked.

4. Widen column F to display a "quick chart".

note

A more expert solution using mixed cell references

In my classroom courses I always teach this lesson as presented here.

I like to keep things simple by solving the problem using a simple formula.

The reason I do this is that many students find mixed cell references challenging (the subject of: *Lesson 3-13: Understand mixed cell references*).

If you completely understood *Lesson 3-13: Understand mixed cell references* you might find it interesting to solve this problem in a more efficient way.

You can apply a single mixed cell reference to all four columns in a single operation:

1. Select columns A to D.

2. Click: Home→Styles→ Conditional Formatting→ New Rule...

3. Select: *Use a formula to determine which cells to format.*

4. Type this formula (note the use of a mixed cell reference) into the *Format values where this formula is true* box:

   =$C1="USA"

5. Click the *Format...* button.

6. Click the *Fill* tab and select a light orange color for the conditional fill.

7. Click OK and OK again.

Lesson 4-18: Create a formula driven conditional format

While the built-in conditional format options are very powerful, you will occasionally have a conditional format requirement that is not catered for.

For example, I've lost count of the number of times I have been asked if it is possible to highlight an entire row, rather than a single cell within a row, based upon the value in one of the row's cells.

This lesson will show you how to achieve this using a formula-driven conditional format.

1 Open *Sales Summary First Quarter 2008* from your sample files folder.

> Our challenge will be to highlight the entire row when the Country column contains the value: *USA*.

2 Apply a conditional format to Column C to change the background color to light orange when the cell contains the text: USA.

> 1. Select column C and apply a *Text that Contains...* conditional formatting rule selecting *Custom Format* as the fill color:

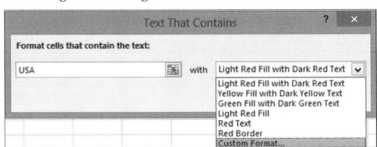

> This was covered in: *Lesson 4-15: Use simple conditional formatting.*

> 2. Click the *Fill* tab and select a light orange color for the conditional fill.

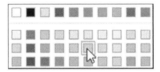

> 3. Click the OK button once, and then again, to close both dialogs.

> Every cell in column C that contains the text *USA* is now shaded light orange.

	B	C	D
40	Familia Arquibaldo	Brazil	100.00
41	Hungry Coyote Import Store	USA	62.40
42	Hungry Coyote Import Store	USA	40.00
43	Wartian Herkku	Finland	146.00

Sales Summary First Quarter 2008

3   Apply a formula-driven conditional format to column B so that the same rows are highlighted.

This is a lot more difficult than the simple conditional format applied to column C.

1. Select column B.

2. Click: Home→Styles→Conditional Formatting→New Rule…

    The *New Formatting Rule* dialog appears.

3. Select *Use a formula to determine which cells to format* from the *Select a Rule Type* list.

4. Type the formula **=C1="USA"** into the formula text box.

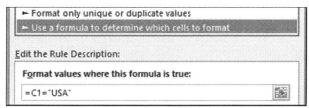

See sidebar for a discussion of this formula.

5. Click the *Format* button, then the *Fill* tab and apply the same light orange fill color.

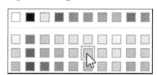

6. Click the OK button once, and then again, to close both dialogs.

    Both columns now have a light orange fill when the country is USA.

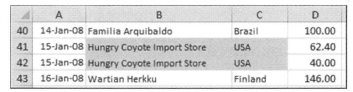

4   Apply the same formula-driven conditional format to columns A and D so that the whole row is highlighted.

5   Save your work as *Sales Summary First Quarter 2008-1*.

tip

Why does the formula relate to cell C1?

At first it seems rather odd that we refer to cell C1 in the conditional formatting formula.

C1 is in the title row so how can this be right?

The answer is to be found in Excel's treatment of absolute and relative cell references (originally explained in: *Lesson 3-12: Understand absolute and relative cell references*).

Excel regards the cell reference to be relative to the first row in the selected range.

Since we selected an entire column, row 1 is the reference row used to adjust the formula for every other row within the column.

In other words, Excel will look at cell C2 when applying conditional formatting to row 2, C3 when applying to row 3… and so on.

This is exactly what we want to happen.

Lesson 4-19: Insert a Sparkline into a range of cells

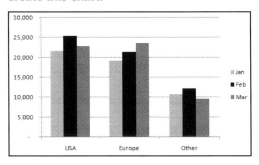

Sparklines were introduced for the first time in Excel 2010. They solve a very common worksheet problem.

In *Lesson 4-17: Bring data alive with visualizations,* you discovered how visualizations can illustrate the differences between values in a single column of data (see example in sidebar).

In: *Session Five: Charts and Graphics*, you will discover Excel's ability to create fantastic charts of all descriptions. These are especially useful when your data has two dimensions (several columns per row). You'll create this chart:

But imagine you had a large number of rows of two dimensional data to compare. This is the case in the sample worksheet for this lesson, where there are 36 rows (one for each branch), each having six values (Jan-Jun):

	A	B	C	D	E	F	G	H
4	Country	Branch	Jan	Feb	Mar	Apr	May	Jun
5	USA	Chicago	671,185	359,811	745,471	685,637	- 16,562	711,009
6	USA	Dallas	708,157	276,972	227,227	482,136	377,175	198,273

The worksheet contains data for 36 branches and would produce a very confusing chart (with 36 data series, one for each branch):

A *Sparkline* is a chart that can be inserted into a single cell, typically charting the values on its left hand side.

Sparklines provide an elegant way to present users with a visual depiction of large two dimensional data sets, even when they contain thousands of rows.

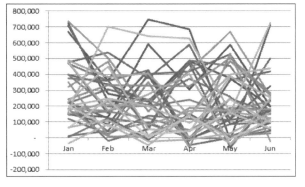

	A	B	C	D	E	F	G	H	I
4	Country	Branch	Jan	Feb	Mar	Apr	May	Jun	
5	USA	Chicago	671,185	359,811	745,471	685,	Sparklines	711,009	
6	USA	Dallas	708,157	276,972	227,227	482,		198,273	

First Half-Year Profit Report

You can also add Sparklines using the Quick Analysis button

Whenever you select a range of cells, a *Quick Analysis* button appears just outside the bottom-right corner of the selected range.

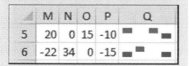

Apr	May	Jun
685,637 -	16,562	711,009
482,136	377,175	198,273
- 2,625	86,518	96,686

When you click the *Quick Analysis* button, the *Quick Analysis* dialog appears.

One of the menu options on this dialog is *Sparklines*.

It is possible to add *Line*, *Column* and *Win/Loss* Sparklines using this dialog.

important

Win/Loss Sparklines depict zero values with a blank space

In the example data for this lesson, all of the branches have either made a profit or a loss.

If you have a data set with zero values, the Win/Loss Sparkline will show blank spaces in the chart to illustrate zero values.

	M	N	O	P	Q
5	20	0	15	-10	
6	-22	34	0	-15	

1   Open *First Half-Year Profit Report* from your sample files folder.

2   Create a *Line Sparkline* in cell I5 that charts the data in cells C5:H5.

   1.   Click in cell I5.

   2.   Click: Insert→Sparklines→Line.

The *Create Sparklines* dialog appears.

   3.   Click in the *Data Range:* box and then select cells C5:H5

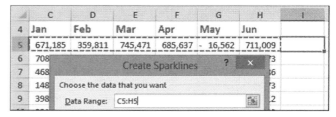

   4.   Click the OK button.

A Sparkline appears in cell I5:

	H	I
4	Jun	
5	711,009	

3   AutoFill the Sparkline to cells I6:I40.

You learned how to do this in: *Lesson 2-14: Use AutoFill for text and numeric series.*

You can now see how Sparklines visualize each branch's performance in a way that is beyond the scope of Visualizations and Charts.

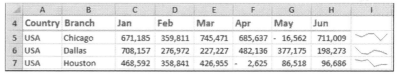

	A	B	C	D	E	F	G	H	I
4	Country	Branch	Jan	Feb	Mar	Apr	May	Jun	
5	USA	Chicago	671,185	359,811	745,471	685,637 -	16,562	711,009	
6	USA	Dallas	708,157	276,972	227,227	482,136	377,175	198,273	
7	USA	Houston	468,592	358,841	426,955 -	2,625	86,518	96,686	

4   Use the same technique to place a *Column Sparkline* in cells J5:J40 that charts the same data range (C5:H5).

5   Use the same technique to place a *Win/Loss Sparkline* in cells K5:K40 that charts the same data range (C5:H5).

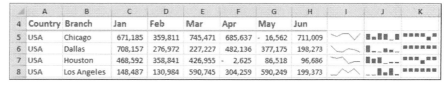

	A	B	C	D	E	F	G	H	I	J	K
4	Country	Branch	Jan	Feb	Mar	Apr	May	Jun			
5	USA	Chicago	671,185	359,811	745,471	685,637 -	16,562	711,009			
6	USA	Dallas	708,157	276,972	227,227	482,136	377,175	198,273			
7	USA	Houston	468,592	358,841	426,955 -	2,625	86,518	96,686			
8	USA	Los Angeles	148,487	130,984	590,745	304,259	590,249	199,373			

The *Column Sparkline* is very similar to the *Line Sparkline* but represents data as a bar chart.

Notice how the *Win/Loss Sparkline* enables you to see at a glance that Chicago and Houston had one loss-making month while Dallas and Los Angeles made a profit every month.

6   Save your work as *First Half Year Profit Report-1.*

Lesson 4-20: Apply a common vertical axis and formatting to a Sparkline group

Consider the following column Sparklines:

	A	B	C	D	E	F	G	H	I
4	Country	Branch	Jan	Feb	Mar	Apr	May	Jun	
5	USA	Chicago	671,185	359,811	745,471	685,637 -	16,562	711,009	▪▪▪▪_▪
28	UK	Manchester	180,988	209,763	203,761	2,201	165,328	124,392	▪▪▪_▪▪

If you only looked at the sparklines (and not the values) you'd guess that Manchester made more profit in the first three months than Chicago.

A glance at the actual profit values shows that Chicago actually made about three times more profit than Manchester.

The *Column* Sparklines are misleading because, by default, Excel only considers each row's values when setting the *Maximum* and *Minimum* values for the bars (also called the *Vertical Axis* values).

In this lesson we'll change this behaviour so that the size of the bars gives a true indication of each branch profit.

1 Open *First Half-Year Profit Report-1* from your sample files folder (if it isn't already open).

2 Delete columns I and K so that only the Column Sparklines remain.

You learned how to do this in: *Lesson 3-1: Insert and delete rows and columns.* Removing the two other Sparklines will help to focus upon the *Column Sparkline.*

3 Set a common Maximum and Minimum value for all Sparklines.

1. Click on any of the Sparklines in column I.

   Notice that a thin blue line has appeared around all of the Sparklines in column I. This happens because Excel views all of the Sparklines as a *Sparkline Group.* This means that when we use any of the *Sparkline Design Tools* on the Ribbon, the settings will apply to all Sparklines in the group.

2. Click: Sparkline Tools→Design→Group→Axis drop-down.

3. Click: Vertical Axis Minimum Value Options→ Same for All Sparklines.

4. Click: Vertical Axis Maximum Value Options→ Same for All Sparklines.

5. Notice the change in the Chicago and Manchester Sparklines:

	F	G	H	I
4	Apr	May	Jun	
5	685,637 -	16,562	711,009	▪▪▪▪_▪
28	2,201	165,328	124,392	▬▬▬▬▬▬

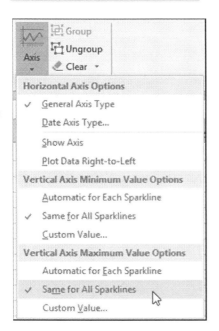

First Half-Year Profit Report-1

note

You can change the size of a Sparkline by re-sizing the cell that contains it

In the lessons in this session, the Sparkline cells have been left at their default size for neatness and to keep the worksheet compact.

If you resize a cell that contains a Sparkline it will automatically resize to fill the cell:

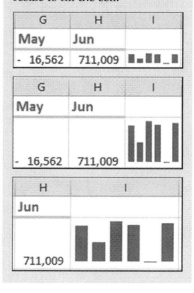

It is now clear, from looking at the bars alone, that in every month (except May) Manchester produced far less profit than Chicago.

4   Explore Sparkline formatting options.

The *Sparkline Tools Design* tab on the Ribbon provides many ways in which you can change the appearance of a group of Sparklines. Try experimenting with them.

1. Use the *Show* and *Marker Color* options.

    The *Show* check boxes allow you to apply a chosen color to any of the following points on a Sparkline.

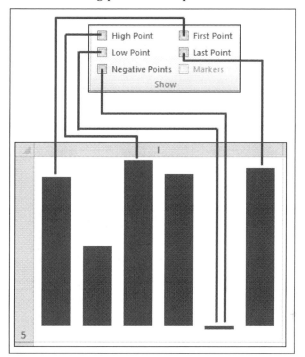

    You can choose a color for each of the points you check from the *Style→Marker Color* drop down.

2. Choose a new *Sparkline Style* from the *Style* gallery.

    Styles allow you to change the color scheme for your Sparkline. Note that the styles use theme colors and will change if you change the current theme. (You learned about themes in: *Lesson 4-8: Understand themes*).

3. Change the *Sparkline Type* to *Line* by clicking: Type→Line.

4. Add *Markers*.

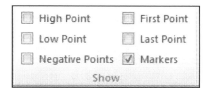

    Click: Sparkline Tools→Design→Show→Markers.

    When the *Sparkline Type* is *Line*, you are able to select the *Markers* option in the *Show* group. Each data point on the Sparkline is then marked with a dot.

5. Click: Sparkline Tools→Design→Style→Sparkline Color.

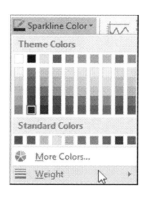

6. Change the line color.

7. Change the line thickness by clicking *Weight*.

5   Close *First Year Profit Report-1* without saving.

Lesson 4-21: Apply a date axis to a Sparkline group and format a single Sparkline

Sometimes you will encounter data that is attached to dates with uneven time intervals. Here's some of the sample data for this lesson:

	A	B	C	D	E	F	G	H
1	Number of Rings to Answer Phone Survey							
2								
3	Country	Branch	01-Mar-11	03-Mar-11	04-Mar-11	07-Mar-11	08-Mar-11	09-Mar-11
4	USA	Chicago	3	1	1	2	3	2
5	USA	Dallas	2	3	1	3	2	1
6	USA	Houston	10	8	11	7	11	5
7	USA	Los Angeles	1	3	2	3	3	1

This company has a policy that the telephone should be answered within three rings. To make sure the staff are hitting this target, head office phone each branch occasionally and record the number of rings taken to answer. You can see that Chicago, Dallas and Los Angeles are doing well but Houston is performing well below standard.

Head office don't phone every day – only when they have time to do so. This means that they didn't phone at all on 2nd, 5th and 6th March.

By default a Sparkline will assume that the data is at equal intervals and chart like this:

	C	D	E	F	G	H	I
3	01-Mar-11	03-Mar-11	04-Mar-11	07-Mar-11	08-Mar-11	09-Mar-11	
4	3	1	1	2	3	2	
5	2	3	1	3	2	1	
6	10	8	11	7	11	5	
7	1	3	2	3	3	1	

… but we'd like the Sparklines to have a common vertical axis and show a gap for the missing dates like this:

	E	F	G	H	I
3	04-Mar-11	07-Mar-11	08-Mar-11	09-Mar-11	
4	1	2	3	2	
5	1	3	2	1	
6	11	7	11	5	
7	2	3	3	1	

1 Open *Phone Survey* from your sample files folder.

2 Insert a Column Sparkline in cell I4 to chart data in cells C4:H4 and AutoFill it to the end of the range.

You learned to do this in: *Lesson 4-19: Insert a Sparkline into a range of cells.*

3 Set the *Vertical Axis Minimum Value* and *Vertical Axis Maximum Value* to be the same for all Sparkilines.

You learned to do this in: *Lesson 4-20: Apply a common vertical axis and formatting to a Sparkline group.*

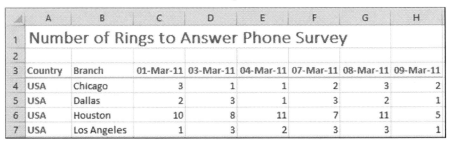

Phone Survey

note

Options for worksheets that contain Hidden and Empty cells

In:

Lesson 5-15: Chart non-contiguous source data by hiding rows and columns

And:

Lesson 5-17: Deal with empty data points

... you will learn the concept of hidden rows and columns, and also learn how to use Excel's *Hidden and Empty Cells* dialog.

You'll then also be able to use these options when you add a Sparkline to worksheets that contain empty cells or hidden rows and columns.

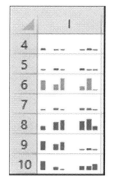

Your worksheet should now look like this:

	D	E	F	G	H	I
3	03-Mar-11	04-Mar-11	07-Mar-11	08-Mar-11	09-Mar-11	
4	1	1	2	3	2	
5	3	1	3	2	1	
6	8	11	7	11	5	
7	3	2	3	3	1	

4 Set the *Sparkline Date Range* to C3:H3.

1. Click any Sparkline in column I to select the Sparkline group.

2. Click:

   Sparkline Tools→Design→Group→Axis→Date Axis Type...

   The *Sparkline Date Range* dialog appears.

3. Select cells C3:H3 with the mouse.

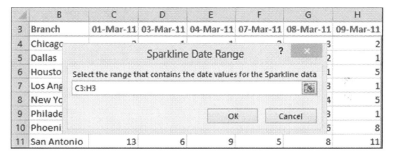

4. Click the OK button.

   The Sparkline is now shown with gaps for the missing dates:

	E	F	G	H	I
3	04-Mar-11	07-Mar-11	08-Mar-11	09-Mar-11	
4	1	2	3	2	
5	1	3	2	1	
6	11	7	11	5	
7	2	3	3	1	

5 Format the *Houston* Sparkline (in cell I6) so that all bars are orange.

To format a single Sparkline it is necessary to *Ungroup* the Sparklines. When Sparklines are ungrouped it is possible to format them individually.

1. Click in cell I6.

2. Click: Sparkline Tools→Design→Group→Ungroup.

3. Click:

   SparklineTools→Design→Style→Sparkline Color→ Orange Accent 2

4. The *Houston* Sparkline is now colored orange, while all other Sparklines remain black.

6 Save your work as *Phone Survey-1*.

Lesson 4-22: Use the Format Painter

The format painter is one of the most useful tools in Microsoft Office.

You can use the format painter in PowerPoint, Word and all other Office products.

I find that at least half of the experienced Excel users who attend my classroom courses have never discovered the format painter. I love it when they gasp in amazement at the enormous amount of time and effort they will save in future when using this tool.

In this lesson we're going to take a worksheet that is partially formatted and use the format painter to quickly copy formatting information (as opposed to values) from one cell to another.

1   Open *Sales Report-FP from* your sample files folder.

This worksheet has been partially formatted.

	A	B	C	D	E
1	Sales Report - 6 Months ended March 2008				
2					
3	Sales By Country			Sales by Category	
4	Country	Total Sales		Category	Total Sales
5	Argentina	762.6		Beverages	70168.1
6	Austria	33462.58		Condiments	24938.055
7	Belgium	6109.48		Confections	31883.54
8	Brazil	20524.42		Dairy Products	49902.95
9	Canada	21306.29		Grains/Cereals	19570.36
10	Denmark	16658.8		Meat/Poultry	35767.63
11	Finland	5525		Produce	17109.18
12	France	26155.54		Seafood	17304.51
13	Germany	28361.38		Grand Total	266644.325
14	Ireland	6157.755			

2   Apply the comma style to all of the values in column B.

This was covered in: *Lesson 4-3: Format numbers using built-in number formats.*

Values are now formatted with two decimal places and a thousand comma separator.

	A	B
9	Canada	21,306.29
10	Denmark	16,658.80
11	Finland	5,525.00

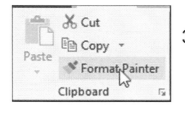

3   Use the format painter to copy formatting from the values in column B to the ranges E5:E13 and E20:E26.

1.   Click any value in column B.

2.   Click: Home→Clipboard→Format Painter. [Format Painter]

The cursor shape changes to a paint brush.

Sales Report-FP

note

Autofill and Paste are also able to match formatting in the same way as the Format Painter

The Format Painter is the fastest and most convenient way to match formatting when you only have to deal with a small range of cells.

Sometimes you'll need to match formatting in very large ranges containing thousands of cells. This would take a long time using the Format Painter but can be quickly achieved using *AutoFill*, or by using *Paste* along with the skills you learned in: *Lesson 2-8: AutoSelect a range of cells.*

AutoFill

AutoFill options were covered in depth in: *Lesson 2-16: Use AutoFill options.*

When you AutoFill using a right-click and drag (or AutoFill and then look at the Smart tag options) you'll notice that there's a *Fill Formatting Only* option.

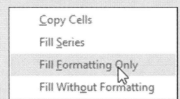

Paste

Copy and Paste were covered in depth in: *Lesson 3-3: Cut, copy and paste.*

When you paste there's also a *Formatting* option in the *Paste Options.*

3. Click and drag across cells E5:E13.

   The format of cells E5:E13 changes to match those of the values in column B.

	D	E
4	Category	Total Sales
5	Beverages	70,168.10
6	Condiments	24,938.06

4. Click on any value in column B.

5. Click: Home→Clipboard→Format Painter.

6. Drag across cells E20:E26.

   All values in this worksheet are now formatted with the comma style.

4 Use the format painter to copy formatting from cell A3 to cells D3 and D18.

This time we will use the format painter in a slightly different way.

If you double-click the format painter icon a *sticky format painter* results. This will stay switched on until you click the format painter icon again to switch it off.

1. Click on cell A3 to make it the active (source) cell.

2. Double-click: Home→Clipboard→Format Painter.

   The cursor shape changes to a paint brush.

3. Click cell D3. The format now matches cell A3 but the cursor remains the same.

4. Click cell D18. The format now matches cell A3 but the cursor remains the same.

5. Click: Home→Clipboard→Format Painter to switch off the format painter. The cursor reverts to the normal shape.

5 Copy formatting from cell A4 to cells D4:E4 and D19:E19 using the format painter.

6 Apply the *Total* style to cell B26.

   This was covered in: *Lesson 4-9: Use cell styles and change themes.*

7 Copy the total style from cell B26 to cells E13 and E26 using the format painter.

8 Save your work as *Sales Report-FP-1.*

Lesson 4-23: Rotate text

1   Open *Top 20 Films from* your sample files folder.

2   Insert a new column to the left of column A.

This was covered in: *Lesson 3-1: Insert and delete rows and columns.*

3   Cut and paste the contents of cell B1 to cell A1.

This was covered in: *Lesson 3-3: Cut, copy and paste.*

4   Apply the *Title* style to cell A1, the *Heading 2* style to cells A3:E3 and the *Heading 4* style to cell D25.

This was covered in: *Lesson 4-9: Use cell styles and change themes.*

5   Type: **Over 400M** into cell A4, **Over 350M** into cell A12 and **Over 300M** into cell A17.

6   Make column A slightly wider so that all text in the column is visible.

This was covered in: *Lesson 2-9: Re-size rows and columns.*

7   Select cells A4:A11.

	A	B	C
3		Title	Year
4	Over 400M	Titanic	1997
5		The Dark Knight	2008
6		Star Wars	1977
7		Shrek 2	2004
8		E.T.: The Extra-Terrestrial	1982
9		Star Wars: Episode I - The Phantom Menace	1999
10		Pirates of the Caribbean: Dead Man's Chest	2006
11		Spider-Man	2002
12	Over 350M	Star Wars: Episode III - Revenge of the Sith	2005

8   Merge the selected cells.

This was covered in: *Lesson 4-6: Merge cells, wrap text and expand/collapse the formula bar.*

9   Rotate the text through ninety degrees.

1.   Click: Home→Alignment→Orientation.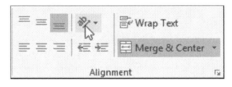

2.   Select *Rotate Text Up* from the drop-down list.

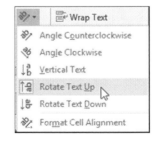

note

Other ways to rotate text

You can also rotate text using the *Format Cells* dialog, though you'll nearly always find the Ribbon method faster and more convenient.

The *Format Cells* dialog is slightly more powerful as it allows you to rotate text by any angle.

1.   Right-click a cell or range and click *Format Cells* from the shortcut menu.

2.   Click the *Alignment* tab.

3.   In the *Orientation* pane either type in the number of degrees of rotation or click and drag the red diamond to set it visually.

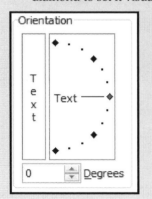

Top 20 Films

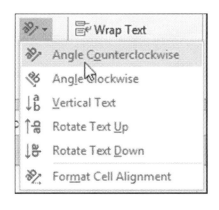

3		Title
4		Titanic
5		The Dark Knight
6		Star Wars
7		Shrek 2
8	Over 400M	E.T.: The Extra-T
9		Star Wars: Episo
10		Pirates of the Ca
11		Spider-Man
12		Star Wars: Episo
13	Over 350M	The Lord of the
14		Spider-Man 2
15		The Passion of t
16		Jurassic Park
17		The Lord of the
18		Finding Nemo
19		Spider-Man 3
20	Over 300M	Forrest Gump
21		The Lion King
22		Shrek the Third
23		Transformers

10 Merge and rotate the text in cells A12:A16 and A17:A23.

Your worksheet should now look like the sidebar.

11 Select cells A4:A17 and set the horizontal alignment to *center* and the vertical alignment to *middle.*

This was covered in: *Lesson 4-5: Horizontally align the contents of cells* and *Lesson 4-7: Vertically align the contents of cells.*

12 Apply the *Heading 4* style to cells A4:A17.

13 AutoFit cells A4:A17 so that they are just wide enough for the text.

This was covered in: *Lesson 2-9: Re-size rows and columns.*

14 Apply the *40% Accent 3* style to cell A4.

This was covered in: *Lesson 4-9: Use cell styles and change themes.*

Note that the cell reference for the old range A4:A11 is now the single cell reference A4.

15 Apply the *40% Accent 6* style to cell A12.

16 Apply the *40% Accent 2* style to cell A17.

17 Widen row 3 so that it is about three times the normal height.

18 Rotate the text in row 3 through 45 degrees.

1. Select row 3.

2. Click: Home→Alignment→Orientation [icon] → Angle Counter Clockwise.

19 Make columns C and E a little wider.

20 Save your work as *Top 20 Films-1.*

Session 4: Exercise

1   Open *House Mortgage* from your sample files folder.

2   Merge and center cells B3:J3.

3   Apply the *Title* style to cell A1, the *Heading 1* style to cell B3, the *Heading 3* style to cells A4:J4 and the *Heading 3* style to cells A10:C10.

4   Apply the *Heading 4* style to cells A5:A8 and cells A11:A15.

5   Apply the *Percentage* style to cells B4:J4.

6   Apply the *Comma* style to cells B5:J8.

7   Apply the *Percentage* style to cells B11:C15 and then increase decimals to one place.

8   Type the word *Average* into cell A16 and use the *Format Painter* to match the formatting to that of the cell above (A15).

9   Horizontally right-align the text in cell A16.

10   Use *AutoSum* to place an *Average* function into cells B16 and C16.

11   Apply the *Percentage* style to cells B16:C16 and then increase decimals to one place.

12   Place a thin black border beneath cells A15:C15.

13   Apply a *20% Accent 1* cell style to cells B4:J4 and B10:C10.

14   Change the theme to *Celestial*.

15   Autofit cells A4:A16 so that they are exactly wide enough to display all text.

16   Save your work as *House Mortgage-1*.

	A	B	C	D	E	F	G	H	I	J
1	House Mortgage Monthly Payments - 25 year term									
2										
3					interest rate					
4	House Value	2.0%	3.0%	4.0%	5.0%	6.0%	7.0%	8.0%	9.0%	10.0%
5	50000	211.93	237.11	263.92	292.30	322.15	353.39	385.91	419.60	454.35
6	100000	423.85	474.21	527.84	584.59	644.30	706.78	771.82	839.20	908.70
7	150000	635.78	711.32	791.76	876.89	966.45	1,060.17	1,157.72	1,258.79	1,363.05
8	200000	847.71	948.42	1,055.67	1,169.18	1,288.60	1,413.56	1,543.63	1,678.39	1,817.40
9										
10	Historical Base/Prime Rates	UK	USA							
11	1990	14.8%	7.3%							
12	1995	6.7%	5.5%							
13	2000	6.0%	5.5%							
14	2005	4.7%	2.3%							
15	2008	5.0%	2.0%							
16	Average	7.4%	4.5%							

House Mortgage

If you need help slide the page to the left ➡

Session 4: Exercise answers

These are the four questions that most students find the most difficult to remember:

Q 14	Q 12	Q 10	Q 8
1. Click Page Layout→ Themes→Themes→ Celestial. This was covered in: *Lesson 4-9: Use cell styles and change themes.*	1. Select cells A15:C15. 2. Click: Home→Font→ Borders→ Bottom Border. This was covered in: *Lesson 4-11: Add borders and lines.*	1. Select cells B16:C16. 2. Click: Home→Editing→ AutoSum→Average 3. Either press the **<Enter>** key or click the AutoSum button again. This was covered in: *Lesson 2-11: Use AutoSum to quickly calculate averages.*	1. Click in cell A15. 2. Click: Home→Clipboard→ Format Painter 3. Click in cell A16. This was covered in: *Lesson 4-22: Use the Format Painter.*

If you have difficulty with the other questions, here are the lessons that cover the relevant skills:

1   Refer to: Lesson 1-5: Download the sample files and open/navigate a workbook.

2   Refer to: Lesson 4-6: Merge cells, wrap text and expand/collapse the formula bar.

3   Refer to: Lesson 4-9: Use cell styles and change themes.

4   Refer to: Lesson 4-9: Use cell styles and change themes.

5,6,7 Refer to: Lesson 4-3: Format numbers using built-in number formats.

9   Refer to: Lesson 4-5: Horizontally align the contents of cells.

11   Refer to: Lesson 4-3: Format numbers using built-in number formats.

13   Refer to: Lesson 4-9: Use cell styles and change themes.

14   Refer to: Lesson 4-9: Use cell styles and change themes.

15   Refer to: Lesson 2-9: Re-size rows and columns.

16   Refer to: Lesson 1-6: Save a workbook.

5

Session Five: Charts and Graphics

In this session you'll learn to present your data in a chart. You'll also learn some valuable "tricks of the trade" to present your data in the most effective way.

Session Objectives

By the end of this session you will be able to:

- Understand chart types, layouts and styles
- Create a simple chart with two clicks
- Move, re-size, copy and delete a chart
- Create a chart using the Recommended Charts feature
- Add and remove chart elements using Quick Layout
- Apply a pre-defined chart style and color set
- Manually format a chart element
- Format 3-D elements and add drop shadows
- Move, re-size, add, position and delete chart elements
- Apply a chart filter
- Change a chart's source data
- Assign non-contiguous source data to a chart
- Understand data series and categories
- Change source data using the Select Data Source dialog tools
- Chart non-contiguous source data by hiding rows and columns
- Create a chart with numerical axes
- Deal with empty data points
- Add data labels to a chart
- Highlight specific data points with color and annotations
- Add gridlines and scale axes
- Emphasize data by manipulating pie charts
- Create a chart with two vertical axes
- Create a combination chart containing different chart types
- Add a trend line
- Add a gradient fill to a chart background
- Create your own chart templates

Lesson 5-1: Understand chart types, layouts and styles

The Excel designers noted that there are three things that control the design of a chart:

Chart Type

There are many different *types* of chart. The most common are: *Column Charts*, *Line Charts* and *Pie Charts*.

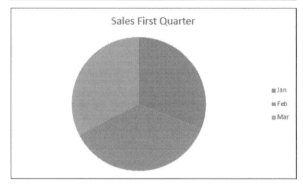

You'll discover how to choose a suitable *Chart Type* in: *Lesson 5-2: Create a simple chart with two clicks.*

Chart Layout

The layout of a chart can be thought of as a list of the *elements* that a chart contains.

Elements are artifacts such as a *Title, Axis Titles or Legend.*

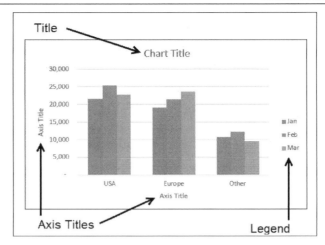

In: *Lesson 5-5: Add and remove chart elements using Quick Layout*, you'll discover how to quickly select a group of common elements for a chart.

Chart Style

The *Chart Style* determines the font, color and positioning of each chart element. Here are two charts that have an identical *Type* and *Layout* but have different styles:

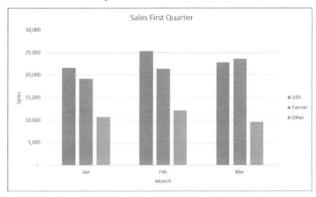

You can see that both charts are of the same type (*Clustered Column*), and that both have the same elements (that include the *Axis Titles, Chart Title* and *Legend* elements).

The differences in appearance (colors, shading of bars, fonts used and position of legend) are collectively referred to as the chart's *Style*.

You'll learn how to change a chart's style in: *Lesson 5-6: Apply a pre-defined chart style and color set.*

Lesson 5-2: Create a simple chart with two clicks

1   Open *World Sales from* your sample files folder.

This is a very simple worksheet containing January, February and March sales data for three regions.

	A	B	C	D
1	Month	USA	Europe	Other
2	Jan	21,600	19,200	10,800
3	Feb	25,400	21,400	12,200
4	Mar	22,800	23,600	9,600

2   Select all of the values and all of the labels (cells A1:D4).

When Excel creates a chart it needs both values and labels. For this reason you must always select the labels *as well as* the values before you create your chart.

Missing the labels is one of the most common errors in my classroom courses.

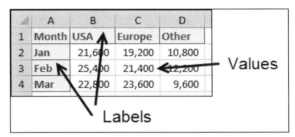

3   Click: Insert→Charts→Insert Column Chart and hover the mouse pointer over some of the charts in the gallery.

As you hover the mouse button over each chart type Excel provides a ScreenTip describing the chart. A preview of how the chart will look is also displayed on the worksheet.

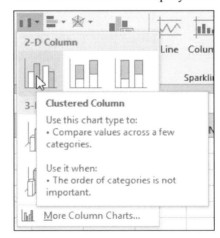

4   Click the left-most 2-D Column chart (the *Clustered Column* chart).

In just two clicks we have created a very presentable chart.

World Sales

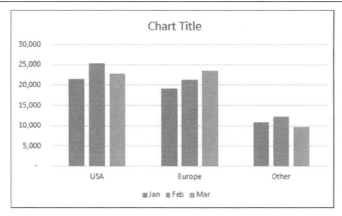

note

Changing the chart type of an existing chart

You may create a chart but later decide that you really need a different chart type.

For example, you might create a *bar chart* but later decide you would have preferred a *pie chart* or *line chart*.

To change the type of an existing chart:

1. Right-click on the chart.

2. Click: *Change Chart Type* from the shortcut menu.

note

Create a chart with the Quick Analysis button

Whenever you select a range of cells, a *Quick Analysis* button appears just outside the bottom-right corner of the selected range.

When you click the *Quick Analysis* button, the *Quick Analysis* dialog appears.

One of the menu options on this dialog is *Charts*.

When you click the *Charts* menu option you are presented with a choice of five recommended charts for the range selected.

This method isn't as versatile as choosing a chart manually (as described in this lesson).

Because you have only specified the chart *Type*, Excel has chosen a default *Layout* and *Style* for you. You'll learn how to change these default choices later in this session.

5   Understand chart activation.

In this example the worksheet only contains one chart.

It is possible that a worksheet will contain more than once chart.

For this reason, you need to indicate to Excel which chart you want to work on. To do this the chart needs to be *activated*.

To activate a chart you simply click anywhere inside the chart.

When the chart is activated two things happen:

1. The *Chart Tools Design* and *Chart Tools Format* tabs appear on the Ribbon:

    CHART TOOLS
    DESIGN   FORMAT

2. A frame (with sizing handles) appears around the chart:

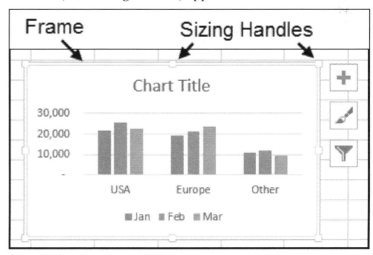

6   Save your work as *World Sales-1*.

tip

Give charts meaningful names to make them easier to find in the Selection and Visibility task pane

If you have more than one chart embedded in a worksheet, it is a good idea to give them more meaningful names than the default *Chart1, Chart2* etc.

To rename a chart you need to first activate it and then change the name in the *Name Box* (at the left of the formula bar):

When charts have meaningful names it is easy to activate them using the *Selection and Visibility* task pane.

To make this task pane appear, first activate the chart and then click:

Chart Tools→Format→ Arrange→Selection Pane

The selection pane will then appear and can be left on screen to quickly activate specific charts.

It is also possible to show or hide charts by clicking the eyeball symbol  to the right of the relevant chart.

Lesson 5-3: Move, re-size, copy and delete a chart

1   Open *World Sales-1* from your sample files folder (if it isn't already open).

2   Move the chart to a different position on screen.

    1.   Click just inside the border of the char to activate it.

       When the chart is activated you will see a frame and corner handles around it.

       Excel also displays the *Chart Tools* group of Ribbon tabs.

    2.   Hover with the mouse cursor just inside the border of the selected chart until you see the four headed arrow cursor shape.

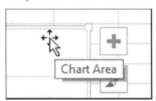

    3.   Click and drag the chart to the required position.

3   Re-size the chart.

    1.   Click just inside the border of the chart to activate it.

    2.   Hover over one of the corner or side sizing handles on the edges of the chart until you see the two-headed arrow cursor shape.

    3.   When you see the two-headed arrow cursor shape, click and drag to re-size the chart.

       If you hold down the **<Shift>** key as you click-and drag one of the corners of the chart, the perspective will remain constant (ie the chart will get proportionately wider as it gets taller).

4   Create a duplicate chart using copy and paste.

    1.   Click just inside the border of the chart to activate it.

    2.   Right-click, on the border of the activated chart (just inside the border works too) and click *Copy* from the shortcut menu.

    3.   Right-click anywhere on the worksheet and click *Paste* from the shortcut menu to create the duplicate chart.

World Sales-1

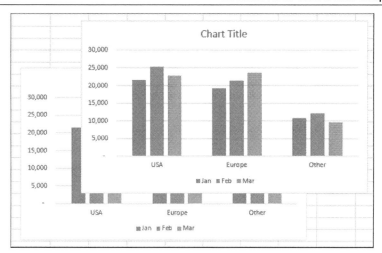

Note that even though the new chart is a duplicate, it is not linked to the original chart in any way. You can freely change any part of either chart and it will never affect the other.

5 Delete one of the charts.

1. Click just inside the border of either of the charts to activate it.

2. Press the **<Delete>** key on the keyboard.

6 Move the chart to its own chart worksheet.

Sometimes it is better to keep charts and data separate by placing a chart in its own *chart worksheet*. A chart worksheet is a special worksheet without any cells that can only contain a single chart.

1. Right-click just inside the border of the chart to activate it and then click *Move Chart...* from the shortcut menu.

2. Click the *New Sheet* option button, name the new sheet *Sales Summary Chart* and click the OK button.

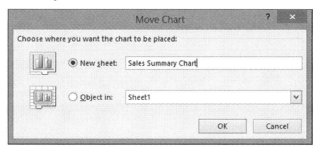

The chart is now displayed within its own dedicated chart worksheet.

7 Move the chart back to its original location.

1. Right-click just inside the border of the chart and click *Move Chart...* from the shortcut menu.

2. Click the *Object in* option button, choose *Sheet1* from the drop down list and click the OK button.

8 Save your work as *World Sales-2*.

Lesson 5-4: Create a chart using the Recommended Charts feature

A new feature for Excel 2013 is its ability to recommend a chart type to use with any specified data.

Excel can now intelligently analyze your data and then try to guess which chart type will do the best job of representing it visually.

1 Open *Hawaii Temperature-1* from your sample files folder.

This worksheet contains temperature data for Honolulu, Hawaii (one of the nicest year-round climates in the world).

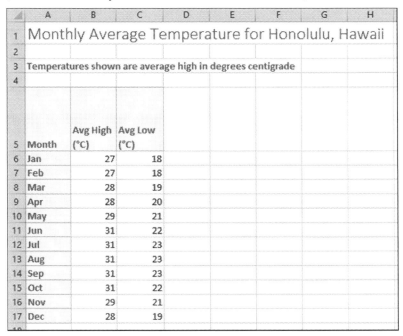

	A	B	C	D	E	F	G	H
1	Monthly Average Temperature for Honolulu, Hawaii							
2								
3	Temperatures shown are average high in degrees centigrade							
4								
5	Month	Avg High (°C)	Avg Low (°C)					
6	Jan	27	18					
7	Feb	27	18					
8	Mar	28	19					
9	Apr	28	20					
10	May	29	21					
11	Jun	31	22					
12	Jul	31	23					
13	Aug	31	23					
14	Sep	31	23					
15	Oct	31	22					
16	Nov	29	21					
17	Dec	28	19					

2 Use *Recommended Charts* to select a suitable chart type.

1. Click anywhere inside the data (in a cell somewhere in the range A5:C17).

   You could also select the range A5:C17, but when you want to chart an entire range it is only necessary to select a single cell within the range.

2. Click: Insert→Charts→Recommended Charts.

3. The *Insert Chart* dialog is displayed with the *Recommended Charts* tab selected.

Hawaii Temperature-1

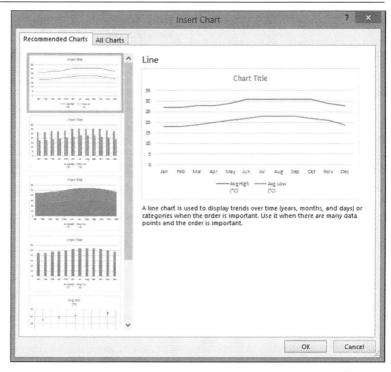

note

You can see a smaller selection of recommended charts using the Quick Analysis button

Whenever you select a range of cells, a *Quick Analysis* button appears just outside the bottom-right corner of the selected range.

31	23	
31	22	
29	21	
28	19	

When you click the *Quick Analysis* button, the *Quick Analysis* dialog appears.

One of the menu options on this dialog is *Charts*.

When you click the *Charts* menu option you are presented with a choice of five recommended charts for the range selected. This is one chart less than when using the Ribbon's *Recommended Charts* button.

Notice that Excel's first choice for an appropriate chart type is a line chart.

This isn't a bad choice but perhaps Excel's second choice, the *Clustered Column* chart, will work better with this data.

4. Click the *Clustered Column* chart (the second recommended chart in the left-hand list).

A preview of the clustered column chart is shown in the right-hand pane of the dialog.

5. Click OK to create a *Clustered Column* chart.

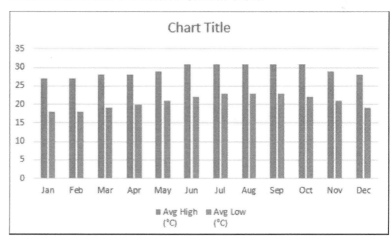

This chart does a very good job of visually showing the temperature range each month in Hawaii.

In: *Lesson 5-5: Add and remove chart elements using Quick Layout,* you'll learn how to change the *Chart Title* element to display appropriate text.

3 Save your work as *Hawaii Temperature-2*.

Lesson 5-5: Add and remove chart elements using Quick Layout

World Sales-2

The term *Layout* can be confusing. It is used to describe the *Elements* that a chart contains. For example, here is a simple chart containing only two elements:

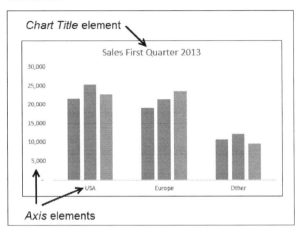

And here's a chart that contains four elements:

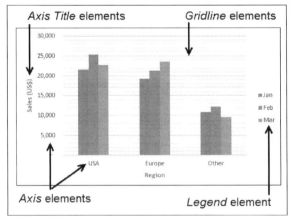

Some layouts also include a *Data Table* showing the source data for the chart:

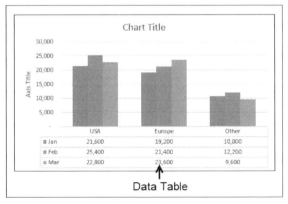

Don't confuse the layout (the elements that a chart contains) with the chart style (the colors and appearance of the chart elements).

In this lesson we use Excel's *Quick Layout* feature to choose from nine common layouts with a single click.

1 Open *World Sales-2* from your sample files folder (if it isn't already open).

2 Change the *Chart Layout* to: *Layout 9*.

1. Click just inside the border of the chart to activate it.

2. Click: Chart Tools→Design→Chart Layouts→Quick Layout.

This gallery contains eleven pre-defined chart layouts. Each layout contains a group of elements.

3. Click: *Layout 9*.

This layout includes a *Chart Title* element, a *Legend* element, two *Axis* elements, two *Axis Title* elements and a *Gridlines* element.

In: *Lesson 5-9: Move, re-size, add, position and delete chart elements*, you'll learn how to add elements one by one.

You can see how much faster it is to select all five elements with a single click instead of individually adding each one.

3 Click the *Chart Title* element and type: **Sales First Quarter**

4 Click the *Vertical Axis Title* element and type: **Sales**

5 Click the *Horizontal Axis Title* element and type: **Region**

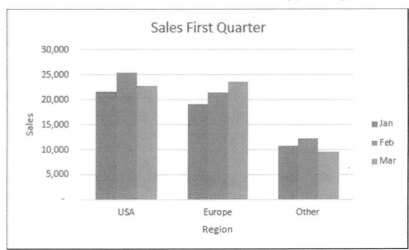

6 Save your work as: *World Sales-3*.

note

Use chart tips to discover chart element names

When you hover the mouse cursor over a chart element, the name of the element is displayed in a chart tip.

If this doesn't work on your machine somebody has switched off the chart tips.

Here's how to switch them back on:

1. Click:

   File→Options→Advanced

2. In the *Chart* section, check the *Show chart element names on hover* check box.

Lesson 5-6: Apply a pre-defined chart style and color set

1   Open *World Sales-3 from* your sample files folder (if it isn't already open).

2   Change the chart style.

1. Click just inside the border of the chart to activate it.
2. Click: Chart Tools→ Design→Chart Styles→ Chart Styles Gallery.

Chart Styles

When you click the *Gallery* button [⊟] you are able to choose a new chart style from 14 pre-defined options. Each chart style uses theme colors, so the chart's appearance will change if you later change the workbook's theme (you learned about themes in: *Lesson 4-8: Understand themes*).

Notice that the chart changes as you hover over each style so that you can preview how your chart will look if the style is chosen.

3. Click a new chart style to change the appearance of your chart.

In the example below I have chosen *Style 8*.

3   Change the chart's color scheme.

In: *Lesson 4-8: Understand themes,* you learned that every theme has a related color set.

In: *Lesson 4-10: Add color and gradient effects to cells (sidebar)* you learned why it is good practice to restrict colors to theme colors.

Excel provides a quick and convenient way to choose new set of colors (from the current theme's color set) for your chart.

World Sales-3

note

Another way to change a chart's style or color set

When you activate a chart (by clicking on it), three small icons appear next to the top-right corner:

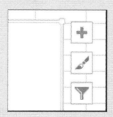

The middle icon 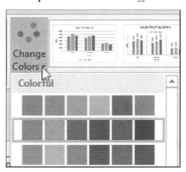 provides a different way to select a style or color set.

The other two buttons allow you to select *Chart Elements* and *Chart Filters*.

You'll learn about Chart Elements later, in: *Lesson 5-9: Move, re-size, add, position and delete chart elements.*

You'll learn about Chart Filters later, in: *Lesson 5-10: Apply a chart filter.*

1. Click just inside the border of the chart to activate it.

2. Click: Chart Tools→Design→Change Colors.

   A set of color palettes (each consisting of six colors) are displayed. All colors belong to the current theme (in this example, the default *Office* theme).

   As you hover the mouse cursor over each palette, the chart changes to preview the effect of choosing the new color set.

3. Click any of the color sets to select. The new color set is applied to the chart.

4 Close the workbook without saving.

   You want to stay with the original default style, so close this workbook without saving. The chart will then retain the default style.

note

Chart titles can display the contents of a specific worksheet cell

Normally you will simply type the text that you need directly into the *Chart Title* element.

It is also possible to link the *Chart Title* to a worksheet cell so that it displays whatever text is in the specified cell.

Here's how it is done:

1. Click the *Chart Title* element.

2. Click inside the formula bar.

3. Type: = to start the formula.

4. Click on cell A1 (or the worksheet cell containing the value you want to be displayed).

5. Press the <Enter> key.

   This will add a fully qualified cell reference such as:

   =Sheet1!$A$1

   This is required when you reference a cell from a *Chart Title* element. A simple reference such as:

   =A1

   ...will not work.

   You'll learn more about fully qualified cell references later, in: *Lesson 6-6: Create cross worksheet formulas.*

   The contents of cell A1 are then displayed in the *Chart Title* element and will change whenever the text in cell A1 changes.

Lesson 5-7: Manually format a chart element

Up until now you've selected a pre-defined chart style and color scheme from a gallery.

Sometimes you may have a requirement that is not catered for within the selection of pre-defined styles offered by the *Chart Styles* gallery.

In this case you will need to manually format one or more chart elements.

Once you have the hang of how to format one element it becomes easy to work with any other element, because the options are broadly the same.

In this lesson you'll manually format the *Chart Title* element.

1   Open *World Sales-3* from your sample files folder (if it isn't already open).

2   Click the *Chart Title* element to select it.

A frame appears:

3   Right-Click the *Chart Title* element and click *Format Chart Title* from the shortcut menu.

The *Format Chart Title* task pane appears.

4   Apply a *Blue Accent 1* fill (background color) to the *Chart Title* element.

1.   Click the *Fill & Line* icon in the *Format Chart Title* task pane.

2.   Click the *Fill* option to display the fly-out menu.

3.   Click the *Solid fill* option button.

4.   Click the *Fill Color* icon.

5.   Click the *Blue, Accent 1* fill color.

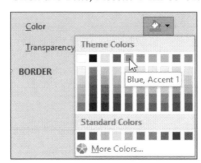

6.   Drag the *Transparency* slider to the right to set the transparency to about 80%.

note

Working with the Format Shape task pane

The *Format Chart Title* task pane you have been working with in this lesson is actually an instance of the more generic *Format Shape* task pane.

The name shown at the top of the *Format Shape* task pane changes depending upon which chart element you are working with.

The *Format Shape* task pane (in common with all other Office task panes) is modeless. (You learned about the difference between modal dialogs and modeless task panes in: *Lesson 3-7: Use the Multiple Item Clipboard – sidebar*).

This means that you can go on working and leave the *Format Shape* dialog happily sitting in the background. Even better, as you select different chart elements, the *Format Shape* task pane will automatically change to show the settings appropriate for the selected element.

This is a huge time saver, especially if you have a large screen (or multiple monitors) enabling you to "park" the task pane out of the way of the worksheet.

Notice that the background color of the *Chart Title* element becomes lighter as you drag to the right, and darker as you drag to the left.

5   Apply a 1pt solid black border to the *Chart Title* element.

1.   Click the *Fill & Line* icon in the *Format Chart Title* task pane.

2.   Click the *Border* option to display the fly-out menu.

3.   In the *Border* section, click the *Solid Line* option button.

4.   Click the *Color* drop-down arrow and select a solid black color.

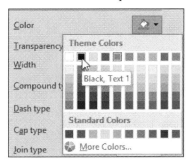

5.   In the *Border* section, set the *Width* to: 1pt

Notice that a solid black border has now been applied to the *Chart Title* element.

6   Close the *Format Chart Title* task pane.

7   Save your work as *World Sales-4*.

Lesson 5-8: Format 3-D elements and add drop shadows

The use of subtle shadows and 3-D formats will add a professional sheen to your work.

1   Open *World Sales-4* from your sample files folder (if it isn't already open) and click just inside the border of the chart to activate it.

2   Select the *Chart Title* element using *Chart Tools.*

Click: Chart Tools→Format→Current Selection→
Chart Elements Drop Down→Chart Title.

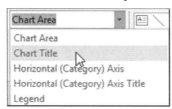

This is an alternative way to select chart elements. The drop-down shows every element in the currently selected chart.

Directly clicking on an element is usually faster but there are some chart elements (such as gridlines) that can sometimes be difficult to select with the mouse.

Here are the elements available in the *Chart Elements* drop-down list for this chart:

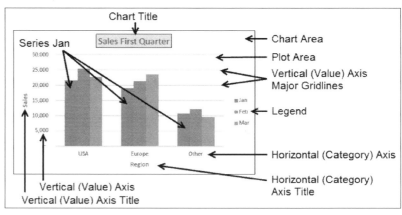

If you do a lot of work with charts it is well worth adding the *Chart Elements Drop-Down List* to the *Quick Access Toolbar* (this was covered in: *Lesson 1-14: Customize the Quick Access Toolbar and preview the printout*).

3   Display the *Format Title* task pane.

Click: Chart Tools→Format→Current Selection→Format Selection.

This is an alternative way to bring up the *Format Title* dialog.

4   Apply an *Offset Diagonal Bottom Right* shadow to the *Chart Title* element.

note

More about data series

A data series is a group of data that is associated with a specific category.

For example, the *Series Jan* data series is a group of values, one for each of the categories *USA, Europe* and *Other.*

In this example there are three data series containing numerical data for each category.

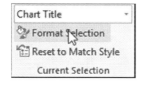

World Sales-4

1. Click the *Effects*  icon in the *Format Chart Title* task pane.

2. Select *Shadow* from the four effects options.

3. Click the *Presets* icon.

   While you can create your own shadows using the *Transparency, Size, Blur, Angle* and *Distance* sliders, you'll probably find that the presets will suffice. Presets will also maintain uniformity between different chart elements.

4. Click the *Offset Diagonal Bottom Right* item in the shadow gallery.

   The effect is applied to the *Chart Title* element.

5 Apply a *Circle top bevel* 3D effect to the *Chart Title* element

Bevel effects make an element look like a button.

1. Click the *Effects*  icon in the *Format Chart Title* task pane.

2. Select *3-D Format* from the four effects options.

3. Click the *Top Bevel* preset button to display the Top Bevel gallery and choose a *Circle* top bevel.

   Just like shadows, you'll probably find what you need in the 3-D presets rather than creating your own custom 3-D effects.

6 Use *Reset to Match Style* to restore the *Chart Title* element to its default state.

We've added a lot of fancy formatting to the *Chart Title* element but haven't really improved the appearance of the element.

Excel provides the *Reset to Match Style* feature to enable you to restore elements back to their original state.

1. Click on the *Chart Title* element to select it.

2. Click: Chart Tools→Format→Current Selection→ Reset to Match Style.

   The *Chart Title* element is restored to its default state.

   Sales First Quarter

   30,000

7 Close the *Format Chart Title* task pane.

8 Save your work as *World Sales-5.*

Lesson 5-9: Move, re-size, add, position and delete chart elements

Several elements such as the *Chart Title*, *Legend* and *Horizontal/Vertical Axis Titles* can be moved by drag and drop.

In this lesson we'll see how to manually move these elements, and how to automatically restore them to their pixel-perfect locations if you change your mind.

We'll also manually remove and add single chart elements. Once you've got the hang of this you'll be able to custom design charts for any specific requirement.

1   Open *World Sales-5* from your sample files folder (if it isn't already open).

2   Click and drag the *Chart Title* element to the left hand side of the chart.

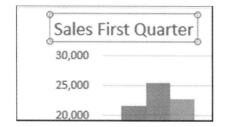

   1.   Click the *Chart Title* element to select it.

   2.   Hover the mouse over the border of the *Chart Title* element until you see a four headed arrow.

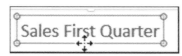

   3.   When you see the four headed arrow, click and drag to move the element to the top left corner of the chart.

3   Move the *Chart Title* element back so that it is above the center of the chart.

You couldn't position this perfectly using the mouse.

   1.   Click on the *Chart Title* element to select it.

   2.   Click: Chart Tools→Design→Chart Layouts→ Add Chart Element→Chart Title→Above Chart.

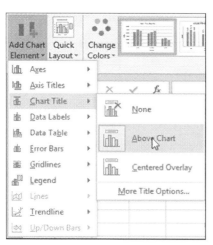

      The *Chart Title* element is restored to the center.

4   Delete the legend.

   1.   Click the *Legend* element to select it

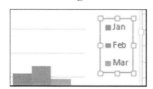

   2.   Press the **<Delete>** key.

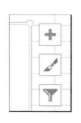

5   Display the legend at the top of the screen.

   1.   Select the chart.

      Notice that a group of three icons appears outside the top right corner of the chart:

World Sales-5

2. Click the *Chart Elements*  icon.

A list of all elements available for the chart is displayed. This is almost the same as the dialog shown when you clicked the *Add Chart Element* button on the Ribbon earlier in this lesson.

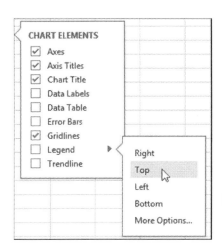

3. Click the arrow button to the right of the word: *Legend* in the list.

Several options for positioning the legend are shown.

4. Click: Top.

The legend moves to the top of the chart.

6 Add a thin black border to the *Legend* element.

This was covered in: *Lesson 5-7: Manually format a chart element.*

7 Resize the *Legend* element so that it spans the entire width of the plot area.

1. Click the *Legend* element to select it. Notice the sizing handles on each corner and edge.

2. Hover over the square sizing handle on the right-hand edge of the element. Notice that the cursor shape changes to a two headed arrow.

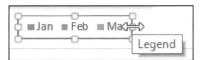

3. When you see the two-headed arrow click and drag to re-size the legend so that it is the same width as the plot area. (You'll have to first re-size the right side and then the left).

8 Increase the size of the font within the *Legend* element.

1. Click the *Legend* element to select it.

2. Click: Home→Font→Font Size Drop-down.

3. Hover the mouse cursor over each font size and note that *Live Preview* allows you to preview the effect of your choice.

4. Select *14 points* for the new text size.

You'll often want to increase text sizes when you create charts for PowerPoint slides.

9 Save your work as *World Sales-6*.

Lesson 5-10: Apply a chart filter

The chart that you have been working with contains three data series and three categories:

- The *data series* are Jan, Feb and Mar. Each of these data series contain three different values, one for each category.

- The *categories* are USA, Europe and Other.

The *Chart Filters* feature (a brand new feature in Excel 2013) allows you to show or hide any of the data series or categories.

1 Open *World Sales-6* from your sample files folder (if it isn't already open).

2 Apply a *Chart Filter* to show sales only for Jan and Feb.

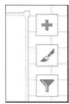

1. Click on the chart to activate it.

A group of three icons appears outside the top right corner of the chart:

2. Click the *Chart Filters* ▼ icon.

A list of all of the data series and categories used in the chart is displayed (see sidebar).

Each data series and category has a check box enabling you to hide or show the relevant item.

3. Uncheck the *Mar* check box so that only the *Jan* and *Feb* data series will be shown on the chart.

4. Click the *Apply* button to apply the filter.

The chart changes so that only *Jan* and *Feb* data is displayed.

World Sales-6

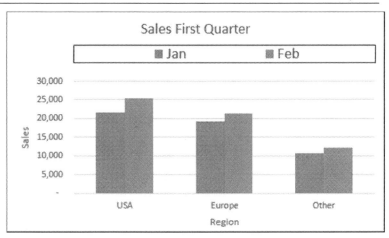

3   Apply *Chart Filters* to show sales for all months, but only in the *USA* and *Europe* categories.

1.   Click on the chart to activate it.

2.   Click the *Chart Filters* 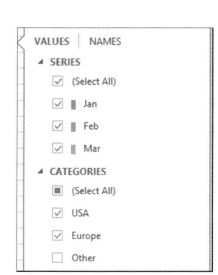 icon.

3.   In the *Series* list check the *(Select All)* item to select all three months.

4.   In the *Categories* list uncheck the *Other* item so that only *USA* and *Europe* categories will be shown on the chart.

5.   Click the *Apply* button to apply the filter.

The chart changes so that only *USA* and *Europe* data is displayed for the months *Jan, Feb* and *Mar.*

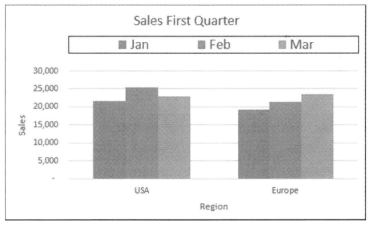

4   Remove all filters so that all data series and categories are displayed.

1.   Select the chart.

2.   Click the *Chart Filters* icon.

3.   Check the *(Select All)* check box in the *Categories* list to select all three categories.

4.   Click the *Apply* button to apply the filter.

Lesson 5-11: Change a chart's source data

You'll often want to chart a small number of columns from a much larger range (that may contain hundreds, or even thousands of columns).

If a range only contains a handful of columns, it may be easier to chart the entire range and then use the *Chart Filters* feature (that you used in: *Lesson 5-10: Apply a chart* filter) to remove the unwanted columns.

When there are a lot of columns you may find it a lot faster to address the issue in the chart's source data using the technique described in this lesson.

1 Open *World Sales-6* from your sample files folder (if it isn't already open).

2 Display the *Select Data Source* dialog.

note

Another way to display the Select Data Source dialog

You can also bring up the *Select Data Source* dialog from the Ribbon by clicking:

Chart Tools→
Design→Data→Select Data

1. Right-click in the *Plot Area* of the chart and click *Select Data...* from the shortcut menu.

The *Select Data Source* dialog appears.

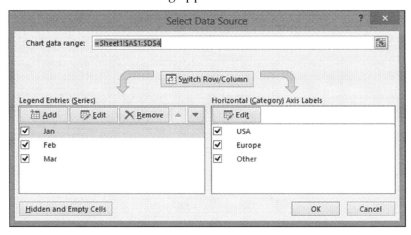

Notice the *Chart data range* shown at the top of the dialog. For the moment this is all that I want you to concentrate upon.

The range is shown as: Sheet1!$A$1:$D$4.

This means the absolute range A1:D4 on the *Sheet1* worksheet.

(Absolute cell references were covered in: *Lesson 3-12: Understand absolute and relative cell references*).

3 Change the *Chart data range* so that only USA sales are charted.

The current range is A1:D4.

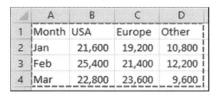

	A	B	C	D
1	Month	USA	Europe	Other
2	Jan	21,600	19,200	10,800
3	Feb	25,400	21,400	12,200
4	Mar	22,800	23,600	9,600

World Sales-6

If we change the range to A1:B4 the *Europe* and *Other* regions will be removed.

You could simply type the new reference into the *Chart data range* text box but it is less error prone if you visually select the data with the mouse.

1. Delete the current contents of the *Chart data range* text box.

2. With the mouse cursor still inside the empty *Chart Data Range* text box, click and drag with the mouse across cells A1:B4.

    The data range displays in both the *Select data range* text box and as a marquee on the worksheet.

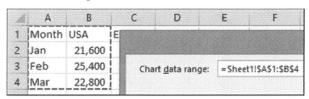

It is very easy to mess up the data range in the text box. If you get an obscure error message, simply delete all of the contents of the *Chart data range* text box and re-select.

Notice that, in the background, the chart has changed to reflect the new data range.

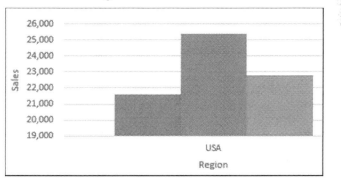

4   Change the *Chart data range* to A1:C4 to chart sales for the USA and Europe.

5   Click OK to view the new chart.

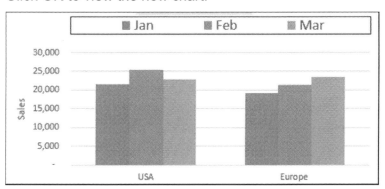

6   Save your work as *World Sales-7*.

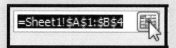

Lesson 5-12: Assign non-contiguous source data to a chart

In the previous lesson it was easy to select the source data because it comprised of a single block (we use the word: *contiguous* for this type of range).

In this lesson we'll take things a little further by selecting data that isn't in a single block (ie non-contiguous data) to show sales for the *USA* and *Other* categories.

1   Open *World Sales-7* from your sample files folder (if it isn't already open).

2   Chart sales for all months in the *USA* and *Other* categories by changing the source data.

    1.   Right-click in the plot area of the chart and click *Select Data* from the shortcut menu.

       The *Select Data Source* dialog appears.

    2.   Delete the current contents of the *Chart data range* text box.

    3.   With the mouse cursor still inside the empty *Chart data range* text box, click and drag with the mouse across cells A1:B4.

    4.   Release the mouse button.

    5.   Hold down the **<Ctrl>** key.

    6.   Select the range D1:D4.

    7.   Click the OK button.

    Selecting non-contiguous ranges was covered extensively in: *Lesson 2-7: Select non-contiguous cell ranges and view summary information.*

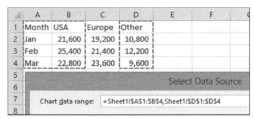

World Sales-7

3   Display the total sales for each month in column E.

Type the word: **Total** into cell E1 and then use AutoSum to place the total for all regions into cells E2:E4.

AutoSum was covered in: *Lesson 2-3: Use AutoSum to quickly calculate totals.*

4   Change the source data so that only the *Total* category is charted.

1. Right-click in the plot area of the chart.

2. Click *Select Data* from the shortcut menu.

3. Delete the current contents of the *Chart data range* text box.

4. With the mouse cursor still inside the empty *Chart data range* text box, click and drag with the mouse across cells A1:A4.

5. Hold down the **<Ctrl>** key.

6. Select cells E1:E4.

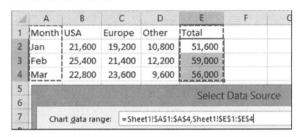

5   Change the source data so that sales for *USA*, *Europe* and *Other* regions are shown (but not the total).

1. Right-click in the plot area of the chart and click *Select Data* from the shortcut menu.

2. Select cells A1:D4.

3. Click OK to close the *Select Data Source* dialog.

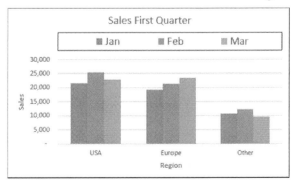

6   Save your work as *World Sales-8*.

Lesson 5-13: Understand Data Series and Categories

In order to use the *Select Data Source* dialog in a more advanced way, you will need to understand how Excel automatically divides a range of data into *data series* and *categories*.

Data series and categories

Here is the data we have been working with for most of this session:

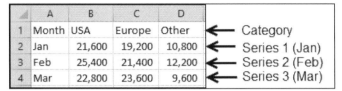

Excel interprets this data as having three data series (Jan, Feb and Mar).

In this example, each data series has three values. For example, the *Jan* data series has the three values 21,600|19,200|10,800.

The values are plotted along the left-hand vertical axis (sometimes referred to as the Y axis).

Each of the values in a data series is associated with a *Category*. This is simply a label that identifies each value in the series. For example, the *Jan* series value of 19,200 belongs to the *Europe* category.

The category is shown along the bottom horizontal axis (sometimes referred to as the X axis).

Showing this on the chart makes things clearer:

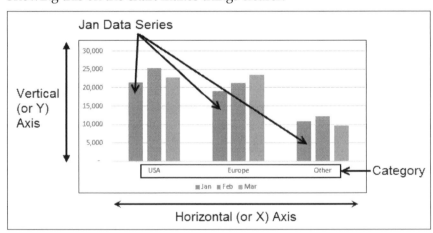

Swapping the Rows and Columns

It is also possible to take a different view of the same data.

The old data series become categories, and the old categories become data series.

World Sales-8

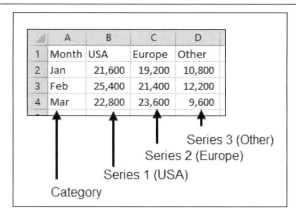

When the data is viewed in this way a different chart will result.

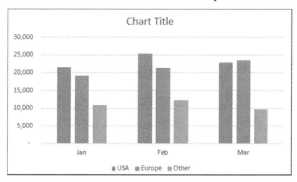

1   Open *World Sales-8* from your sample files folder (if it isn't already open).

At present Excel regards months as data series, and regions as categories:

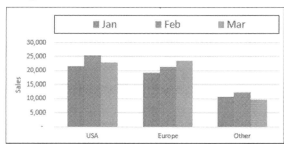

2   Switch the rows and columns so that the X Axis shows months instead of regions.

1.   Click just inside the border of the chart to select it.

2.   Click: Chart Tools→Design→Data→Switch Row/Column

Excel now regards the regions as data series, and the months as categories.

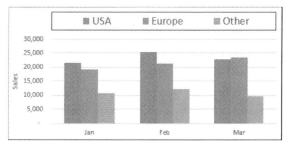

3   Save your work as *World Sales-9*.

Lesson 5-14: Change source data using the Select Data Source dialog tools

1 Open *World Sales-9* from your sample files folder (if it isn't already open).

2 Display the *Select Data Source* dialog.

1. Right-click in the *Plot Area* of the chart and click *Select Data* from the shortcut menu.

The *Select Data Source* dialog appears.

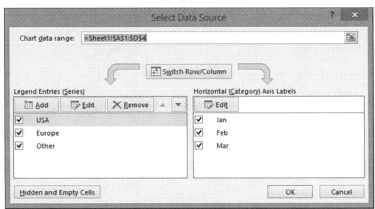

Notice that there are check boxes next to each series and category.

You can check and uncheck these boxes to apply a chart filter (a different way to do the same thing that you did in: *Lesson 5-10: Apply a chart filter*).

3 Add a *Total* data series.

Click the *Add* button in the *Legend Entries (Series)* pane.

1. Type: **Total** for the series name.

2. Delete any text currently appearing in the *Series values* text box.

3. Select the range E2:E4 for the *Series values*.

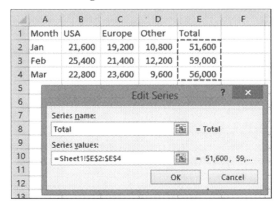

4. Click OK.

The series is added to the dialog.

note

An alternative method for selecting source data

The *Select Data Source* dialog is by far the best way to set and modify source data for charts.

An alternative (and less intuitive) way is to copy a data range, activate the chart, and then click:

Home→Clipboard→Paste→ Paste Special...

A *Paste Special* dialog is then displayed that is specifically designed for charts:

World Sales-9

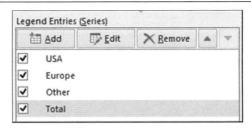

The series also appears on the chart.

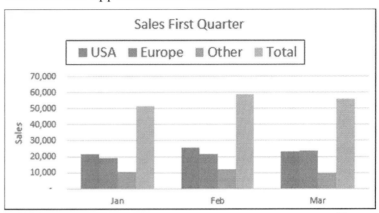

4   Delete the *Total* data series.

   1.   Click the *Total* data series in the *Legend Entries (Series)* list to select it.

   2.   Click the Remove button. ✕ Remove

   The series is removed from the dialog.

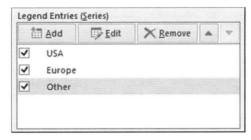

   The series has also been removed from the chart.

5   Switch the rows and columns so that the X Axis shows regions instead of months.

   You learned how to do this using the Ribbon in: *Lesson 5-13: Understand Data Series and Categories.*

   You can do the same thing by clicking the *Switch Row/Column* button on the *Select Data Source* dialog.

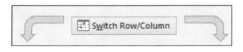

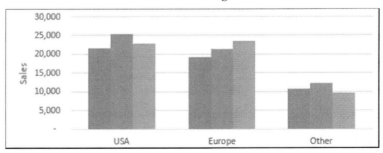

6   Save your work as *World Sales-10.*

Lesson 5-15: Chart non-contiguous source data by hiding rows and columns

In this lesson you'll look at an alternative method of charting a non-contiguous range simply by hiding the data elements that you don't want to chart.

Excel allows you to hide rows and columns in a worksheet by effectively setting their width to zero. The default behavior of charts is to ignore these hidden rows and columns.

It is also possible to override this default behavior and instruct Excel to chart hidden rows and columns.

1   Open *World Sales-10 from* your sample files folder (if it isn't already open).

2   Remove the *Europe* series from the chart by hiding column C.

   1.   Right-click on the column header button at the top of column C.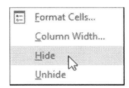

   2.   Click *Hide* from the shortcut menu.

   | Format Cells... |
   | Column Width... |
   | Hide |
   | Unhide |

   The *European* sales data is no longer shown on the chart.

3   Remove the *February* data from the chart by hiding row 3.

   1.   Right-click on the row header button on the left of row 3.

   2.   Click *Hide* from the shortcut menu.

   February data is no longer shown on the chart.

4   Display the hidden data in the chart.

Excel allows you to chart hidden data if you want to.

World Sales-10

1. Right-click in the plot area of the chart and click *Select Data...* from the shortcut menu.

   The *Select Data Source* dialog appears.

2. Click the *Hidden and Empty Cells* button on the bottom left corner of the dialog.

   The *Hidden and Empty Cells* dialog appears.

3. Check the *Show data in hidden rows and columns* check box and click the OK button.

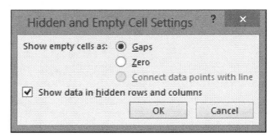

note

The Hidden and Empty Cell Settings dialog can also be used with Sparklines

If you select a Sparkline group and click:

Sparkline Tools→Design→ Sparkline→Edit Data→ Hidden & Empty Cells

... you will see the same *Hidden and Empty Cell Settings* dialog that is used in this lesson to deal with hidden rows and columns in charts.

You can use it in exactly the same way to deal with hidden rows and columns in Sparklines.

You learned how to create Sparkline groups in: *Lesson 4-19: Insert a Sparkline into a range of cells.*

4. Click the OK button twice to dismiss the dialogs.

   The previously hidden chart data re-appears.

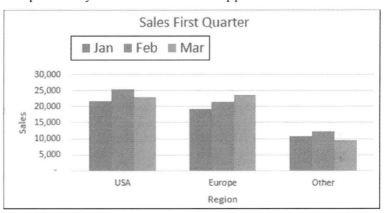

5 Unhide the hidden rows and columns.

   1. Click any cell in the worksheet to de-activate the chart.

   2. Click the *Select All* button at the top left corner of the worksheet to select every cell.

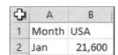

   3. Click: Home→Cells→Format→Hide & Unhide→Unhide Rows.

   4. Click: Home→Cells→Format→Hide & Unhide→Unhide Columns.

6 Save your work as *World Sales-11.*

Lesson 5-16: Create a chart with numerical axes

Sometimes Excel gets a little confused when it attempts to automatically generate a chart.

Problems usually occur when you need to plot numerical information along the horizontal axis. Excel sees the numerical labels and assumes that they are a series.

In this lesson you'll use such a worksheet to confuse Excel and then fix things up manually using the *Select Data Source* dialog.

1 Open *Annual Sales Summary* from your sample files folder.

2 Display the range as a clustered column chart.

    1. Click on any single cell inside the range.

       Note that it isn't necessary to select the range when you want to chart all of it.

       If you simply click any cell inside the range, Excel will automatically select the entire range for the chart's source data.

    2. Click: Insert→Charts→Insert Column Chart→ 2D Column→Clustered Column.

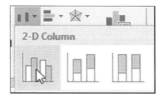

       The range is displayed as a chart, but there's a problem. Excel has assumed that the numbers in the *Year* column are a data series.

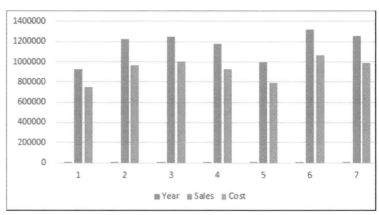

       Note that the numbers for the *Year* data are so small in relation to the *Sales* and *Cost* data that you can hardly see their bars in the bar chart. The bars are there, but they are so short that they are almost invisible.

3 Right-click just inside the plot area of the chart and click *Select Data…* from the shortcut menu.

    The *Select Data Source* dialog is displayed.

Annual Sales Summary

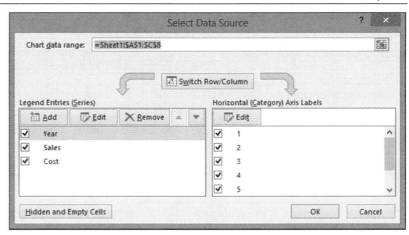

The problem is immediately apparent. Excel has wrongly identified the year as series data rather than as category axis labels.

4   Remove the Year *data series* and add the *Year* data as *Horizontal (Category) Axis Labels*.

1. Click *Year* in the left hand pane of the dialog and then click the Remove button. [✗ Remove]

2. Click the *Edit* button [✎ Edit] on the right hand pane.

3. Select cells A2:A8 for the *Axis label range* (the year data but not the column header).

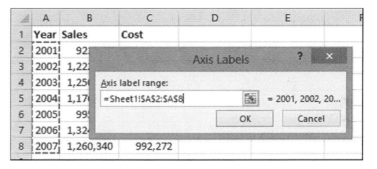

4. Click the OK button twice to close both dialogs.

    The chart now displays correctly.

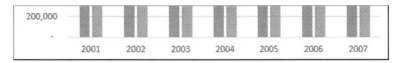

5   Save your work as *Annual Sales Summary-1*.

Lesson 5-17: Deal with empty data points

Sometimes you'll only have partial data for a series.

In the worksheet used for this lesson I'll share a secret with you. I weigh myself every day and keep a chart on my bathroom wall to make sure that I'm staying at a healthy weight.

Sometimes I'm away travelling and can't weigh in as usual. When I get back I need to fill in the gaps.

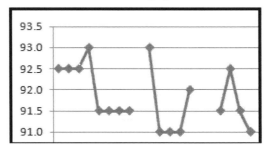

I use a line chart for my weight, so the best solution is to simply draw a line connecting the last data point recorded before I went away with the first recorded upon my return.

For a column chart, the best solution would be to show no columns for the missing days. In other words, there would be gaps for each date when there was a missing bar.

1   Open *Weight 2008* from your sample files folder.

       This is a simple worksheet showing my weight in kilograms for each date in July 2008. Notice that there are missing days when I was away from home.

2   Display the range as a *Line with Markers* chart.

       1.   Click on any of the date values within the range.

       2.   Click: Insert→Charts→Insert Line Chart→Line with Markers.

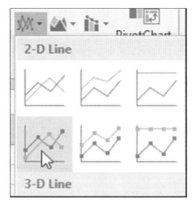

       The chart displays, but there are gaps for the missing entries.

Weight 2008

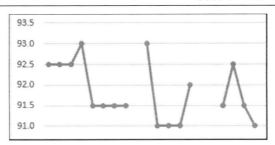

3   Tell Excel to connect the gaps in the chart with a line.

1. Right-click just inside the plot area of the chart and click *Select Data* from the shortcut menu.

    The *Select Data Source* dialog is displayed.

2. Click the *Hidden and Empty Cells* button at the bottom left corner of the dialog.

    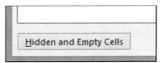

    The *Hidden and Empty Cells* dialog appears.

3. Click the *Connect data points with line* option button.

note

The Hidden and Empty Cell Settings dialog can also be used with Sparklines

If you select a Sparkline group and click:

Sparkline Tools→Design→ Sparkline→Edit Data→ Hidden & Empty Cells

... you will see the same *Hidden and Empty Cell Settings* dialog that is used in this lesson to deal with empty data points in charts.

You can use it in exactly the same way to deal with empty data points in Sparklines.

You learned to create Sparkline groups in: *Lesson 4-19: Insert a Sparkline into a range of cells.*

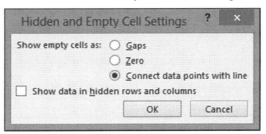

4. Click the OK button and OK again to dismiss both dialogs

    All data points are now connected with a line.

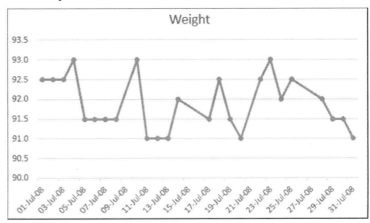

4   Save your work as *Weight 2008-1.*

Lesson 5-18: Add data labels to a chart

It is possible to approximate the values that are displayed in a chart by looking at the vertical axis.

Sometimes you will need to convey the precise values that are being charted. There are three ways of doing this:

- Embed the chart in the worksheet containing the source data so that the user can see both the chart and data.

- Add data labels to each point on the chart.

- Add a *Data Table* chart element to the bottom of the chart.

1 Open *Annual Sales Summary-1* from your sample files folder.

2 Change the source data so that only sales (not costs) for 2004 to 2007 are charted.

This will allow you to test your understanding of the skills learned in: *Lesson 5-12: Assign non-contiguous source data* , *Lesson 5-14: Change source data using the Select Data Source dialog tools*, and *Lesson 5-16: Create a chart with numerical axes*.

1. In the *Select Data Source* dialog select this range for *the Chart data range*:

	A	B	C	D	E
1	Year	Sales	Cost		
2	2001	923,859	755,087		
3	2002	1,222,054	961,643		
4	2003	1,250,365	1,008,292		
5	2004	1,176,787	925,430		
6	2005	995,720	788,576		
7	2006	1,324,534	1,067,627		
8	2007	1,260,340	992,272		
9					
10				Select Data Source	
11		Chart data range:	=Sheet1!$A$1:$B$1,Sheet1!$A$5:$B$8		
12					

2. In the *Select Data Source* dialog, select this data range for the *Horizontal (Category) Axis Labels*.

You learned how to do this in: *Lesson 5-16: Create a chart with numerical axes.*

Axis Labels

Axis label range:

=Sheet1!$A$5:$A$8   = 2004, 2005, 20...

OK   Cancel

3. In the *Select Data Source* dialog delete the *Year* item from the *Legend Entries (Series)*.

The *Select Data Source* dialog should now look like this:

tip

Data labels can be moved and formatted just like any other element

When preparing a chart for a PowerPoint presentation, the data labels are often too small to be visible at the back of the room.

You may also want to fine-tune the positioning of data labels.

For most formatting options, right-click a data label to select the entire series and then click *Format Data Labels* from the shortcut menu.

If you need to change the font size, select the series of data labels and then click:

Home→Font→Font Size

If you need to re-position or format a single data label, click once to select the data label series and then a second time to select the individual label you want to work with.

Annual Sales
Summary-1

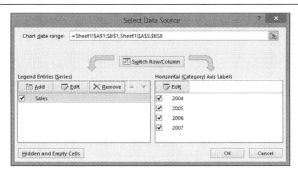

... Resulting in the following chart:

4. Click the OK button to close the dialog.

3 Add data label elements outside the end of each bar.

1. Activate the chart by clicking just inside the chart's border.

2. Click the *Chart Elements* icon ⊞ that appears outside the top-right corner of the chart.

3. Click: Data Labels→Outside End.

Data labels are now shown outside the end of each bar:

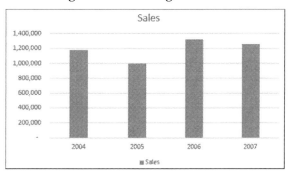

4 Switch off the data labels.

1. Activate the chart by clicking just inside the chart's border.

2. Click the *Chart Elements* icon ⊞ that appears outside the top-right corner of the chart.

3. Uncheck the *Data Labels* check box.

5 Add a *Data Table* element to the bottom of the chart.

1. Activate the chart by clicking just inside the chart's border.

2. Click the *Chart Elements* icon ⊞ that appears outside the top-right corner of the chart.

3. Check the *Data Table* check box.

A table is displayed below the chart:

6 Save your work as *Annual Sales Summary-2*.

Lesson 5-19: Add data labels from a range

In: *Lesson 5-18: Add data labels to a chart*, you added data labels to a column chart to show the precise value represented by each column.

This is the most common use for data labels.

Excel 2013 has a brand new feature that allows you to add data labels that can display any type of information.

The values to be used for the data labels are placed in a range on the worksheet. It is then possible to specify this range as the source for the data labels to be displayed.

In this lesson we'll use a bar chart to show the actual mark achieved in an examination. Data labels will then be added to show the grade that corresponds to each mark:

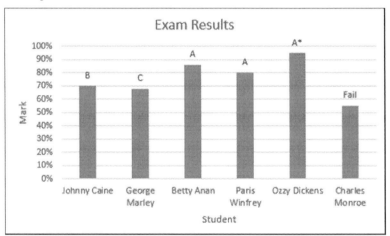

You can see how this adds value to the chart. It is easy to see at a glance that although Betty Annan and Paris Winfrey both achieved a grade A pass, Betty actually had a higher mark.

1 Open *Exam Results-1* from your sample files folder.

2 Create a column chart showing the student name and percentage mark.

    1. Select the range A3:B9.

    2. Click: Insert→Charts→2D Column→Clustered Column.

3 Add *Axis Title* elements to the chart.

    You learned how to do this in: *Lesson 5-9: Move, re-size, add, position and delete chart elements.*

4 Change the *Vertical Axis Title* text to: **Mark**, the *Horizontal Axis Title* text to: **Student** and the *Chart Title* text to: **Exam Results**.

Exam Results-1

You learned how to do this in: *Lesson 5-5: Add and remove chart elements using Quick Layout.*

5   Add data labels to show the student grade above each bar.

1.   Click anywhere on the chart to activate it.

2.   Chick the *Chart Elements* icon  that appears just outside the top right-hand corner of the chart.

3.   Click the fly out menu button to the right of *Data Labels.*

4.   Click: *More Options…* from the fly out menu.

The *Format Data Labels* task pane appears.

5.   Click the *Label Options* icon.

6.   Click the fly out menu button to the left of *Label Options.*

7.   In the *Label Contains* list, uncheck any checked check boxes and then check *Value From Cells.*

The *Data Label Range* dialog appears.

8.   Click inside the *Data Label Range* text box.

9.   Select Cells C4:C9 with the mouse.

10. Click the OK button.

Your chart should now look like this:

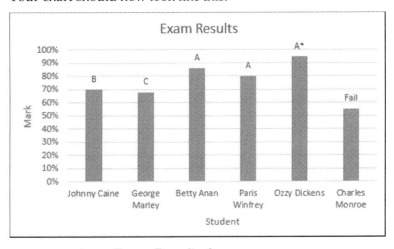

6   Save your work as *Exam Results-2.*

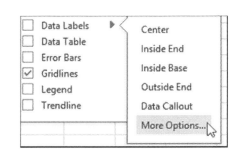

tip

Text boxes are more flexible than the built-in Chart Title elements

This lesson shows you how to add Text Boxes to a chart.

Elements such as *Chart Title* and *Horizontal (Category) Axis Title* appear to have sizing handles but you cannot, in fact, re-size them. The only way to make them wider is to type in more text or change the font.

Text boxes have no such restrictions. For this reason you may sometimes find that it is preferable to substitute a text box for a *Chart Title* element.

Lesson 5-20: Highlight specific data points with color and annotations

A single value within a data series is often referred to as a *data point*.

Sometimes you will want to emphasize a specific data point in a series. For example, you may want to color a single column differently to its neighbors to emphasize some special attribute of the data point.

Color alone cannot convey why the data point is special. You will normally want to also add a text box to the chart to explain the reason for its different color.

In this lesson we'll imagine that the company is a hotel, and that 2005 was the centenary year in a competing resort, leading to an expectation of decreased sales. To mark this, we'll color the 2005 bar orange and add an annotation saying *Centenary Year* to the bar.

1 Open *Annual Sales Summary-2 from* your sample files folder (if it isn't already open).

2 Change the color of the 2005 bar to orange.

　1. Click the 2005 bar once. Notice that the entire data series is selected.

　2. Click the 2005 bar once more. This time only the 2005 bar is selected.

　3. Click: Chart Tools→Format→Shape Styles→ Shape Fill→Orange, Accent 2.

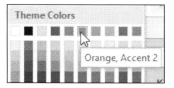

　4. The 2005 bar is now colored orange. The legend has also changed to give a further visual prompt that the orange bar relates to 2005.

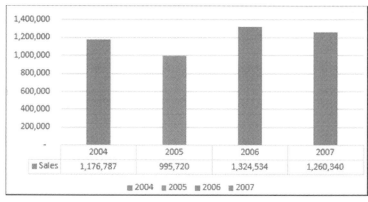

3 Add a text box above, and to the right of, the 2005 bar containing the text: **Centenary Year**.

　1. Click just inside the border of the chart to activate it.

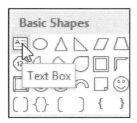

2. Click: Chart Tools→Format→Insert Shapes→
    Shapes Gallery→Basic Shapes→Text Box.

3. Click on the chart, above the orange 2005 bar, and type
    Centenary, then press **<Shift>+<Enter>** and then type **Year.**
    (The **<Shift>+<Enter>** key combination moves you to the next
    line in a text box).

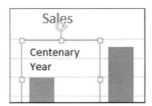

4   Add a border and fill to the text box.

Click the text box to select it and then click:

Drawing Tools→Format→Shape Styles→
Shape Styles Gallery→Subtle Effect – Blue, Accent 1

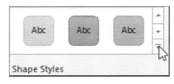

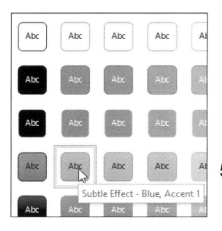

This effect is the second on row four (see sidebar).

5   Resize the text box.

Click the text box once to select it and then drag the sizing handles
to resize so that the text fills the box.

6   Move the text box.

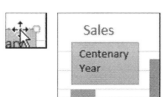

Click the text box once to select it and then hover over any part of
the border that is not a sizing handle. You will see the four-headed
arrow cursor shape (see sidebar). When you see the four-headed
arrow, click and drag to move the text box to an ideal position.

7   Add an arrow pointing from the text box to the red 2005 bar.

1. Click the chart to activate it. (Make sure that you click just
    inside the border of the chart and not on the text box. The
    Chart Tools tab will not be displayed when the text box is
    selected).

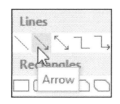

2. Click: Chart Tools→Format→Insert Shapes→
    Shapes Gallery→Lines→Arrow.
    (see sidebar).

3. Click and drag to draw an arrow pointing from the text box to
    the orange bar.

4. With the arrow selected, click: Drawing Tools→Format→
    Shape Styles→Gallery drop-down.

5. Choose an attractive style for the arrow.

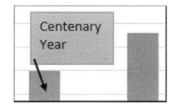

8   Save your work as *Annual Sales Summary-3.*

Lesson 5-21: Add gridlines and scale axes

In this session we'll manipulate the vertical axis of a sales chart to give two entirely different views of a company's sales. Each chart emphasizes one of the following true statements.

- It is true that sales are increasing every month.

- It is true that sales are almost completely flat.

You'll see how we can manipulate a column chart to visually convey each of these "truths" to an audience. After this session you'll never look at a chart again without paying close attention to the vertical axis!

1   Open *Sales First Quarter* from your sample files folder.

	A	B
1	Month	Sales
2	Jan	80,010
3	Feb	80,040
4	Mar	80,080

This worksheet shows sales that are almost completely flat. Sales increased by 0.04% in February and by 0.05% in March.

A twentieth of a percent increase isn't anything at all.

2   Create a chart that illustrates flat sales.

Imagine you are the sales director of the company and need to have a pep talk with your salespeople.

You want to show them a chart that demonstrates the lack of sales growth in order to motivate them to do better in April.

1. Click inside the data range.

2. Click: Insert→Charts→Insert Column Chart→ 2-D Column→Clustered Column.

The following chart is automatically generated:

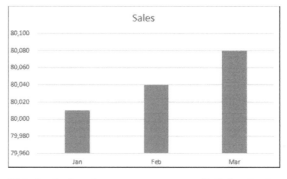

This isn't the chart you want at all. Sales look rather good!

The reason that the chart isn't as honest as it should be is because the vertical axis begins at 79,960. We're looking at the tips of columns that are very long.

Sales First Quarter

To fix things up we need a more honest vertical axis, one that begins at zero.

3. Right-click the vertical axis and select *Format Axis...* from the shortcut menu.

    The *Format Axis* task pane appears.

4. Change the *Minimum* value to zero and press the **<Enter>** key.

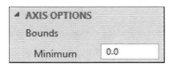

The chart now depicts a more honest representation of flat growth.

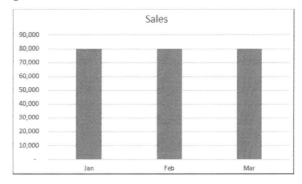

Look at the task pane and notice how Excel has automatically managed the other settings. *Major units* for gridlines (the interval between numbers on the vertical axis) have now changed to 10,000.

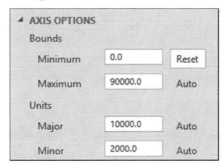

5. Change the *Minor unit* gridline value to 5000 (without the comma as Excel has a problem with commas in this task pane). We will enable the display of minor gridline elements in a moment and will expect to see one minor gridline between each major gridline.

3 **Add minor horizontal gridlines to the chart.**

1. Activate the chart by clicking just inside the chart's border.

2. Click the *Chart Elements* icon outside the top right of the chart.

3. Click: Gridlines→Primary Minor Horizontal.

    Minor gridlines are now displayed on the chart (see sidebar).

4 **Save your work as *Sales First Quarter-1*.**

tip

Use gridlines sparingly

Too many gridlines can make a chart difficult to read.

This lesson's chart looks cluttered with minor gridlines and might even look cleaner without any gridlines.

When you do use gridlines, always choose a light color to focus attention upon foreground elements.

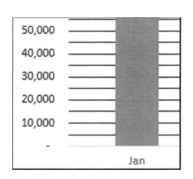

Lesson 5-22: Emphasize data by manipulating pie charts

In the last session we saw how a column chart could visually reinforce different characteristics of the same data.

Pie charts also offer several techniques to present data in a way that will best convey your objectives. Designers of pie charts often use the presentation methods described in this lesson to make one value in a series seem bigger or smaller in relation to its neighbors.

1 Open *Competitor Analysis* from your sample files folder (if it isn't already open).

	A	B	C
1	Splendid Supplies Competitor Analysis		
2			
3	Competitor	Annual Sales (Millions)	Market Share
4	Cheapo discount stores	22.2	28%
5	Budget supplies	16.3	21%
6	Lo Cost warehouse	24.5	31%
7	Splendid Supplies	16.2	20%

This worksheet has been compiled by Splendid Supplies to monitor the activity of their three competitors. Splendid aren't doing so well. In fact, they have the lowest market share of the four.

There's a big investor meeting coming up and Splendid would like to make their market share seem a little more impressive!

2 Create a 3-D pie chart for the range A3:B7.

1. Select the range A3:B7.

2. Click: Insert→Charts→Insert Pie or Doughnut Chart→3-D Pie (see sidebar).

   A pie chart is displayed, illustrating the market share of the four companies.

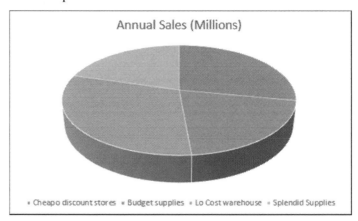

Splendid Supplies don't look very impressive on this chart. Let's use our first presentational technique to make things seem a little better.

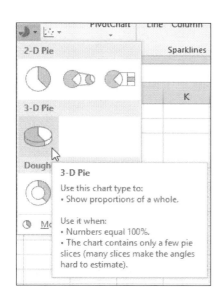

Competitor Analysis

3   Rotate the pie chart so that Splendid Supplies sales are at the front.

Because of the perspective of a 3-D pie, the slice at the front always seems the biggest (especially if you keep the perspective angle high).

1. Right-click in the plot area of the pie chart. To do this you'll need to click just outside one of the pie chart's slices.

2. Click *Format Plot Area* on the shortcut menu. If you don't see *Format Plot Area* in the shortcut menu it is because you have right-clicked in the wrong place. In this case try again, making sure that you click just outside one of the pie chart's slices.

   The *Format Plot Area task pane* appears.

3. Click the *Effects* icon  at the top of the task pane.

4. In the *3-D rotation* section, click the *X Rotation* spin button until the Splendid Supplies (yellow) slice is at the front of the pie chat (about 220 degrees).

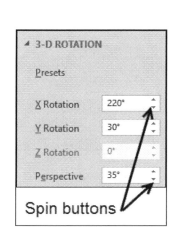

4   Change the pie chart's perspective to emphasize Splendid Supplies' sales.

In the 3-D rotation section, click the *Perspective* spin button to make the Splendid Supplies sales seem as large as possible. I found that a setting of 35 degrees worked well.

5   Pull the Splendid Supplies slice slightly out of the pie.

A very common pie chart presentational technique is to pull the slice that you want to emphasize away from the pie chart. This slice then appears to be larger in relation to the other slices.

1. Click just inside the chart border to activate the chart.

2. Click one of the slices on the chart once to select the entire pie.

3. Click the Splendid Supplies slice once to select it.

4. Click and drag the slice slightly out of the pie.

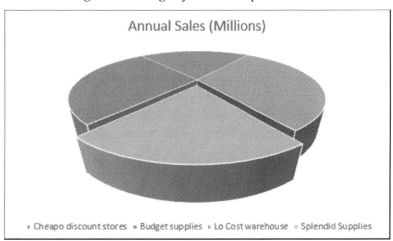

You'd never guess now that Splendid Supplies actually have the lowest market share.

6   Save your work as *Competitor Analysis-1*.

Lesson 5-23: Create a chart with two vertical axes

Sometimes you'll have two data series that are very different in magnitude but you still want to show them on the same chart.

The examples used in this lesson are *UK Average House Prices* and *Bank Base Rates*. Analysts have noticed that when interest rates come down, house prices go up. To test this theory, we will create a chart showing UK bank base rates against average house prices for the twelve years up to 2008.

During the twelve year period, house prices ranged from 68,788 to 199,021 while base rates fluctuated between 3.5% and 6.75%. We need two different vertical axes to make this chart work.

1 Open *UK House Prices* from your sample files folder.

2 Create a default *Line with Markers* chart from the range.

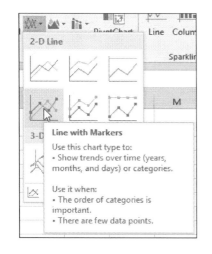

   1.   Click anywhere within the data.

   2.   Click: Insert→Charts→Insert Line Chart→2-D Line→ Line with Markers.

       The default chart is displayed.

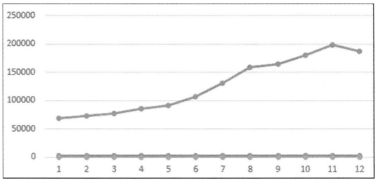

3 Remove the *Year* data series and show the years 1997 to 2008 along the *Horizontal Axis*.

You learned how to do this in: *Lesson 5-16: Create a chart with numerical axes.*

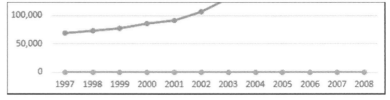

4 Select the *Min Base Rate* series.

Because the *Min Base Rate* series is in almost the same place as the horizontal axis, this can be difficult with the mouse (though it is possible).

You may find it easier to select the chart and then click:

Chart Tools→Format→Current Selection→
Chart Elements drop down→Series "Min Base Rate"

UK House Prices

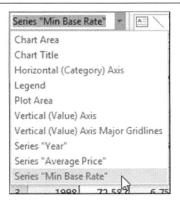

5   Move the *Min Base Rate* series to a secondary axis.

1. With the *Min Base Rate* series selected, click:

    Chart Tools→Format→Current Selection→Format Selection

    The *Format Data Series* task pane is displayed.

2. Click the *Series Options* icon.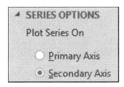

3. Click the *Secondary Axis* option button.

    ▲ SERIES OPTIONS
    Plot Series On
    ◯ Primary Axis
    ⦿ Secondary Axis

    The chart is displayed with two vertical axes and Excel even auto-scales the new axis for you.

6   Save your work as UK House Prices-1.

Lesson 5-24: Create a combination chart containing different chart types

Excel allows you to allocate a different chart type to each data series. This opens up many interesting possibilities such as superimposing a *Clustered Column* chart on top of an *Area* chart.

In this lesson we'll chart the Hawaii climate as a combination Clustered Column/Area chart with clustered columns for high/low temperature and an area chart for rainfall.

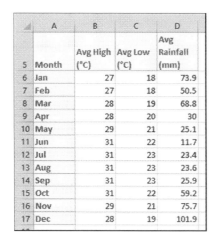

1   Open *Hawaii Climate-1* from your sample files folder.

This workbook documents the temperature range and rainfall in Hawaii for each month of the year.

2   Create a combination chart showing temperature as a *clustered column* chart type and rainfall as an *area* chart type.

1. Click in any cell within the range.

    Because we want to chart the entire data range, there's no need to select the range of cells.

2. Click: Insert→Charts→Insert Combo Chart→ Create Custom Combo Chart…

    The *Insert Chart* dialog appears with the *Combo* chart type chosen in the left-hand menu bar.

3. Set the chart types to *Clustered Column* for both *Temperature* series and to *Area* for the *Avg Rainfall (mm)* series.

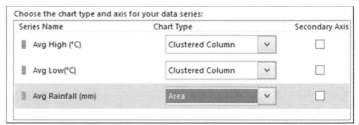

4. Click the OK button.

    The combination chart is created:

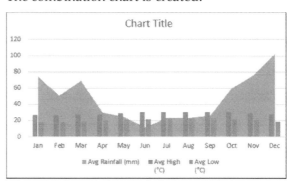

Hawaii Climate-1

The chart isn't bad but it could be improved. Because there is only one axis, the rainfall's *Area* chart type dominates the chart.

Adding a second vertical axis will solve this problem.

3   Add a secondary axis for rainfall.

You could do this using the technique learned in: *Lesson 5-23: Create a chart with two vertical axes.*

Instead we'll use a different technique by recalling the *Insert Chart* dialog (this time it will be called *Change Chart Type*).

1.   Right click anywhere on the chart and click: *Change Chart Type...* from the shortcut menu.

     The *Change Chart Type* dialog appears.

2.   Click the *Secondary Axis* check box next to *Avg Rainfall (mm)*.

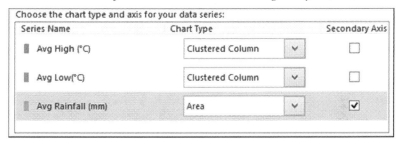

3.   Click OK.

     The chart now looks a lot better with two axes (one for temperature and one for rainfall).

4   Add *Axis Title* elements and give them (along with the *Chart Title* element) appropriate names.

You learned how to do this in: *Lesson 5-9: Move, re-size, add, position and delete chart elements* and *Lesson 5-5: Add and remove chart elements using Quick Layout.*

The chart now looks professional:

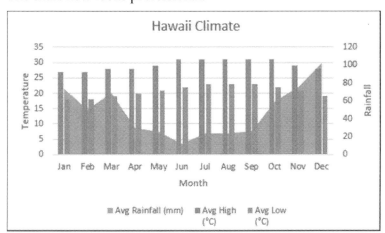

5   Save your work as *Hawaii Climate-2*.

Lesson 5-25: Add a trend line

> It is impossible to demonstrate empirically that a cause produces an effect. Just because the sun has risen every day since the beginning of the Earth does not mean that it will rise again tomorrow. However; it is impossible to go about one's life without assuming such connections, and the best that we can do is to maintain an open mind and never presume that we know any laws of causality for certain.
>
> *David Hume (1711-1776),*
> *Scottish philosopher, economist, and historian.*
> *From "An Enquiry Concerning Human Understanding".*

Trend analysis applies the science of mathematics to the art of fortune telling.

If a value has been increasing for a long time, trend analysis would suggest that it will go on increasing. Some would say that the reverse is true, but Excel remains healthily optimistic that we can predict the future from the past!

Excel provides several different types of trend analysis. We're going to use a linear trend line and a two-period moving average to decide whether it was a good idea to buy a house in 2008.

1   Open *UK House Prices-1* from your sample files folder (if it isn't already open).

2   Remove the *Min Base Rate* data series from the chart.

> This was covered in: *Lesson 5-14: Change source data using the Select Data Source dialog tools.*

3   Add a linear trend line element to forecast where property prices will be in the year 2014.

   1.   Activate the chart by clicking just inside the chart's border.

   2.   Click the *Chart Elements* icon ⊞ outside the top right of the chart.

   3.   Click: Trendline→More Options…

        The *Format Trendline* task pane appears.

   4.   Click the *Trendline Options* icon. 📊

   5.   Make sure that the *Linear Trendline* type is selected (this is the default).

   6.   As 2014 is 6 periods after 2008, enter 4 in the *Forecast Forward* text box and then press the **<Enter>** key.

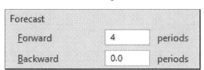

Forecast		
Forward	4	periods
Backward	0.0	periods

UK House Prices-1

Notice the trend line shown on the chart.

Excel confidently predicts that that a house purchased for 187K in 2008 will be worth over a quarter of a million by 2014 (though David Hume would have advised you not to bet on it).

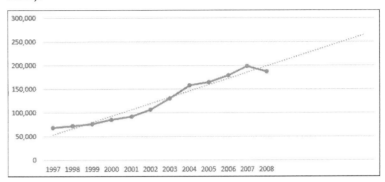

4   Remove the trend line.

1.   Click on the trendline to select it.

2.   Press the **<Delete>** key on the keyboard.

5   Add a two period moving average.

Moving averages are one of the most loved instruments of speculators who predict the future values of shares, currencies and commodities based entirely upon charts. The theory is that when the price crosses beneath the moving average it is time to sell.

1.   Activate the chart.

2.   Click the *Chart Elements* icon ⊕ outside the top right of the chart.

3.   Click: Trendline→Two Period Moving Average.

This time the analysis shows that, for the first time in ten years, 2008 was the year to sell up because the price has moved below the moving average.

6   Save your work as *UK House Prices-2.*

Lesson 5-26: Add a gradient fill to a chart background

When you prepare a chart for a PowerPoint presentation, or for inclusion in a high quality color publication, you want the chart to look professional and interesting. A *Gradient* background fill will put the finishing touch to your chart so that it looks like it was produced by a professional graphic artist.

1 Open *World Sales* from your sample files folder.

2 Create a *Clustered Column* chart from the entire range.

    1. Click anywhere in the range.

    2. Click: Insert→Charts→Insert Column Chart→2-D Column→ Clustered Column.

    The chart is created:

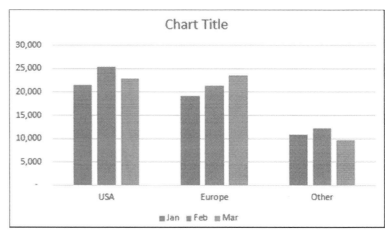

Switch Row/Column

3 Switch Rows/Columns to transpose the *Legend* and *Regions*.

You learned how to do this in: *Lesson 5-13: Understand Data Series and Categories.*

The regions are now listed in the legend and the months are shown along the horizontal axis.

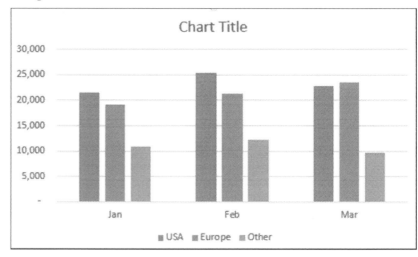

World Sales

4 Add a gradient fill to the chart background.

1. Right-click on the *Chart Area* element (just inside the border of the chart).

2. Click *Format Chart Area* from the shortcut menu.

   The *Format Chart Area* task pane appears.

3. Click the *Fill & Line* icon.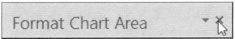

4. Click the *Fill* menu item.

5. Click the *Gradient Fill* option button.

6. Choose one of the preset gradients (I chose *Light Gradient – Accent 4*).

7. Explore the *Type/Direction/Angle/Transparency* and other settings until you are happy with the fill.

8. Click the *Close* button to close the *Format Chart Area* task pane.

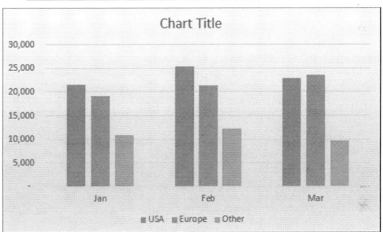

5 Save your work as *Gradient Fill*.

Lesson 5-27: Create your own chart templates

> ## note
>
> ### You can also change chart text font sizes with the mini toolbar
>
> When you want to change attributes such as font type and size for a single piece of text (such as the Chart Title) it is quicker to use the mini toolbar.
>
>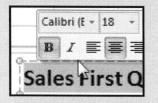
>
> The mini toolbar pops up when you first select text within an element.

If you use charts a lot you may find yourself applying the same fonts, fills, layouts and other attributes over and over again. If you find this happening, it is time to create a chart template.

Chart Templates can be used just like the built-in gallery charts. You can use templates to create a unique, personal, or corporate chart style that will enable you to produce consistently styled work.

In this lesson we'll develop a useful chart template with larger fonts to enable them to be more readable when incorporated into a PowerPoint presentation. We can then use this template in future for any chart that is destined to be used in a presentation.

1   Open *Gradient Fill* from your sample files folder (if it isn't already open).

2   Increase the font size of the *Chart Title* element to 28 Points.

    1.   Select the *Chart Title* element

    2.   Click: Home→Font→Font Size Drop-Down→28 Points.

3   Increase the font size of the *Vertical (Value) Axis*, *Horizontal (Category) Axis* and *Legend* elements to 14 points.

    Select each element in turn and set the font in the same way as in the previous step.

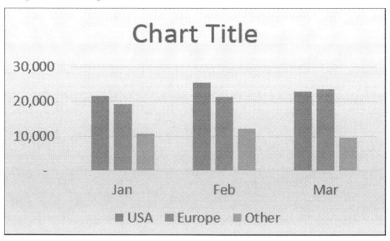

The chart now has labels that will be readable by viewers at the back of the room when projected onto a screen.

4   Save the chart design as a template.

    1.   Right-click in the *Chart Area* (just inside the border of the chart).

    2.   Select *Save as Template…* from the shortcut menu.

    3.   Type **PowerPoint Clustered Column with Title and Gradient Fill** as the *File Name*.

    4.   Click the *Save* button.

5   Delete the chart.

Gradient Fill

Click once, just inside the border of the chart, to select it and then press the **<Delete>** key.

6   Create a new chart from the template.

1.   Click anywhere inside the data range A1:D4.

2.   Click: Insert→Charts→Dialog Launcher.

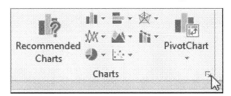

The *Insert Chart* dialog is displayed.

3.   Click the *All Charts* tab at the top of the *Insert Chart* dialog.

4.   Click the *Templates* category on the left of the dialog.

A single icon is displayed on the right hand side of the dialog showing a preview of the template you just saved:

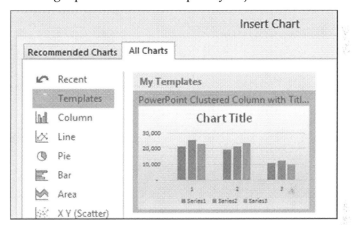

Notice that when you hover the mouse cursor over the icon a larger preview is shown.

5.   Either double-click the template icon, or click it once to select, and then click the OK button.

A chart is displayed with all of the attributes of your template.

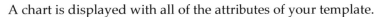
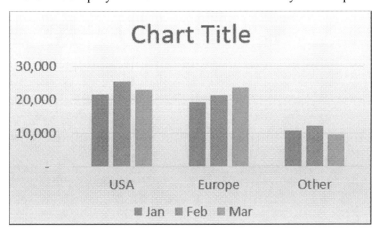

7   Save your work as *PowerPoint Template.*

Session 5: Exercise

1   Open *Exercise 5* from your sample files folder.

2   Click any cell in the range A3:F8.

3   Click: Insert→Charts→Insert Column Chart→2-D Column→Clustered Column.

      The chart will look strange at first as there are many errors to correct.

4   Switch rows and columns so that the European country names are shown in the *Legend*.

5   Use the *Select Data Source* dialog to remove the *Year* series and place the years along the *Horizontal (Category) Axis*.

6   Change the scale of the vertical axis so that it has a *Minimum* value of 15 and a *Maximum* value of 50.

7   Format the *Legend* so that a solid line black border appears around it.

8   Apply a *Chart Filter* so that sales are only shown for the UK, Spain and Italy.

9   Increase the font size of the legend to 12 points.

10   Change the *Chart Title* text to: *European Sales.*

11   Add a gradient fill to the *Chart Area* element using the *Light Gradient – Accent 5* preset.

12   Save your work as *Exercise 5-1.*

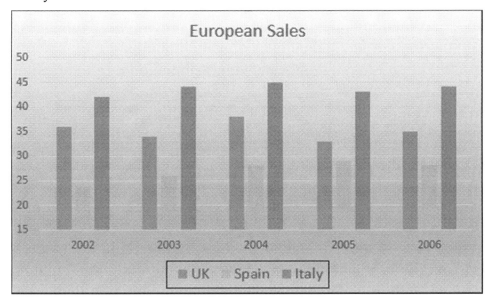

Exercise 5

If you need help slide the page to the left

Session 5: Exercise answers

These are the four questions that most students find the most difficult to remember:

Q 11	Q 8	Q 6	Q 5
1. Right-click just inside the border of the chart and click *Format Chart Area...* from the shortcut menu. 2. Click *Format Chart Area* from the shortcut menu. 3. Choose the *Fill & Line* icon in the *Format Chart Area* task pane. 4. Click the *Fill* menu item. 5. Click the *Gradient Fill* option button. 6. Select the *Light Gradient – Accent 5* preset gradient. This was covered in: *Lesson 5-26: Add a gradient fill to a chart background*	1. Click just inside the border of the chart to select it. 2. Click the *Chart Filters* icon at the top right of the chart. 3. Uncheck the *France* and *Germany* check boxes. 4. Click the *Apply* button. This was covered in: *Lesson 5-10: Apply a chart filter.*	1. Click the vertical axis to select it. 2. Right-click the vertical axis and click *Format Axis...* from the shortcut menu. 3. Click the *Axis Options* icon in the *Format Axis* task pane. 4. Type the value **15** in the *Minimum* text box and press the **<Enter>** key. Make sure that **50** is shown in the *Maximum* value text box. This was covered in: *Lesson 5-21: Add gridlines and scale axes.*	1. Right-click just inside the border of the chart and click *Select Data...* from the shortcut menu. 2. Click the *Year* item in the *Legend Entries (Series)* list and then click the *Remove* button. 3. Click the *Edit* button on top of the *Horizontal (Category) Axis Labels* list. 4. Select cells A4:A8. 5. Click the OK button on each dialog. This was covered in: *Lesson 5-16: Create a chart with numerical axes.*

If you have difficulty with the other questions, here are the lessons that cover the relevant skills:

1   Refer to: *Lesson 1-5: Download the sample files and open/navigate a workbook.*

2   Refer to: *Lesson 1-5: Download the sample files and open/navigate a workbook.*

3   Refer to: *Lesson 5-2: Create a simple chart with two clicks.*

4   Refer to: *Lesson 5-13: Understand Data Series and Categories.*

7   Refer to: *Lesson 5-7: Manually format a chart element.*

9   Refer to: *Lesson 5-9: Move, re-size, add, position and delete chart elements.*

10   Refer to: *Lesson 5-5: Add and remove chart elements using Quick Layout.*

12   Refer to: *Lesson 1-6: Save a workbook.*

Session Six: Working With Multiple Worksheets and Workbooks

> There are no big problems; there are just a lot of little problems.
>
> *Henry Ford (1863-1947)*
> *American industrialist and pioneer of assembly-line production*

Henry Ford knew that big problems are really just a lot of little problems bundled together.

Often you will find that a worksheet is getting over-complicated and difficult to work with. This session will give you the skills needed to quickly break one very complex worksheet into many smaller and easier to manage worksheets.

This session will also show you how to view different parts of large worksheets at the same time and how to create cross-worksheet formulas that summarize data from several different worksheets.

Session Objectives

By the end of this session you will be able to:

- View the same workbook in different windows
- View two windows side by side and perform synchronous scrolling
- Duplicate worksheets within a workbook
- Move and copy worksheets from one workbook to another
- Hide and unhide a worksheet
- Create cross worksheet formulas
- Understand worksheet groups
- Use find and replace

Lesson 6-1: View the same workbook in different windows

Excel allows you to view the same worksheet in two separate worksheet windows. This is useful when you need to compare different areas of the same worksheet.

1 Close any Excel workbooks that are currently open.

2 Open *Sales First Quarter 2008* from your sample files folder.

This workbook has only one worksheet containing 242 rows of data.

3 Open a new window to see February 2008 and January 2008 sales at the same time.

Click: View→Window→New Window.

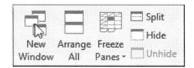

Nothing seems to have happened except that the Title bar now reads: *Sales First Quarter 2008:2*

Two views of the same workbook are now open at the same time but, because they are both maximized, you can only view one at a time which isn't very useful.

4 View both windows at the same time.

Click: View→Window→Arrange All.

The *Arrange Windows* dialog appears:

5 Select the *Horizontal* option and then click the OK button.

Both worksheets are displayed in the worksheet window, one below the other. You are able to freely scroll to any position in either window.

Sales First Quarter 2008

You will now appreciate the importance of closing any open workbooks in step 1. If you had several workbooks open, you would now be viewing all of them in multiple windows.

In the screen grab below I've scrolled the bottom window down to see February sales:

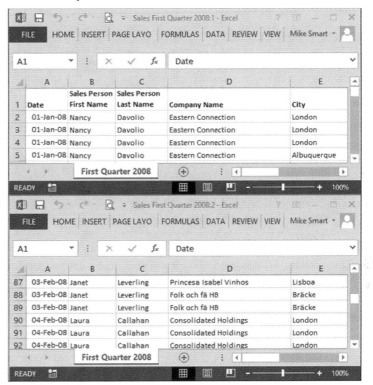

It's important to realize that we are not looking at two different worksheets, but two different views of the same worksheet.

If you change a value in one of the views, you'll immediately see the changed value in the other.

6 Close the *Sales First Quarter 2008:2* window and maximize the *Sales First Quarter 2008:1* worksheet.

1. Click in the *Sales First Quarter 2008:2* window. Notice how the title bar and border changes color to indicate that this is now the active window.

2. Click the *Close* button in the top right hand corner of the worksheet.

3. Click the *Maximize* button in the top right-hand corner of the *Sales First Quarter 2008* worksheet.

Lesson 6-2: View two windows side by side and perform synchronous scrolling

When only two workbooks are open, the *Arrange All* method covered in the previous lesson will work just fine.

It is more likely that you will have many workbooks (or views of the same workbook) open and will want to see two specific workbooks on screen at the same time.

You may sometimes be given a workbook that somebody else has changed and need to identify what has been altered. We'll use Excel's synchronous scrolling feature to make this task easier.

1   Close any Excel workbooks that are currently open.

2   Open *Exercise 6* from your sample files folder.

3   Open *Sales First Quarter 2008 Revised* from your sample files folder.

4   Open *Sales First Quarter 2008* from your sample files folder.

Only the last workbook opened: *Sales First Quarter 2008* is visible on screen.

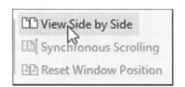

5   Click: View→Window→View Side By Side.

The *Compare Side By Side* dialog is displayed.

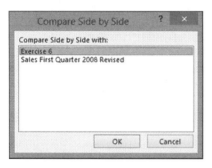

6   Select *Sales First Quarter 2008 Revised* as the workbook that you want to view with the current workbook and then click the **<OK>** button.

The workbooks should display one above the other.

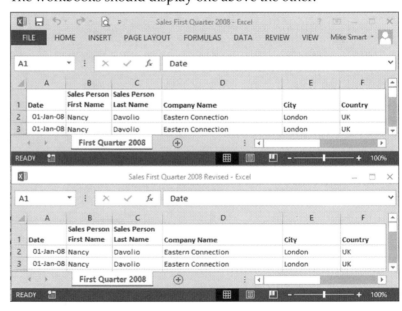

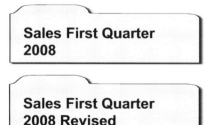

Sales First Quarter 2008

Sales First Quarter 2008 Revised

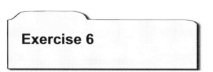

Exercise 6

If you don't see this, click:

View→Window→Reset Window Position.

This is often needed when the workbooks have been moved or re-sized.

Notice that when you use the scroll bars to move up and down the list (scroll) in one window, the other window scrolls at the same time. This is called *synchronous scrolling*.

7 **Unlock the windows so that they no longer scroll together.**

1. Click: View→Window→Synchronous Scrolling to switch synchronous scrolling off. You are now able to freely scroll each window independently.

2. Scroll each window to the top (so that row 1 is at the top of each window).

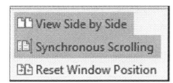

3. Click: View→Window→Synchronous Scrolling to switch synchronous scrolling back on so that both windows automatically scroll together.

8 **Identify differences between the two workbooks.**

Scroll down so that you can see row 77. Notice that row 78 has gone out of synchronization because one of the 29-Jan-08 sales to Hungry Owl has been deleted from the *Revised* workbook.

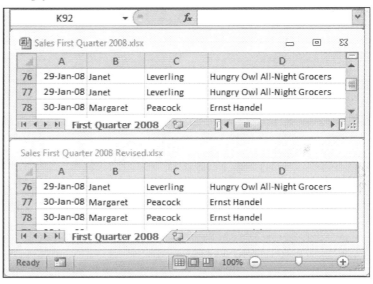

9 **Re-synchronize the windows.**

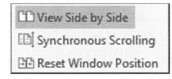

1. Click: View→Window→Synchronous Scrolling to switch Synchronous Scrolling off.

2. Scroll so that the first transaction on 30th Jan 2008 is on the first row in both windows.

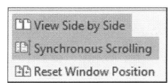

3. Click: View→Window→Synchronous Scrolling to switch Synchronous Scrolling back on.

10 **Close all open workbooks without saving.**

Lesson 6-3: Duplicate worksheets within a workbook

In this lesson you're going to disassemble a large worksheet and make it into three smaller worksheets.

You'll often find that data is easier to work with if you divide it into logically separated sections.

1   Open *Sales First Quarter 2008* from your sample files folder.

This workbook shows all sales completed in January, February and March 2008. Your task will be to split them into separate months.

2   Create a new worksheet and name it *January*.

This skill was covered in *Lesson 1-9: View, move, add, rename, delete and navigate worksheet tabs.*

3   Select every cell in the *First Quarter 2008* worksheet.

1.   Click the *First Quarter 2008* worksheet tab.

There's a special button at the top left corner of every worksheet called the *Select All* button.

⊕	A	B	C
1	Date	Sales Person First Name	Sales Person Last Name
2	01-Jan-08	Nancy	Davolio

2.   Click the *Select All* button to select every cell in the worksheet.

4   Copy all selected cells.

The easiest way to do this is to right-click within the selected range and then click *Copy* from the shortcut menu.

5   Paste the copied cells into the *January* worksheet beginning at cell A1.

Click the *January* tab, right-click in cell A1 and select *Paste* from the shortcut menu.

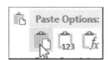

6   Create another copy of the worksheet using *Move or Copy*.

Excel provides a simpler way to duplicate a worksheet.

1.   Right-click the *First Quarter 2008* worksheet tab and choose *Move or Copy...* from the shortcut menu.

The *Move or Copy* dialog appears.

2.   Select *(move to end)* in the *Before sheet* list.

3.   Check the *Create a copy* check box.

4.   Click the *OK* button.

Sales First Quarter 2008

Notice that Excel has named the new worksheet: *First Quarter 2008 (2)*.

7   Change the name of the new worksheet to *February*.

This skill was covered in *Lesson 1-9: View, move, add, rename, delete and navigate worksheet tabs.*

8   Create another copy of the worksheet using *drag and drop*.

There's an even quicker way to create a duplicate worksheet.

1.   Click once on the *First Quarter 2008* tab to select it.

2.   Hold down the **<Ctrl>** key.

3.   Click and hold the mouse button on the *First Quarter 2008* tab.

The cursor changes shape to a page with a plus sign:

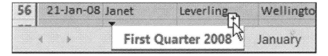

4.   Drag to the right until you see a black insertion arrow to the right of the *February* tab.

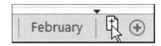

When you release the mouse button another copy of the worksheet is created.

9   Change the name of the new worksheet to *March*.

10   Remove rows from the January, February and March workbooks so that only the named month's transactions remain.

This was covered in: *Lesson 3-1: Insert and delete rows and columns.*

11   Save your work as *Sales First Quarter 2008-1*.

Lesson 6-4: Move and copy worksheets from one workbook to another

In *Lesson 6-3: Duplicate worksheets within a workbook*, you worked with a single workbook.

It is also possible to move and copy worksheets between different workbooks using a similar technique.

1   Close any workbooks that are currently open.

2   Open *Sales First Quarter 2008-1* from your sample files folder (if it isn't already open).

3   Open *First Quarter Sales and Bonus* from your sample files folder.

4   Arrange the windows *Horizontally* in the Excel window.

Click: View→Window→Arrange All→Horizontal.

The two workbooks are now shown together.

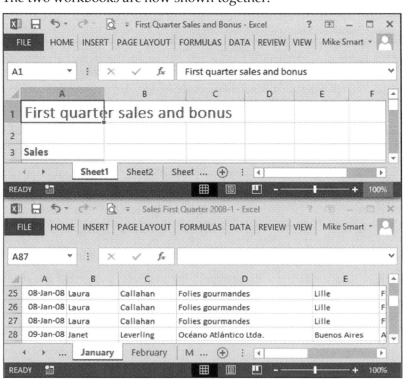

5   Rename *Sheet1* in the *First Quarter Sales and Bonus* workbook to *Bonus*.

This was covered in: *Lesson 1-9: View, move, add, rename, delete and navigate worksheet tabs.*

6   Hold down the **<Ctrl>** key and drag and drop the *Bonus* sheet from the *First Quarter Sales and Bonus* workbook to the *Sales First Quarter 2008-1* workbook.

First Quarter Sales and Bonus

Sales First Quarter 2008-1

A copy of the *Bonus* worksheet is created in the *Sales First Quarter 2008-1* workbook.

7 Drag and drop the *Sheet3* worksheet from the *First Quarter Sales and Bonus* workbook to the *Sales First Quarter 2008-1* workbook.

You will have to click the *First Quarter Sales and Bonus* workbook once to activate it before you can drag and drop the sheet tab.

This time, because you didn't hold the **<Ctrl>** key down, the worksheet is moved rather than copied.

8 Change the name of the moved worksheet from *Sheet3* to *Summary*.

This skill was covered in: *Lesson 1-9: View, move, add, rename, delete and navigate worksheet tabs.*

9 If necessary, move the worksheet tabs in the *Sales First Quarter 2008-1* workbook so that they appear in the following order:

		First Quarter 2008	January	February	March	Summary	**Bonus**

This was covered in: *Lesson 1-9: View, move, add, rename, delete and navigate worksheet tabs.*

10 Maximize the *Sales First Quarter 2008-1* workbook window.

This was covered in: *Lesson 1-4: Maximize, minimize, re-size, move and close the Excel window.*

11 Save your work as *Sales First Quarter 2008-2*.

Lesson 6-5: Hide and unhide a worksheet

Sometimes you'll want to prevent users from viewing and changing one or more worksheets.

In this case you will want to *Hide* the worksheet.

A hidden worksheet becomes invisible to the user but is still there. You can bring back hidden worksheets by *Unhiding* them.

1   Open *Sales First Quarter 2008-2* from your sample files folder (if it isn't already open).

In this workbook you may not want viewers to see the *First Quarter 2008* worksheet as the information is already contained in the *January/February/March* worksheets.

You might also want to hide the *Bonus* worksheet as it contains confidential information. Note that you should not rely upon hidden worksheets to secure confidential information (see sidebar).

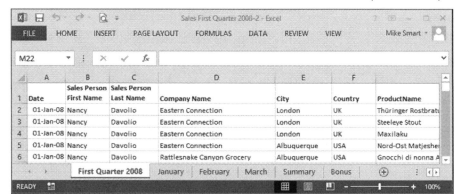

2   Select the *First Quarter 2008* and *Bonus* worksheets.

1.   Click on the *First Quarter 2008* worksheet tab.

2.   Hold down the **<Ctrl>** key.

3.   Click on the *Bonus* worksheet tab.

Both worksheet tabs should now be highlighted:

3   Hide the *First Quarter 2008* and *Bonus* worksheets.

The easiest way to do this is to right click either of the selected tabs and then click *Hide* from the shortcut menu.

The worksheets vanish.

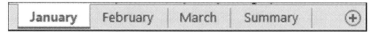

It's also possible to do this from the Ribbon less efficiently (see sidebar).

4   Unhide the *Bonus* worksheet.

Excel will never allow you to hide all of the worksheets, so this method of unhiding sheets will always work.

1. Right-click on any of the visible worksheet tabs.

2. Click *Unhide* from the shortcut menu.

   The *Unhide* dialog is displayed:

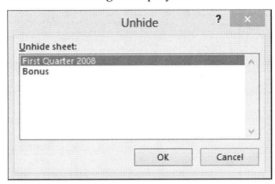

3. Click *Bonus* and then click the OK button.

   You can also unhide the worksheets less efficiently using the Ribbon (see facing page sidebar).

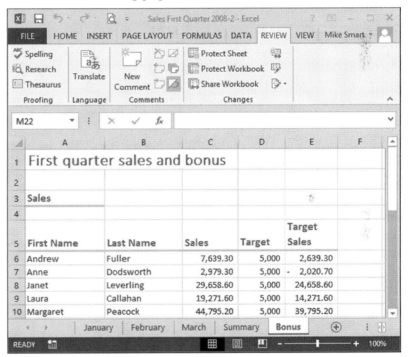

5   Save your work as *Sales First Quarter 2008-3*.

Lesson 6-6: Create cross worksheet formulas

You'll often want to summarize information from multiple worksheets within a workbook.

This can be done by simply prefixing the cell reference with the worksheet name followed by an exclamation mark.

1 Open *Sales First Quarter 2008-3* from your sample files folder (if it isn't already open).

2 Select the *January* tab and scroll to the bottom of the range.

3 Type the word **Total:** into the first empty cell in column G (cell G87).

4 Right-Align cell G87.

This was covered in: *Lesson 4-5: Horizontally align the contents of cells.*

5 Bold-face all of row 87.

This was covered in: *Lesson 1-15: Use the Mini Toolbar, Key Tips and keyboard shortcuts.*

6 Use AutoSum to add totals to columns H and J.

This was covered in: *Lesson 2-3: Use AutoSum to quickly calculate totals.*

	G	H	I	J
85	Gumbär Gummibärchen	10	24.90	249.00
86	Tourtière	40	5.90	236.00
87	Total:	2,401		66,692.80

7 Add similar totals to the *February* and *March* worksheets.

8 Select the *Summary* tab.

9 Type the text: **First Quarter Summary** into cell A1 and apply the *Title* cell style.

This was covered in: *Lesson 4-9: Use cell styles and change themes.*

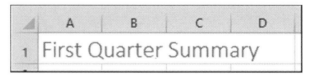

10 Type **Month**, **Units** and **Price** into cells A3, B3 and C3.

11 Type **Jan** into cell A4 and then AutoFill down two cells to add Feb and Mar.

This was covered in: *Lesson 2-14: Use AutoFill for text and numeric series.*

12 Apply the *Heading 2* style to cells A3:C3.

Sales First Quarter 2008-3

13 Apply the *Heading 4* style to cells A4:A6.

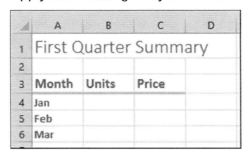

14 Add a formula to cell B4 to display the total units sold in January.

1. Click cell B4.

2. Press the equals key on your keyboard (**=**) to begin a formula.

3. Click on the *January* tab.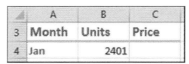

4. Scroll to the bottom of the screen using the scroll bars or arrow keys, being careful not to click on any cell.

5. Click on cell H87 (the cell with the total units in it).

6. Press the **<Enter>** key on the keyboard.

The total is shown on the *Summary* sheet.

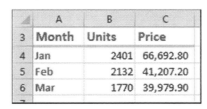

15 Use the same technique to add summary totals to **Units** and **Price** for all three months.

	A	B	C
3	Month	Units	Price
4	Jan	2401	66,692.80
5	Feb	2132	41,207.20
6	Mar	1770	39,979.90

16 Examine the formulas that Excel has created.

Click in cell B4 and then look at the formula bar at the top of the screen. Note that the formula is:

The formula is simply the worksheet name, followed by an exclamation mark, followed by the cell reference.

Note the important sidebar information regarding worksheet names that contain spaces.

17 Save your work as *Sales First Quarter 2008-4*.

---

important

You must use quotation marks if a worksheet name contains spaces

The example worksheet names used in this session do not contain any spaces.

If you had a worksheet called *January Sales* you would have to construct your formula like this:

Because worksheet names with spaces are more difficult to work with, many Excel users prefer to name their sheets without spaces by capitalizing the first letter of every word.

Example:

JanuarySales
EuropeIncludingSouthAfrica

Lesson 6-7: Understand worksheet groups

A very interesting (and little known) feature of Excel is its ability to group worksheets into a three-dimensional array of worksheet cells.

When worksheets are grouped, it is possible to perform a single operation upon all of the worksheets in the group. This can be very useful when you need to:

- Print out all of the worksheets in the group.

- Enter data into the same cell for all worksheets in the group.

- Apply formatting to the same cell or range for all worksheets in the group.

1 Open *Widget Supplies Price List* from your sample files folder.

The formatting of this workbook leaves a lot to be desired. It consists of three worksheets all showing similar information but lacking any style.

	A	B	C	D	E	F	G
1	Price List						
2	Prices Effe	20th March 2008					
3	When calculating prices the following exchange rates will be used						
4							
5		USD	GBP	EUR	JPY		
6	USD	1	1.8383	1.4708	0.00911		
7							
8	Descriptic	Dollars	Pounds	Euros	Yen		
9	Standard \	3.75	2.039928	2.549633	411.6356		
10	Premium	5.5	2.991895	3.739462	603.7322		
11	De-luxe g	7.95	4.324648	5.405222	872.6674		

We're going to use the magic of grouping to format all three worksheets at the same time.

2 Select all three worksheets to create a worksheet group.

1. Click the *Widgets* worksheet tab.

2. Hold down the **<Shift>** key and click the *Sprockets* worksheet tab.

All three tabs now have a white background to show that they are selected.

Something else has also happened. The title bar at the top of the screen now indicates that the worksheets form a worksheet group.

Widget Supplies Price List [Group] - Excel

3 Apply formatting to the *Sprockets* worksheet to make it look attractive.

Widget Supplies Price List

When you have grouped every worksheet in a workbook, you have a little problem. You can't switch between worksheets and still keep the group selected. As soon as you click a selected sheet the other two are de-selected.

To work-around this we'll have to insert a new blank worksheet. The sheet's only purpose is to allow you to switch between sheets in the selected group.

1. Add a worksheet called *Dummy*.

2. Select the *Widgets, Grommets* and *Sprockets* group as before.

3. Click on the *Sprockets* tab. The group remains selected and the *Sprockets* worksheet is now active.

4. Apply the comma style to the range B9:E11. This was covered in: *Lesson 4-3: Format numbers using built-in number formats.*

5. Adjust the widths of all columns so that they fully display their contents. This was covered in: *Lesson 2-9: Re-size rows and columns.*

6. Apply the *Title* style to cell A1, the *Heading 4* style to cells A2, A6 and A9:A11 and the *Heading 3* style to cells B5:E5 and A8:E8. This was covered in: *Lesson 4-9: Use cell styles and change themes.*

7. Adjust the height of rows 2, 3 and 4 to tidy the top part of the price list.

8. Click on each of the other two tabs to ensure that columns are also wide enough for their content. Adjust if needed.

4   With the group still selected, change some exchange rates and the *Prices Effective* date.

I saved the best bit for last. You can now update the exchange rates for all three price lists at the same time. This would be regularly needed as exchange rates fluctuate. When a group of worksheets are selected, any change made to one worksheet is also made to all of the others.

5   Save your work as *Widget Supplies Price List-1*.

Lesson 6-8: Use find and replace

note

Other ways to display the Find and Replace dialog

Find

Use the <Ctrl>+<F> keyboard shortcut.

Replace

Use the <Ctrl>+<H> keyboard shortcut.

Excel's find and replace tool is amazingly powerful. There are several special features that can massively shorten many common tasks.

This lesson will explore all of the special features and suggest useful ways in which they can be used to solve real-world problems.

1 Open *Sales First Quarter 2008-4* from your sample files folder (if it isn't already open).

2 Use *Find and Replace* to change the text *Davolio* to *O'Reilly* throughout the workbook.

Nancy Davolio has married Sean O'Reilly and she is very proud of her new name. She's made a special request for you to change her name throughout the workbook too!

1. Click: Home→Editing→Find & Select→Replace. The *Find and Replace* dialog is displayed.

2. Type **Davolio** in the *Find what:* text box and **O'Reilly** in the *Replace with:* text box.

3. Click the *Options>>* button.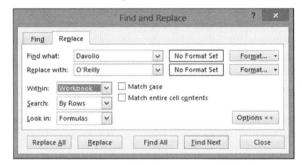

   We don't want to only look in the current worksheet, but in all of the worksheets in this workbook so select the *Within: Workbook* option.

note

Searching only part of a worksheet

If you only select a single cell, *Find and Replace* will search the entire worksheet.

If you select a range of cells, *Find and Replace* will only search within that range.

4. Click the *Find Next* button. The first instance of *Davolio* is found on the worksheet.

5. Click the *Replace* button to replace just this one instance. The cursor moves to the next instance found.

6. Click *Replace All* to replace all remaining instances of *Davolio* with *O'Reilly*. Excel prompts that it has made 28 replacements.

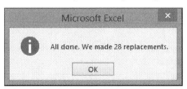

7. Click the *OK* and *Close* buttons to close both dialogs.

8. Examine the worksheets. Notice that Nancy's surname has now changed in every worksheet.

Sales First Quarter 2008-4

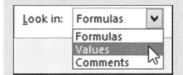
3 Apply the *Good* style to cell G21 on the *January* worksheet.

   1. Click cell G21 to select and then click:

   2. Home→Styles→Cell Styles→Good

   The *Good* cell style has a light green background and dark green text.

4 Apply the same style to every other mention of *Boston Crab Meat* in the workbook.

   1. With cell G21 still visible on the workbook click:

      Home→Editing→Find & Select→Replace…

   2. Type **Boston Crab Meat** in the *Find what:* text box.

   3. Delete the current contents of the *Replace with* box.

   4. Click the *Format* button alongside *Replace with:* and select *Choose format from Cell…* from the drop-down menu.

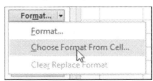

   It is really important that you click the lower of the two *Format* buttons. If you get it wrong click:

   Format→Clear Find Format

   …to start again.

   The cursor shape changes to an eye-dropper. Click on cell G21.

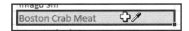

   The same format now appears in the *Replace with:* format text box on the *Find and Replace* dialog

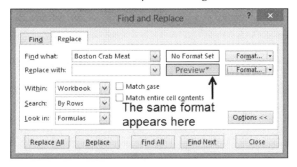

   5. Click *Replace All* to re-format all instances of *Boston Crab Meat* to the *Good* cell style. Excel advises that it has changed the format of seven cells.

   6. Click the *OK* and *Close* buttons to close both dialogs.

   7. Examine all of the worksheets and notice that every cell containing the text *Boston Crab Meat* has now turned green.

5 Save your work as *Sales First Quarter 2008-5*.

Session 6: Exercise

1   Close any workbooks that are open.

2   Open *Exercise 6* from your sample files folder.

3   View two copies of the worksheet in different windows stacked horizontally.

4   Scroll one of the windows so that the first USA sale is visible in the first row.

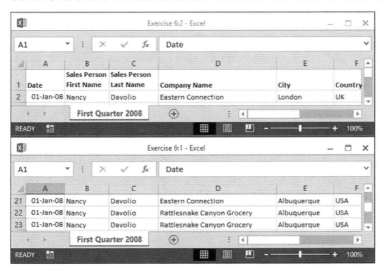

5   Close the *Exercise 6:2* window and maximize the *Exercise 6:1* window.

6   Make two duplicate copies of the *First Quarter 2008* worksheet and name them *USA* and *UK*.

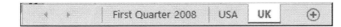

7   Delete all of the non USA rows from the USA worksheet and all of the non UK rows from the UK worksheet.

8   Hide the *First Quarter 2008* worksheet tab.

9   Use AutoSum to create a total at the bottom of Columns H and J (*Quantity* and *Total*) for both the *USA* and *UK* worksheets.

10   Add a new worksheet and name it *Summary*.

11   Complete the summary sheet as illustrated below using cross-worksheet formulas to calculate the totals.

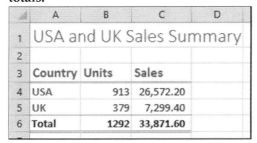

12   Save your work as *Exercise 6-End*.

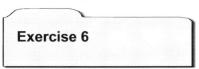

Exercise 6

If you need help slide the page to the left

Session 6: Exercise answers

These are the four questions that most students find the most difficult to remember:

Q 11	Q 8	Q 6	Q 3 and 4
In the example the following styles were used: A1 Title A3:C3 Heading 2 A4:A5 Heading 4 A6:C6 Total 1. Click cell B4 and type an equals sign into it (=). 2. Click the *USA* tab. 3. Use the scroll bars to make the total cell (cell H27) visible, being careful not to click in the cell area. 4. Click cell H27 and then press the **<Enter>** key. This was covered in: *Lesson 6-6: Create cross worksheet formulas.*	1. Right-click the *First Quarter 2008* worksheet tab. 2. Click *Hide* on the shortcut menu. This was covered in: *Lesson 6-5: Hide and unhide a worksheet.*	1. Click on the *First Quarter 2008* worksheet tab to select it. 2. Hold down the **<Ctrl>** key. 3. Click and drag the *First Quarter 2008* worksheet tab to the right. 4. Double-click the duplicated worksheet's tab and type the tab's new name. This was covered in: *Lesson 6-3: Duplicate worksheets within a workbook.*	1. Click: View→Window→ New Window 2. Click: View→Window→ Arrange All 3. Click the *Horizontal* option in the *Arrange Windows* dialog. 4. Click the OK button. 5. Scroll one of the windows to the first USA sale (Row 21). This was covered in: *Lesson 6-1: View the same workbook in different windows.*

If you have difficulty with the other questions, here are the lessons that cover the relevant skills:

1   Refer to: Lesson 1-4: Maximize, minimize, re-size, move and close the Excel window.

2   Refer to: Lesson 1-5: Download the sample files and open/navigate a workbook.

5   Refer to: Lesson 6-1: View the same workbook in different windows.

7   Refer to: Lesson 3-1: Insert and delete rows and columns.

9   Refer to: Lesson 2-3: Use AutoSum to quickly calculate totals.

10   Refer to: Lesson 1-9: View, move, add, rename, delete and navigate worksheet tabs.

12   Refer to: Lesson 1-6: Save a workbook.

Session Seven: Printing Your Work

As we move towards the paperless office printing will become less important.

In the last three years, screen and rendering technology have improved to the extent that I now prefer to read on-screen rather than from paper.

Apple now claim that their "retina" display has such a high pixel density that the human eye is unable to notice pixelation at a typical viewing distance. This suggests that there is no longer any quality advantage in printing on paper.

Perhaps we are not far from the time when all communication will be done electronically, but we're not quite there yet.

Excel has a range of tools that will allow you to present your work as polished and professional printed reports. This session will give you all of the skills you need to control every aspect of printing your work on paper.

Session Objectives

By the end of this session you will be able to:

- Print Preview and change paper orientation

- Use Page Layout view to adjust margins

- Use Page Setup to set margins more precisely and center the worksheet

- Set paper size and scale

- Insert, delete and preview page breaks

- Adjust page breaks using Page Break Preview

- Add auto-headers and auto-footers and set the starting page number

- Add custom headers and footers

- Specify different headers and footers for the first, odd and even pages

- Print only part of a worksheet

- Add row and column data labels and grid lines to printed output

- Print several selected worksheets and change the page order

- Suppress error messages in printouts

Lesson 7-1: Print Preview and change paper orientation

1 Open *Sales Report* from your sample files folder.

Make sure that you open the Session 7 *Sales Report* file as there's also a sample file of the same name in an earlier session.

2 *Print Preview* the worksheet to see how it will look on paper.

1. Click: File→Print.

The *Backstage View* appears, showing a preview of the printed page in the right-hand pane.

2. Click the *Next Page* and *Previous Page* buttons to page through the document.

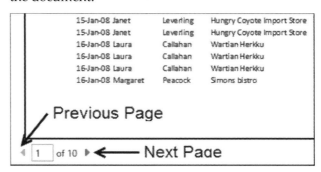

Notice that the paper isn't wide enough to show all of the columns. Excel tries to help out by printing the left-most columns across the first five or six pages followed by the right-most columns on the next five or six pages.

Sales Report for First Quarter 2008

Date	Sales Person First Name	Sales Person Last Name	Company Name	City	Country
01-Jan-08	Nancy	Davolio	Eastern Connection	London	UK
01-Jan-08	Nancy	Davolio	Eastern Connection	London	UK
01-Jan-08	Nancy	Davolio	Eastern Connection	London	UK

Product Name	Qty	Unit Price	Total
Thüringer Rostbratwurst	21	99.00	2,079.00
Steeleye Stout	35	14.40	504.00
Maxilaku	30	16.00	480.00

You would have to take the two pages, cut them with scissors, and tape them together in order to see all of the rows and columns.

3 Change the paper orientation to *Landscape* in order to print more columns on each sheet of paper.

Click the drop-down arrow next to *Portrait Orientation* in the center pane of the *Backstage View* and then click on *Landscape Orientation*.

Sales Report

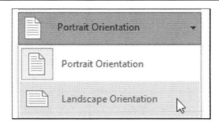

In *Landscape* orientation the paper is printed as if it had been put into the printer sideways.

The printout is very nearly there now, but we still have a problem with the last column which prints out all on its own.

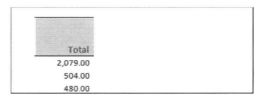

Sales Report for First Quarter 2008

Date	Sales Person First Name	Sales Person Last Name	Company Name	City	Country	Product Name	Qty	Unit Price
01-Jan-08	Nancy	Davolio	Eastern Connection	London	UK	Thüringer Rostbratwurst	21	99.00
01-Jan-08	Nancy	Davolio	Eastern Connection	London	UK	Steeleye Stout	35	14.40
01-Jan-08	Nancy	Davolio	Eastern Connection	London	UK	Maxilaku	30	16.00

Total
2,079.00
504.00
480.00

We'll discover a solution to this problem later in: *Lesson 7-2: Use Page Layout view to adjust margins.*

4   Print a copy of the worksheet.

If you'd like to save the forests (and save the cost of sixteen sheets of paper) you may wish to skip this step.

Click the *Print* button.

Print

Even if you didn't actually print the worksheet, I'm sure you will believe that the print out would not have been very good. You'd be back to the scissors and tape if you wanted the pages to show that missing last column.

The printout would have been in *Landscape* orientation because you've told Excel to do that.

5   Save your work as *Sales Report-1*.

Lesson 7-2: Use Page Layout view to adjust margins

You discovered how to change between Excel's three "views" in: *Lesson 1-16: Understand views.*

Page Layout View is a bit like *Print Preview* as you can see just how your page prints. The big difference is that, unlike *Print Preview,* you can edit a worksheet in this view. You can also set up many page layout features including margins, headers, footers and page numbering.

We'll be exploring all of this view's features in coming lessons. This lesson will focus upon changing the page margins (the blank areas at the top, bottom, left and right of the printout).

1   Open *Sales Report-1* from your sample files folder (if it isn't already open).

2   Display *Page Layout* view.

The fastest way to do this is to click the *Page Layout* button on the status bar at the bottom right of the screen.

You can also do this from the Ribbon by clicking:

View→Workbook Views→Page Layout

Page layout shows almost exactly how the worksheet will print.

The missing *Total* problem is immediately obvious.

3   Make sure that the rulers are visible.

Unless you've turned them off, you'll see a ruler at the top and left of the page that contains the active cell.

Click cell A1, to make it the active cell, and look for the rulers.

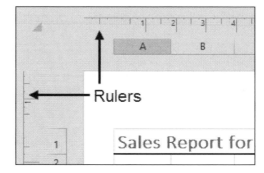

Sales Report-1

If you don't see the rulers, switch them on by clicking:

View→Show→Ruler

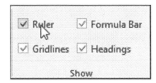

4   Adjust the left margin using the rulers.

1. Select column A.

    Notice how a portion of the ruler above column A is shaded green. This gives you a visual indication of where the margin begins.

2. Hover the mouse cursor over the left-hand side of the ruler's green shaded section.

    The cursor shape changes to a double headed arrow and the current left-hand margin size is displayed. (See sidebar if the margin doesn't display in centimeters)

3. When you see the double-headed arrow, click and drag to the left to reduce the margin to about one centimeter. You'll probably find it impossible to set exactly 1.0 centimeters with this method and will have to settle for 1.01.

    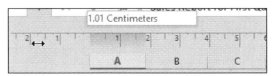

    All of the columns now fit onto one page.

Sales Report for First Quarter 2008									
Date	Sales Person First Name	Sales Person Last Name	Company Name	City	Country	Product Name	Qty	Unit Price	Total
01-Jan-08	Nancy	Davolio	Eastern Connection	London	UK	Thüringer Rostbratwurst	21	99.00	2,079.00
01-Jan-08	Nancy	Davolio	Eastern Connection	London	UK	Steeleye Stout	35	14.40	504.00

5   Save your work as *Sales Report-2*.

Lesson 7-3: Use Page Setup to set margins more precisely and center the worksheet

In the last lesson you adjusted the left margin using the horizontal ruler, and that's often the best way. It is quick and easy and you can immediately see the results of the change on the printed output.

Sometimes you will want the pages in your report to have precise margins. This would be the case when you were going to insert the report into another report (perhaps prepared in Word) and you need the margins to be consistent throughout the publication.

Another common requirement is the need to center the report on the printed page.

1   Open *Sales Report-2* from your sample files folder (if it isn't already open).

2   Display *Page Layout view* (if you aren't already in it).

This was covered in: *Lesson 7-2: Use Page Layout view to adjust margins.*

3   Set margins to the *Narrow* preset.

1. Click: Page Layout→Page Setup→Margins.

A rich menu appears showing three preset margin setups along with the last custom margins applied.

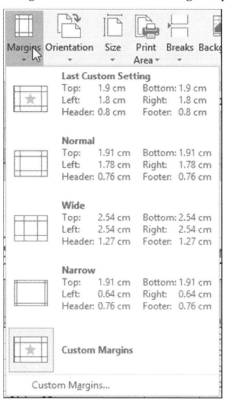

2. Click the *Narrow* option to apply left and right margins of 0.64cm.

Notice that all of the margins have now changed to the *Narrow* specification.

4 **Set a custom left and right margin of exactly one centimeter.**

Let's imagine that this report will be bound within another that uses margins of one centimeter.

Since there's no suitable preset you'll have to apply the margins manually using the *Custom Margins* options.

1. Click:

    Page Layout→Page Setup→Margins→Custom Margins…

    The *Page Setup* dialog appears with the *Margins* tab selected.

2. Type directly into the text boxes, or use the spin buttons, to set the left and right margins to exactly one centimeter.

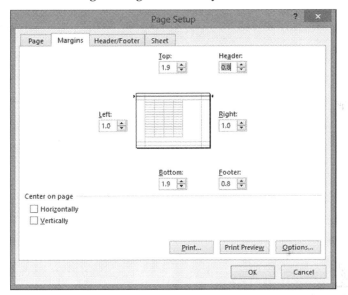

3. Click the OK button.

5 **Horizontally center the printout on the page.**

The page would look better centered.

1. Bring up the *Page Setup* dialog again by clicking:

    Page Layout→Page Setup→Margins→Custom Margins…

2. Check the *Center on page Horizontally* check box.

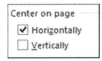

3. Click the OK button.

    The page is now perfectly centered, both on the screen and on any hard copy printed.

6 **Save your work as *Sales Report-3*.**

Lesson 7-4: Set paper size and scale

Let's imagine that *Landscape* orientation isn't an option for you.

You need *Portrait* orientation and you simply must get all of the columns on each page.

There's only two ways you can achieve this.

1. Buy some bigger paper. As long as your printer can accept it, you will have a larger area upon which to print.

2. Print everything in a smaller font.

The second option often works well (as long as you have good eyesight).

You'll be relieved to know that you don't have to manually re-format every font on the page. You can automatically scale the existing fonts to fit.

1 Open *Sales Report-3* from your sample files folder (if it isn't already open).

2 Display *Page Layout* view (if you aren't already in it).

This was covered in: *Lesson 7-2: Use Page Layout view to adjust margins.*

3 Change the paper orientation back to *Portrait*.

Click: Page Layout→Page Setup→Orientation→Portrait.

Notice that the columns no longer fit upon one sheet of paper.

4 Change the paper size to A3.

You will not see an A3 paper option if there are no printer drivers installed on your machine that support A3 (see sidebar).

Click: Page Layout→Page Setup→Size→A3.

In the USA and Canada the nearest equivalent of A3 is ANSI B 17X11 (see sidebar on the facing page for more on this). For the purposes of this lesson you should still set the size to A3 if you are able to.

That works fine. All columns now fit across one sheet of A3 paper.

But what if you don't have an A3 printer, or if the report has to fit on a sheet of A4 (or Letter sized) paper?

5 Change the paper size to A4 (or Letter) sized.

In every country in the world except the USA and Canada the normal business paper size is A4.

important

The paper sizes that are available depend upon the printers installed on your machine

Excel sensibly restricts your choice of paper sizes to those that are supported by your printer(s).

If you do not have a printer driver installed that supports A3 paper you will not see this in the list when you click:

Page Layout→Page Setup→ Size

Sales Report-3

trivia

A4 and Letter paper size

A long time ago everybody used different sizes of paper until the Germans produced a DIN standard (Din 476) in 1922.

So good and great was their DIN standard (that defined the familiar A0, A1, A2, A3, A4... A8 sizes) that it was gradually adopted by every country in the world except the United States and Canada. It is also the official United Nations document format.

As Din 476 was now a world standard, it was ratified in 1975 as ISO 216.

The genius behind the guiding principle of ISO 216 was the German scientist George Lichtenburg (1742-1799). George noticed that if a sheet of paper with an aspect ratio of the square root of two was folded in half, each half would also have the same aspect ratio.

The wonderful thing about this system is that paper merchants only need stock one size of paper (A0) to be able to cut A1, A2, A3, A4...A8 without any waste. It also means that a document designed in any A size will perfectly scale to all other sizes in the series.

A0 has an area of 1 square metre. Fold it in half and you have A1. Fold that in half for A2, then in half again for A3 and so on.

The USA and Canada are the only major countries that use a different system.

In 1995 the American National Standards institute defined a series of paper sizes based upon 8.5"X11" *Letter sized* paper. Unlike the ISO standard, the arbitrary size means that the series has alternating aspect ratios for other derivative sizes.

The ANSI A size (8.5X11) is the nearest to ISO A4 and the ANSI B size (17X11) is nearest to A3.

In the USA and Canada the slightly narrower and longer Letter size (or ANSI A) is the most common.

Click: Page Layout→Page Setup→Size→A4.

6 Make the report fit on a sheet of A4 (or Letter size) paper by scaling the print.

Click the Page Layout→Scale to Fit→Scale spin button. Each time you reduce the percentage the worksheet shrinks until it fits the page at about 70%.

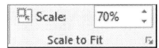

Bear in mind that, even though it fits the page, the information on the page may not be very easy to read at such a small type size.

Another method of achieving the same result would have been to set the *Width* to one page.

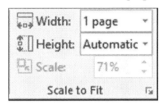

The advantage of this approach is that the content will perfectly fit between the page margins. This will look better and will avoid the need to center the printout on the page.

7 Save your work as *Sales Report-4*.

Lesson 7-5: Insert, delete and preview page breaks

note

If you don't see the dotted line page breaks, somebody has switched them off

By default, automatic page breaks are shown as dotted lines in *Normal* view. Manually inserted page breaks are shown as solid lines.

Like so many features in Excel, Microsoft has given users the ability to switch this feature off, though I can't imagine why anybody would want to.

If you don't see the dotted lines, somebody has done just that on your machine.

To bring the dotted lines back click:

File→Options→
Advanced→
Display Options for This Worksheet→Show Page Breaks

This check box needs to be checked in order to display page breaks in *Normal* view.

After you've either printed a worksheet (or entered *Page Layout* view or *Page Break Preview* and then returned to *Normal* view), you will see thin dotted lines indicating where the page will break.

Sometimes you need to take control of page breaks. This lesson will show you how.

1   Open *Sales Analysis Chart* from your sample file folder.

Note that no page breaks are shown. This is because the worksheet has never been printed or previewed.

2   Use the *Backstage Print* view to Print Preview the worksheet.

Click: File→Print.

The *Print Preview* reveals that the printout will cut the pie chart in half:

09-Oct-07 Germany	Dairy Products	1,112.00	USA
10-Oct-07 Spain	Condiments	422.40	Venezuela
10-Oct-07 Spain	Grains/Cereals	249.60	Grand Total
10-Oct-07 Spain	Beverages	310.00	
11-Oct-07 Sweden	Beverages	304.00	
11-Oct-07 Sweden	Dairy Products	672.00	
11-Oct-07 Sweden	Seafood	579.60	

We need to solve this problem by inserting a vertical page break.

3   Return to *Normal* view and notice that page breaks are shown as dotted lines.

Click the *Back Button* ⬅ at the top left of *Backstage View* to return to *Normal* view and notice the dotted lines showing the vertical and horizontal page breaks.

If you don't see any dotted lines, somebody may have disabled them. See the sidebar for instructions on how to switch them back on.

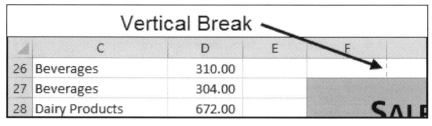

It is immediately clear where the problem lies. The vertical break needs to occur at the left of column E to solve the problem.

4   Insert a page break to the left of column E.

1. Click cell E1. It is important to choose row 1, otherwise both a horizontal and vertical page break would be inserted.

2. Click: Page Layout→Page Setup→Breaks→Insert Page Break.

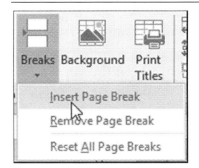

A solid line appears to the left of the active cell to show the new position of the vertical page break. When you see a solid line (rather than a dotted line) you know that the break was manually inserted (rather than automatically added by Excel).

5 Confirm that the worksheet will now print correctly.

1. Click: File→Print to Print Preview the worksheet (or view the page in *Page Layout* view) to confirm that the worksheet will now print correctly.

2. Click the *Back Button* ⬅ at the top left of *Backstage View* to return to *Normal* view.

6 Insert a horizontal page break above row 78.

Row 78 displays the first sale for November 2007.

75	31-Oct-07	Germany	Beverages	216.00
76				37,515.73
77				
78	01-Nov-07	USA	Condiments	616.00

For presentational reasons you want November's sales to begin on a new page, so you need to insert a page break above row 78.

1. Click in cell A78. It's important to click in column A otherwise both a horizontal and vertical page break would be inserted to the left of, and above the active cell.

2. Click: Page Layout→Page Setup→Breaks→Insert Page Break.

A solid line appears above the active cell (row 78) to show the position of the new (manually inserted) horizontal page break.

	A	B	C	D
76	Horizontal page break			37,515.73
77				
78	01-Nov-07	USA	Condiments	616.00

7 Confirm that the worksheet will now print correctly.

Print Preview the worksheet or view the page in *Page Layout* view.

The page now breaks at row 77 and a new page begins for row 78.

8 Remove the horizontal page break above row 78.

1. Click anywhere in row 78 except cell E78. If you were to select cell E78 you would remove both the horizontal and vertical page breaks.

2. Click: Page Layout→Page Setup→Breaks→Remove Page Break.

The solid line disappears indicating that the page will no longer break before row 78.

9 Save your work as *Sales Analysis Chart-1*.

Lesson 7-6: Adjust page breaks using Page Break Preview

In the last lesson you learned how to adjust page breaks in *Normal* view. Many users also like to adjust page breaks in *Page Layout* view.

Microsoft recommends that you don't use either. There's a purpose-built view just to handle page breaks called *Page Break Preview* view.

I tie my tongue in knots during my classes just trying to say *Page Break Preview view*!

This view allows you to click and drag page breaks (something that you can't do with the other views).

1   Open *Sales Analysis Chart-1* from your sample file folder (if it isn't already open).

2   Display *Page Break Preview* view.

Click the *Page Break Preview* button at the bottom right of the screen.

You can also select this view from the Ribbon by clicking:

View→Workbook Views→Page Break Preview

Just like *Normal View*, *Page Break Preview* allows you to see which breaks are manual and which are automatic. Breaks shown as solid lines were manually inserted. Breaks shown as dotted lines were automatically inserted by Excel.

48	21-Oct-07	France	Confections	100.00
49	22-Oct-07	Ireland	Beverages	85.12
50	22-Oct-07	Ireland	Dairy Products	200.00
51	22-Oct-07	Ireland	Dairy Products	122.88

Notice that your manually inserted vertical break (to the left of column E) is shown as a solid line while Excel's automatic page break (after row 49) is shown as a dotted line.

3   Move the automatic break from between rows 99 and 100 to between rows 77 and 78.

1.   Move the mouse cursor over the dotted blue line between rows 99 and 100 until you see the double-headed arrow cursor shape.

| 99 | 12-Nov-07 | Portugal | Meat/Poultry |
| 100 | 13-Nov-07 | Austria | Dairy Products |

2.   When you see the double-headed arrow, click and drag to move the page break up the page so that the line is between rows 77 and 78.

Sales Analysis Charts-1

When you release the mouse button, the page break is shown as a solid blue line.

4   Automatically scale the sheet so that all of November's sales fit on one sheet.

An interesting feature of *Page Break Preview* is its ability to scale a page to fit the paper. We did this manually in: *Lesson 7-4: Set paper size and scale*. The process is far more intuitive in this view.

1. Scroll to row 127. Notice that there is an automatic page break between rows 127 and 128.

2. Drag this page break to a new position between rows 145 and 146.

    Excel hasn't inserted another automatic break anywhere in Page 3 even though Page 3 is now a lot longer than it was before. The only way that Excel can possibly print Page 3 is by automatically scaling it down to fit the page.

3. Click: File→Print to Print Preview the worksheet and notice that the fonts for the entire report have been reduced. Excel cannot scale a single page in isolation; it scales all pages to keep the font size of all report pages consistent.

4. Click the *Back Button* ⊖ at the top left of *Backstage View* to return to *Page Break Previewl* view

5   Remove all manually applied page breaks.

Excel's automatic scaling system means that it is easy to lose track of what is happening. Sometimes you want to set everything back to the way it used to be and start again.

Click: Page Layout→Page Setup→Breaks→Reset All Page Breaks.

All solid lines disappear and Excel's automatic page breaks (shown as dotted lines) reappear.

6   Save your work as *Sales Analysis Chart-2*.

Lesson 7-7: Add auto-headers and auto-footers and set the starting page number

Headers and footers are displayed at the top and bottom of each printed page.

If you are printing a long report it is very useful to add page numbers. Other items commonly added to page headers and footers include:

- A title.
- The date and time that the report was printed.
- The report author's name.
- The name of the Excel file that was used to generate the report.
- The full path to the Excel file.
- A company logo.
- Copyright notices.
- A distribution list or the security level of the document (for example you may want to include the word: *Confidential*).

1   Open *Sales Report-4* from your sample files folder.

2   Display *Page Layout* view (if you aren't already in it).

This was covered in: *Lesson 7-2: Use Page Layout view to adjust margins.*

3   Click in the Page Header area at the top of the screen.

The page header area contains the text: *Click to add header*.

When you click in this area a new tab appears on the Ribbon.

You will use this tab to access Excel's *Auto Header and Footer* feature.

4   Add an Auto-header that will display page numbers at the top of each page in the format: *Page 1*.

When you click in the header area you are able to access the *Header & Footer Tools Design* tab.

1. Click:

   Header & Footer Tools→Design→Header & Footer→Header

2. Choose the option *Page 1* (see sidebar). Page numbers are now shown at the top of each page.

Sales Report-4

5 Add an Auto-footer to show the filename at the bottom of the page.

1. Click in the *Click to add footer* area at the bottom of the page.

2. Click:

Header & Footer Tools→Design→Header & Footer→Footer

3. Choose the *Sales Report-4* item from the drop down list (see sidebar).

The filename is now shown at the bottom of every page in the report.

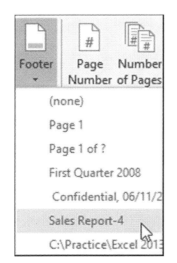

note

You can edit a header and footer on any page

It doesn't matter which page you add your header and footer to.

You can add or edit header and footer information on any page and it will then automatically apply to every other page.

Later in this session (in: *Lesson 7-9: Specify different headers and footers for the first, odd and even pages*) we'll explore a technique that will allow you to have multiple headers and footers in a single worksheet.

6 Change the page numbering so that numbering begins at page ten.

It is very common to print an Excel report and then collate it into another report (perhaps produced using Word). If the pages were to be inserted after page nine we would want Excel to begin numbering at page ten.

1. Click: Page Layout→Page Setup→Dialog Launcher.

2. Click the *Page* tab and type the number 10 into the *First page number* text box.

Click the OK button. Page numbering now begins at Page 10.

7 Save your work as *Sales Report-5*.

Lesson 7-8: Add custom headers and footers

Auto-headers and footers provide a quick and convenient method when your needs are simple. Custom headers allow you to combine your own text with report fields (such as page numbers). You are also able to add text to three different sections in the header and footer areas (Left, Right and Center).

1 Open *Sales Report-5* from your sample files folder (if it isn't already open).

2 Display *Page Layout* view (if you aren't already in it).

This was covered in: *Lesson 7-2: Use Page Layout view to adjust margins*.

3 Click on the *Page Header* area.

Notice that when you click the *Page Header* area the contents change from **Page 10** to **Page &[Page].**

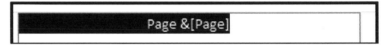

The Ampersand (&) is called an *escape character*. It tells Excel that whatever text follows is a field rather than literal text. The field &[Page] tells Excel to insert the current page number.

4 Change the page header to: *The Gourmet Food Company*.

Click in the center of the header area (where you currently see the page number) and type **The Gourmet Food Company**

5 Place the date and time on the left-hand part of the page header.

There's no Auto-header for date and time. In this case you'll have to create your own custom header field.

1. Click in the **left-hand** section of the header area.

2. Type the text **Printed on:** followed by a space.

3. Click: Header & Footer Tools→Design→ Header & Footer Elements→Current Date.

4. Type a space followed by **at:** and then another space.

5. Click: Header & Footer Tools→Design→ Header & Footer Elements→Current Time.

The left-hand section of the header bar now contains the following text:

Header
Printed on: &[Date] at: &[Time]

Sales Report-5

note

Adding a graphical header

Sometimes you will need a page header that requires more sophisticated formatting than Excel is capable of. The solution is to create the header as a graphic using a program such as Adobe Photoshop.

When the graphic has been prepared click:

Header & Footer→Design→ Header & Footer Elements→ Picture

You are then able to insert the graphic into the header.

When a graphic appears in the header a new *Format Picture* button appears in *the Header & Footer Elements* group.

When you click away from the header section the date and time are displayed. The date is displayed in a format dictated by the locale of your operating system. In this example it is the date: 6th Nov 2013 displayed in UK format (day/month/year):

> Printed on: 06/11/2013 at: 16:06

6   Place the page number on the right-hand side of the page header.

There is an *Auto Header* for this purpose but you can't use it. Auto headers may only be used in the center section of the header. You'll have to make your own using the *Header & Footer Elements* just as you did for the date and time.

1. Click in the right hand part of the page header and type **Page:** followed by a space (the last space won't appear on screen but don't worry, it is there).

2. Click: Header & Footer Tools→Design→ Header & Footer Elements→Page Number.

3. The right hand section of the header bar now contains the following text:

> Page: &[Page]

When you click away from the header section, the current page number is displayed:

> Page: 10

Printed on: 06/11/2013 at: 16:09   The Gourmet Food Company   Page: 10

---

7   Apply an attractive format to the page header section.

1. Click the left-hand section of the header. The text is automatically selected.

> Header
> Printed on: &[Date] at &[Time]

note

Good design practice

It is always a good idea to restrict your font choice to one of the two provided by the current theme.

The reasons for this are discussed in *Lesson 4-10: Add color and gradient effects to cells* (sidebar).

2. Click: Home→Font→Font and set the font face to *Calibri Light 10 Point Bold*. Note that, following good design practice, this is one of the two theme fonts (see sidebar).

3. Click: Home→Font→Font Color and set the color to the *Blue-Gray, Text 2* theme color.

4. Apply the same format to the right-hand section of the header.

5. Format the center section of the header as *Calibri Light, 28 point, Blue-Gray, Text 2*.

Printed on: 06/11/2013 at: 16:15   The Gourmet Food Company   Page: 10

---

8   Save your work as *Sales Report-6*.

Lesson 7-9: Specify different headers and footers for the first, odd and even pages

If you look at the pages in this book, you'll notice that there's a different header and footer for odd and even pages. The first page of each session is also different.

If the sample worksheet needed to be inserted into a publication similar to this one, you'd need to specify three different headers and footers, one for odd pages, one for even pages, and one for the first page.

1   *Open Sales Report-6* from your sample files folder (if it isn't already open.

2   Display *Normal* view (if you aren't already in it).

     Click the normal view button at the bottom right of the screen.

3   Insert five blank rows above row 1.

     This was covered in: *Lesson 3-1: Insert and delete rows and columns.*

4   Insert a manual page break above row 6.

     This was covered in: *Lesson 7-5: Insert, delete and preview page breaks.*

     A solid line appears above row 6.

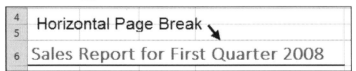

5   Merge and center cells A2:J2 and enter the text: **Sales Report Jan-Mar 2008** into the merged cell.

     This was covered in: *Lesson 4-6: Merge cells, wrap text and expand/collapse the formula bar.*

6   Apply the *Title* style to the newly added text.

     This was covered in: *Lesson 4-9: Use cell styles and change themes.*

7   Merge and center cells A3:J3 and enter the text: **Private & Confidential.**

8   Apply the *Heading 4* style to the newly added text.

9   Apply a fill color of *Blue, Accent1, Lighter 80%* to cells A2:A3.

10   Resize Row 1 so that it is three or four centimeters deep.

11   *Print Preview* the worksheet.

     Click: File→Print.

Sales Report-6

You can see that you've created a cover sheet for the report. It doesn't look bad but the header and footer are spoiling things. You need to suppress the header and footer from the cover sheet.

12 Remove the header and footer from the first (cover) page.

1. Click the *Back Button* ⬅ at the top left of *Backstage View* to return to *Normal View*.

2. Change the view to *Page Layout View*.

3. Click in the *Header* area of the first page.

4. Click: Header & Footer Tools→Design→ Options→Different First Page.

   The header and footer information vanishes from the cover page.

13 Set a different odd and even page header and footer.

1. Click in the *Header* area.

2. Click Header & Footer Tools→Design→ Options→Different Odd & Even Pages.

   The header and footer information vanishes from odd pages but remains on even pages.

14 Remove all header and footer information.

You're going to replace the existing page header and footer, so delete the contents of all header and footer sections.

15 Add odd and even page footers so that the page number appears on the right of all odd pages and on the left of all even pages.

If you look at the footer of this book, you will see that the page numbers are arranged in this manner.

1. Click in the footer area of any of the pages except the first page.

   Notice that when you click in the footer area, Excel indicates which footer you are editing (odd or even).

2. Insert a page number into the odd and even page footer area.

If you're wondering why Excel thinks that even pages are odd, and odd pages are even, see the sidebar for an explanation.

While a cover page is useful in all reports, the different odd and even page headers will only improve the presentation of reports that will be printed on both sides of the paper and then bound.

16 Save your work as *Sales Report-7*.

Important

Page numbering confusion

You have set this workbook to begin its page numbering at page 10 (an even page).

As far as Excel is concerned the "real" starting page number is page one (an odd page).

This can cause a little confusion as you will find:

Even Page Header

... at the top of the second page in this report even though it has a page number of eleven and is thus an odd page.

Excel uses the "real" page numbers when it labels the page header and footer areas.

note

Print areas do not have to be contiguous

You may want to print several different sections from your worksheet.

Simply select the non-contiguous (non-adjacent) ranges (covered in: *Lesson 2-7: Select non-contiguous cell ranges and view summary information*) and then use either of the techniques discussed in this lesson to print the selected cells.

trivia

Origins of the term: "One-off"

Many years ago, I studied engineering and spent part of my time discovering the joys of lathes, milling machines, grinders and all of the other paraphernalia found in machine shops.

Sometimes I would wander around the factory where the lathe operators would sit next to their machines – usually reading a book.

They would have a specification drawing next to them with something like "600 Off" written on it. This would mean that they would make 600 parts to the defined specification.

A *One-off* would be quite unusual as it would be expensive to set-up the lathe to produce just one part.

The term "one-off" is now commonly used in the UK to describe something that happens, or is made, only once.

Sales Report-7

Lesson 7-10: Print only part of a worksheet

Sometimes you will want to print a selection of cells from a worksheet.

Excel provides two ways to do this. The first method is applicable when the requirement is a one-off. In other words, the next time you print, the entire worksheet will be printed in the usual way.

The second method involves setting a print area. If you then save the worksheet, the defined print area will remain until you clear the print area.

In this lesson you'll explore both methods.

1   Open *Sales Report-7* from your sample files folder (if it isn't already open.

2   Display *Normal* view (if you aren't already in it).

Click the *Normal* view button at the bottom right of the screen.

Imagine that you need to print a listing for all of January's sales.

3   Select all of the transactions for January 2008 (cells A8:J93).

4   Print only the selected cells.

1.   Click: File→Print.

The *Backstage Print* view is displayed showing many print settings along with a print preview.

Notice the first option in the *Settings* list currently shows:

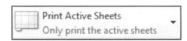

2.   Click the drop-down arrow and select *Print Selection* from the drop-down list:

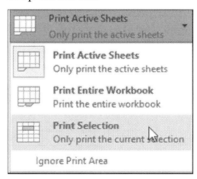

Notice that only January transactions (cells A8:J93) are now displayed in the right-hand *Print Preview* window.

If you were to click the *Print* button at this stage only January sales would be printed.

5   Save, close and re-open the workbook and then enter *Backstage Print* view.

1. Save and close *Sales Report-7.*

2. Re-open *Sales Report-7.*

3. Click: File→Print to return to *Backstage Print* view.

    Notice that the print settings have reverted to *Print Active Sheets*.

    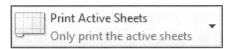

    In other words, the instruction to only print the selected cells is lost when the workbook is closed.

    But consider the case of a worksheet where you will only ever want to print a selected range. In this case you'd like the print settings to be saved with the workbook.

6 Set the print area to cells (A8:J93).

1. Click the *Back Button* ⊖ at the top left of *Backstage View* to return to *Normal View.*

2. Select cells A8:J93.

3. Click: Page Layout→Page Setup→Print Area→Set Print Area.

    When you set the print area it remains set even if you close and re-open a workbook.

4. Click: File→Print to return to *Backstage Print* view.

    Notice that only January sales are shown in the preview in the right pane of the window.

7 Save, close and re-open the workbook and then enter *Backstage Print* view.

1. Save and close *Sales Report-7.*

2. Re-open *Sales Report-7.*

3. Click: File→Print to return to *Backstage Print* view.

    Notice that only January sales are still shown in the preview in the right pane of the window, proving that the print area was saved with the workbook

8 Clear the print area.

1. Click the *Back Button* ⊖ at the top left of *Backstage View* to return to *Normal View.*

2. Click: Page Layout→Page Setup→Print Area→ Clear Print Area.

9 Print preview to prove that the full worksheet will be printed in future.

Click: File→Print to enter *Backstage Print* view.

Notice that the cover sheet along with all sales are now shown in the preview in the right pane of the window.

10 Save *Sales-Report 7.*

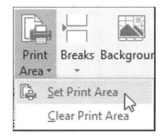

note

The print area is implemented using a named range

Excel has a feature called "named ranges". The definition and use of named ranges is an expert-level skill covered in the next book in this series: *Learn Excel 2013 Expert Skills with The Smart Method.*

When you set a print area, Excel simply creates a sheet-level named range called *Print Area* for the currently active worksheet. Each worksheet can have its own print area.

If you do progress to become an Excel Expert, it is possible to define this named range manually and to use it in formulas.

Lesson 7-11: Add row and column data labels and grid lines to printed output

1   Open *Sales Report-7* from your sample files folder (if it isn't already open).

2   View the worksheet in *Page Layout* view.

There's a slight problem with this worksheet. The first page is easy to understand as it has a column header row to indicate which data is in each column (such as Date, City and Company Name):

Sales Report for First Quarter 2008				
	Sales Person First Name	Sales Person Last Name		
Date	First Name	Last Name	Company Name	City
01-Jan-08	Nancy	Davolio	Eastern Connection	London
01-Jan-08	Nancy	Davolio	Eastern Connection	London

The second page isn't so easy to understand because the column header row is missing:

23-Jan-08	Robert	King	Mère Paillarde
23-Jan-08	Robert	King	Mère Paillarde
24-Jan-08	Michael	Suyama	La maison d'Asie
24-Jan-08	Michael	Suyama	La maison d'Asie

3   Add column headings to each printed page.

1. Click: Page Layout→Page Setup→Print Titles.

   The *Page Setup* dialog is displayed with the *Sheet* tab selected.

2. Click inside the *Rows to repeat at top* text box.

3. Select all of Row 8 by clicking anywhere in row 8.

   The row reference appears in the dialog.

   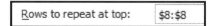

Rows to repeat at top:	$8:$8

   Note that you could enter these manually if you wanted to. For example, to print rows 6 to 8 on each page you would enter: **6:8** (or **$6:$8**).

   The dollar signs denote an absolute reference. You learned about absolute references in: *Lesson 3-12: Understand absolute and relative cell references.*

4. Click the OK button

   Notice that the column headings now appear for every page in the printout.

Sales Report-7

		Sales	Sales	
		Person	Person	
	Date	First Name	Last Name	Company Name
75	23-Jan-08	Robert	King	Mère Paillarde
76	23-Jan-08	Robert	King	Mère Paillarde

4 Add gridlines to the printout.

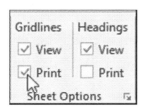

Sometimes it is difficult for the eye to track across printed lines. For this type of report it is useful to print gridlines onto the printed page in a similar way to the ones displayed on the worksheet.

Click: Page Layout→Sheet Options→Gridlines→Print.

5 Print Preview the worksheet.

Click: File→Print to enter *Backstage Print* view.

The *Print Preview* in the right-hand pane shows that gridlines will be printed upon each page:

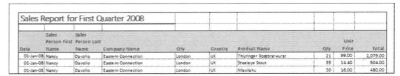

6 Add row and column headings to the printout.

You may want to send a printed worksheet to a colleague and then discuss it on the telephone. It would be useful to be able to ask "what do you think of the value in cell H11?" This isn't possible because row and column headers are not normally shown on the printed page.

1. Click the *Back Button* ⊖ at the top left of *Backstage View* to return to *Normal View*.

2. Click: Page Layout→Sheet Options→Headings→Print.

7 *Print Preview* the worksheet.

Click: File→Print to enter *Backstage Print* view.

The *Print Preview* in the right-hand pane shows that row and column headers will be printed on each page:

	A	B	C	D	E	F
6	Sales Report for First Quarter 2008					
7						
8	Date	Sales Person First Name	Sales Person Last Name	Company Name	City	Country
9	01-Jan-08	Nancy	Davolio	Eastern Connection	London	UK
10	01-Jan-08	Nancy	Davolio	Eastern Connection	London	UK
11	01-Jan-08	Nancy	Davolio	Eastern Connection	London	UK

8 Remove the gridlines and column headers from the printout.

1. Click the *Back Button* ⊖ at the top left of *Backstage View* to return to *Normal View*.

2. Clear the check boxes that were ticked in the previous steps.

9 Save your work as *Sales Report-8*.

Lesson 7-12: Print several selected worksheets and change the page order

1   Open *Palace Hotel Bar Activity* from your sample files folder.

2   Print Preview the worksheet.

    1. Click: File→Print to enter *Backstage Print* view.

    2. Use the *Next Page* button  at the bottom left of *the Print Preview* window to view each page in the report.

       Notice that the worksheet prints first downward (listing all activity between 11:00 AM and 4:00 PM for all days).

       When it reaches the bottom of the list it moves across to print all activity between 5:00 PM and 10:00 PM and so on.

3   Change the view to *Page Break Preview*.

    1. Click the *Back Button* at the top left of *Backstage View* to return to *Normal View.*

    2. Click the *Page Break Preview* button at the bottom right of the screen.

       In this view it is easy to see the page order by looking at the watermarks on each page (the watermark is the transparent large gray text saying Page 1, Page 2 etc).

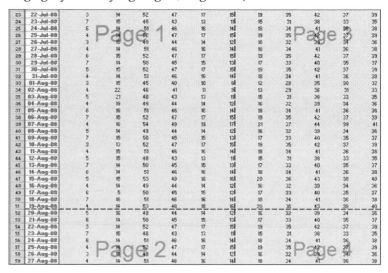

But what if you don't want to print in this order? Perhaps you would like to first print all activity for all times. In other words, you want the above display to make the existing Page 3 into Page 2.

Palace Hotel Bar Activity

---

4   Change the print order to *Over, then down*.

    1.   Click: Page Layout→Page Setup→Dialog Launcher.

    2.   Click the *Sheet* tab.

    3.   Click the *Over, then down* option button.

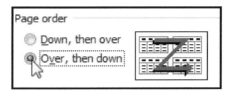

    4.   Click the OK button.

        It can be seen from the page break preview that the page order has now changed.

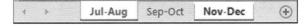

5   Print the headcount for Jul-Aug and Nov-Dec in one printout.

You can print several worksheets at the same time and they needn't be adjacent.

    1.   Click the *Jul-Aug* tab.

    2.   Hold down the **<Ctrl>** key and click the *Nov-Dec* tab.

        Both tabs are now colored white

    3.   Click: File→Print.

        The *Backstage Print* view is displayed.

    4.   Note that when more than one sheet is selected, the first item in the *Settings* list has the *Print Active Sheets* option selected.

    5.   Click the *Next Page* button at the bottom left of the print preview to confirm that the contents of the *Jul-Aug* and *Nov-Dec* worksheets would have been printed.

    6.   Click the *Back Button* ![back button] at the top left of *Backstage View* to return to *Page Break Preview*.

6   Save your work as *Palace Hotel Bar Activity-1*.

Lesson 7-13: Suppress error messages in printouts

Excel has several built-in error messages such as the divide by zero error:

Sometimes you're quite happy to have these errors appear in a worksheet. For example, divide by zero errors could be quite normal when there is incomplete data.

Even though the errors are fine in the worksheet, you may not want them to appear in your printed output.

1 Open *Average Revenue per Sale* from your sample files folder.

2 View the worksheet in *Normal* view.

	A	B	C	D	E
1	Average Revenue Per Sale				
2					
3	First Name	Last Name	Sales	Units	Average Revenue per Sale
4	Andrew	Fuller	7,639.30	15	509.29
5	Anne	Dodsworth	-	-	#DIV/0!
6	Janet	Leverling	29,658.60	60	494.31
7	Laura	Callahan	19,271.60	40	481.79
8	Margaret	Peacock	44,795.20	90	497.72
9	Michael	Suyama	4,109.80	8	513.73
10	Nancy	Davolio	-	-	#DIV/0!
11	Robert	King	21,461.60	43	499.11
12	Steven	Buchanan	2,634.40	5	526.88
13		Total:	129,570.50	261.00	

This is an example of a worksheet with errors. In actual fact, you are simply waiting for Anne Dodsworth and Nancy Davolio to send you their sales figures, so they aren't really errors.

Divide by zero errors occur when you attempt to divide any number by zero.

You want to print out this interim report but replace the ugly #DIV/0 errors with a blank space on the printed page.

3 Replace errors with a blank space in printed output.

1. Click: Page Layout→Page Setup→Dialog launcher.

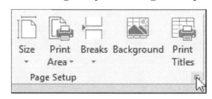

The *Page Setup* dialog appears.

2. Click the *Sheet* tab.

Average Revenue per Sale

3. Click the *Cell errors as* dropdown list and then click *<blank>*.

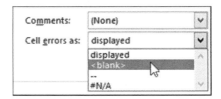

4. Click the OK button.

4 *Print Preview* the worksheet.

1. Click: File→Print to open *Backstage Print* view.

   The errors are no longer printed. Blank spaces are substituted for the divide by zero errors.

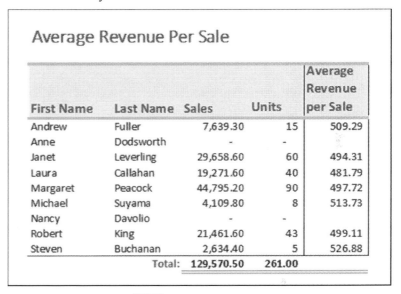

2. Click the *Back Button* at the top left of *Backstage View* to return to *Normal View*.

5 Save your work as *Average Revenue per Sale-1*.

Session 7: Exercise

1   Open *Exercise 7* from your sample files folder.

2   Change to *Page Layout* view.

3   Change the left margin to about 1.0 cm using the click and drag method.

4   Click: Page Layout→Page Setup→Margins and use the *Custom Margins...* option to set top and bottom margins to precisely 2.0 cm and the left and right margins to precisely 1.0 cm.

5   Horizontally center the printout on the page.

6   Change the page orientation to landscape.

7   Change the view to *Page Break Preview*.

8   Insert a horizontal page break between rows 27 and 28.

9   Move the page break so that it now occurs between row 24 and 25.

10   Change to *Page Layout* view.

11   Add an auto-header to match the following:

> Page 1 of 3

12   Make the data labels in row 1 repeat on every page.

13   Set the print area to A1:J12 and then *Print Preview* to prove that only these cells would be printed.

14   Clear the print area.

15   Add gridlines to the printout.

16   *Print Preview* to prove that gridlines would be printed.

	Sales Person First Name	Sales Person Last Name	Company Name	City	Country	
						Page 2 of 4
Date						
08-Jan-08	Laura	Callahan	Folies gourmandes	Lille	France	
08-Jan-08	Laura	Callahan	Folies gourmandes	Lille	France	

17   Save your work as *Exercise 7-End*.

Exercise 7

If you need help slide the page to the left ➡

Session 7: Exercise answers

These are the questions that most students find difficult to remember:

Q 13	Q 12	Q 8	Q 5
1. Select cells A1:J12. 2. Click: Page Layout→ Page Setup→ Print Area→ Set Print Area This was covered in: *Lesson 7-10: Print only part of a worksheet.*	1. Click: Page Layout→ Page Setup→Print Titles 2. Click the *Sheet* tab. 3. Click in the *Rows to repeat at top* text box. 4. Either click in row 1 with the mouse or type 1:1 into the box. This was covered in: *Lesson 7-11: Add row and column data labels and grid lines to printed output.*	1. Click in cell A28. 2. Click: Page Layout→ Page Setup→ Breaks→ Insert Page Break This was covered in: *Lesson 7-5: Insert, delete and preview page breaks.*	1. Click: Page Layout→ Page Setup→ Dialog launcher 2. Click the *Margins* tab. 3. Check the *Center on page horizontally* check box. This was covered in: *Lesson 7-3: Use Page Setup to set margins more precisely and center the worksheet.*

If you have difficulty with the other questions, here are the lessons that cover the relevant skills:

1   **Lesson 1-5: Download the sample files and open/navigate a workbook.**

2,3   **Lesson 7-2: Use Page Layout view to adjust margins.**

4   **Lesson 7-3: Use Page Setup to set margins more precisely and center the worksheet.**

6   **Lesson 7-1: Print Preview and change paper orientation.**

7   **Lesson 7-6: Adjust page breaks using Page Break Preview.**

9   **Lesson 7-6: Adjust page breaks using Page Break Preview.**

10   **Lesson 7-2: Use Page Layout view to adjust margins.**

11   **Lesson 7-7: Add auto-headers and auto-footers and set the starting page number.**

14   **Lesson 7-10: Print only part of a worksheet.**

15   **Lesson 7-11: Add row and column data labels and grid lines to printed output.**

16   **Lesson 7-1: Print Preview and change paper orientation.**

17   **Lesson 1-6: Save a workbook.**

Session Eight: Cloud Computing

> I have computers at Apple, at NEXT, at Pixar and at home. I walk up to any of them and log in as myself… I've got my stuff wherever I am. And none of that is on a local hard disk.
>
> *Steve Jobs, (from a 1997 speech at the WWD Conference).*
> *Co-founder and CEO of Apple Inc. (1955-2011)*

Until very recently it was normal for applications (such as Excel) to be installed onto the computer's local hard disk drive. It was also normal to save files (such as Excel workbooks) onto the computer's local hard disk drive (or a local networked hard disk drive).

In the world of cloud computing, both applications and files are stored on remote servers that are accessed (via the Internet) using web-based computing services. Steve Jobs' vision is now a reality!

Cloud computing provides many advantages:

- Files can be accessed from anywhere in the world, from any device that has a supported web browser (such as a smartphone, tablet or PC).

- Applications (such as Excel) do not need to be installed upon the hard drive of the device. You are able to run Office on any device, anywhere, providing that it has a supported web browser.

In this session you will learn how *Office on Demand, OneDrive* and *Office Online* work together to enable you to access Excel, and all of your files, on any device, anywhere.

Cloud computing support is by far the most important new feature of Excel 2013. This session will show you how to make the most of this exciting new way of working.

Session Objectives

By the end of this session you will be able to:

- Save a workbook to a OneDrive

- Open a workbook from a OneDrive

- Understand operating systems

- Understand Excel Online

- Open a workbook using Excel Online

- Share a link to a workbook

- Edit a workbook simultaneously with other users using Excel Online

note

OneDrive subscriptions

If you purchased Excel 2013 using a Microsoft Office 365 annual subscription, you will have a 1 Terabyte OneDrive subscription included as part of the Office 365 package.

At the time of writing (June 2014) Microsoft also offered a free 15 GB ad-supported OneDrive subscription (though some may find the advertisements annoying).

www.OneDrive.com has all of the details that you need to open a free OneDrive account.

trivia

OneDrive used to be called SkyDrive

OneDrive was called *SkyDrive* between 2008 and 2013.

The British television broadcaster BskyB objected that the use of the word *Sky* within the *Sky Drive* brand name was a breach of their trademark.

Microsoft agreed to change the name and, on January 27th 2014, announced that the service would, in future, be called *OneDrive*.

You may still read older articles on the Internet that refer to the *OneDrive* service using the old *SkyDrive* name.

Lesson 8-1: Save a workbook to a OneDrive

In order to complete this lesson you will need a OneDrive account. At the time of writing (June 2014) a free subscription was available. See sidebar for more information about different OneDrive subscriptions.

A OneDrive can be visualized as a "hard drive in the sky". Saving a workbook to a OneDrive means you'll be able to access it from any device, anywhere in the world.

The files are usually stored on one of Microsoft's servers (accessed via the Internet). Some corporate users may prefer to store their OneDrive files on their own servers for security reasons (see sidebar facing page).

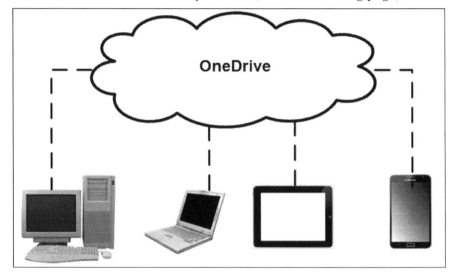

1   Open *Smartphone Sales* from your sample files folder.

2   Save the workbook to your OneDrive in a folder called: *Documents\Excel\Practice.*

1. Click the *File* button **FILE** at the top-left of the screen.

2. Click: *Save As* **Save As** in the left-hand list.

3. Click *OneDrive* **M Smart's OneDrive** in the *Save As* menu.

   You may be prompted to sign in to your OneDrive account if you are not already logged in.

   There may also be a *sign up* link that will enable you to create a *Microsoft Account* if you don't already have one.

4. Click *Browse* **Browse** under the *One Drive* folder list on the right-hand side of the screen.

Smartphone Sales

note

OneDrive security concerns

When you store a file on your local hard drive, you can be reasonably sure that nobody else can access the contents (provided that they cannot gain access to your computer).

When you upload a file to a Microsoft OneDrive server you may worry that the file contents are vulnerable to theft.

Because a very reliable encryption method called SSL (Secure Sockets Layer) is used to transport files to and from the OneDrive, there isn't any realistic possibility of your file being intercepted when travelling to and from the Microsoft Servers.

Because your files are not encrypted upon Microsoft's servers, the main security worry might be that their servers could be compromised and that your files could be accessed by others.

There are two potential solutions for users who have security concerns:

1. Encrypt your files before saving them to the OneDrive.

The *Expert Skills* book in this series comprehensively covers encryption of security-sensitive Excel files.

2. Host your own private OneDrive using *Microsoft SharePoint* along with the *OneDrive for Business* SharePoint component.

SharePoint is mainly used by corporations and is usually installed upon a corporate server by the IT department.

Once installed, *OneDrive for Business* can be used to store files on corporate servers in exactly the same way as upon Microsoft's own OneDrive servers.

A *Save As* dialog appears showing the contents of your OneDrive folder.

By default, the OneDrive has three folders called: *Documents, Pictures* and *Public*.

5. Double-click the *Documents* folder.

The empty *Documents* folder is displayed:

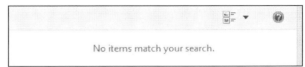

In *Lesson 1-8: Pin a workbook and understand file organization*, you learned why it is a good idea to place your Excel files into a separate folder within your local *Documents* folder. We will also create an *Excel* folder beneath the *Documents* folder on your OneDrive.

6. Right-click in the empty *Documents* folder and click:

New Folder

…from the shortcut menu.

7. Type **Excel** as the name of the new folder.

If you have difficulty doing this, right-click on the folder and click *Rename* from the shortcut menu.

In *Lesson 1-8: Pin a workbook and understand file organization*, you learned why it is a good idea to further organize your Excel files within the *Excel* folder. You will create a *Practice* folder inside the *Excel* folder to do the same thing on your OneDrive.

8. Create a new OneDrive *Practice* subfolder inside the newly created *Excel* folder.

9. Click: *Save* to save the *Smartphone Sales* workbook into the new OneDrive\Documents\Excel\Practice folder.

The workbook is saved and you are returned to the main Excel screen.

3   Close Excel.

note

Beware of the "lunchtime lock"

The lunchtime lock happens when you do this:

1. Open a OneDrive file on your home computer.

2. Leave your computer switched on with the file open and go to work.

3. Open the same OneDrive file on your work computer.

When you try to open the file at work you will see a dialog telling you that the file is "locked" and cannot be worked upon.

IT staff call this problem the "lunchtime lock".

A common support problem occurs when a team member goes out to lunch leaving a shared file open. This prevents anybody else on the team from editing the same file.

Later, in: *Lesson 8-7: Edit a workbook simultaneously with other users using Excel Online,* you'll discover how to share files using the cloud-based *Excel Online.*

Excel Online is, in this respect, more sophisticated than the *Excel desktop app* (the version of Excel you've been using up to now) as it allows several users to read and edit a workbook at the same time. This means that the lunchtime lock scenario cannot occur.

Lesson 8-2: Open a workbook from a OneDrive

Once a workbook has been saved to a OneDrive it can be opened from absolutely anywhere, provided you are connected to the Internet.

In: *Lesson 8-5: Open a workbook using Excel Online,* you'll discover that you can also open a workbook from any device that has a web browser (even if Excel 2013 is not installed on the device). This includes smartphones and tablets such as the iPad.

In sthis lesson we'll consider the scenario where you have a Windows PC at your office, and another Windows PC at home.

You simply want to be able to view and edit the same workbook on both computers.

1   Open Excel.

The start-up screen is displayed.

2   Open the *Smartphone Sales* sample file from your OneDrive.

1.   Click: *Open Other Workbooks*  from the left-hand menu bar.

2.   Click: *OneDrive* 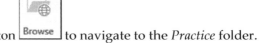 in the *Open* menu.

If you haven't already signed in to your OneDrive account you will now be prompted for an e-mail address and password.

You should see the *Practice* folder in the *Recent Folders* list:

3.   If it is there, click on the *Practice* folder. If not, use the *Browse* button to navigate to the *Practice* folder.

You should see the previously saved *Smartphone Sales* file in the folder:

Smartphone Sales.xlsx

4.   Click on the *Smartphone Sales* file to select it.

5.   Click on the *Open* button to open the workbook.

The *Smartphone Sales* workbook opens from the OneDrive:

Smartphone Sales

note

OneDrive alternatives

Excel 2013 integrates OneDrive features for the first time.

You can save a file to your OneDrive as easily as saving to your local hard drive.

There are similar rival services to OneDrive offered by Dropbox, Google Drive and Amazon Drive, but none integrate with Office as seamlessly as OneDrive.

note

The advantages of using a OneDrive instead of a local drive

1. You can access your workbooks from any Internet connected device, anywhere in the world.

This means that you can work with your tablet device, smartphone or laptop when travelling, without having to copy files between devices.

2. You can share files with other users without having to e-mail the files to them.

You do this by sending a hyperlink to the other user rather than the file itself.

You'll discover more about this later, in: *Lesson 8-6: Share a link to a workbook*.

3. You can collaborate more easily with other users by giving certain users the right to edit your files.

4. You can allow users who do not have Excel 2013 installed upon their device to view, or even edit, your workbook.

You'll discover more about this later, in: *Lesson 8-4: Understand Excel Online*.

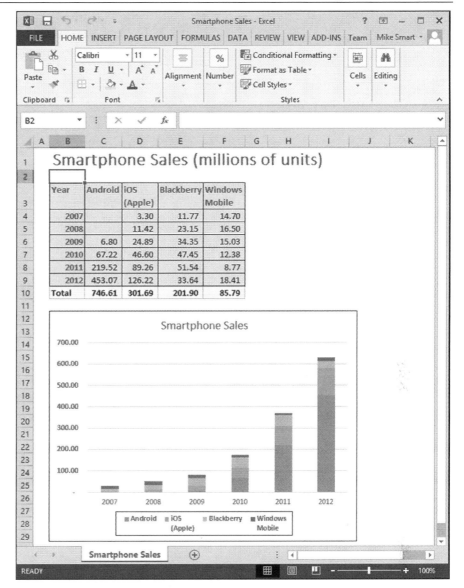

You can use this technique to open a workbook using any computer that has Excel 2013 installed.

3   Close Excel.

Lesson 8-3: Understand operating systems devices and Office versions

What is an operating system?

You are probably using Excel 2013 on a Windows 7 or Windows 8.1 personal computer. Windows is an *operating system*.

When Excel 2013 needs to do something (such as open or save a file) it does so by sending a request to the Windows operating system.

The same request under Apple's OS X operating system (used on an Apple computer) would be very different. This is the reason that you cannot install Office 2013 (or any other Windows application) onto an Apple computer.

Microsoft actually produce a (re-written) version of Office that runs on the Apple's OS X operating system. As a result the Apple versions are very different to their Windows counterparts.

The new *Excel Online* application (that you'll learn about later, in: *Lesson 8-4: Understand Excel Online*) enables you to enjoy the Excel 2013 user interface on an Apple computer (and other non-Windows devices) for the first time. This is possible because an online application doesn't communicate directly with the operating system.

What is a smartphone?

A smartphone is a mobile telephone that also includes a computer and a touch screen.

Lightweight mobile operating systems have been specially designed for smartphones. Small programs (commonly referred to as *apps*) have been developed to run on these mobile operating systems.

There are three common smartphone operating systems: Apple's *iOS*, Google's *Android* and Microsoft's *Windows Phone*. Some apps have been released in three different versions so that a version is available for all three operating systems.

What is a tablet computer?

Apple's iPad (launched in 2010) was the first mass-market modern tablet computer.

A tablet computer is similar to a very large smartphone (though most do not have telephony capability).

Screen sizes are typically 7 or 10 inches and, like a smartphone, they are usually controlled via a touchscreen. Some tablet computers have an optional keyboard and mouse available as an add-on.

note

Windows 8 and Windows 8 RT

ARM and Intel processors

Windows 8 and Windows 8 RT are different operating systems. Their similar-sounding names often cause confusion.

Windows 8 RT is a special lightweight version of the Windows 8 operating system that is designed for mobile devices (such as tablet computers).

Windows 8 RT tablet devices are designed for processors made by ARM.

The Windows 8 operating system will only run on processors made by Intel.

Until very recently ARM processors offered longer battery life than Intel processors due to lower power consumption.

Intel's latest *Atom* processors now provide a battery life that is comparable with ARM processors (typically over 8 hours).

The major drawback of Windows 8 RT is its inability to run regular Windows desktop applications.

The future of Windows RT

Intel's latest Atom processors have enabled tablet manufacturers to produce devices that can run the full version of Windows 8. This means that it is also possible to run all Windows desktop applications (including the full version of Office 2013).

Some have speculated that the availability of Intel-based tablet devices, running the full version of Windows 8, may eventually cause Windows RT tablet devices to become obsolete.

Tablet operating systems are similar to their smartphone counterparts: Apple's *iOS,* Google's *Android* and a special Windows 8 version called *Windows 8 RT.*

Office 2013 Versions

- **Office 2013 Desktop Version**

  The *Office 2013 desktop version* is the full version of Office that you probably have installed on the hard drive of your PC. The *Office 2013 desktop version* will only run on the Windows 7 and Windows 8 (or later) operating systems.

  There is also a version of Office 2013 that runs on the Windows 8 RT operating system (see sidebar). This is almost identical to the desktop version, but there are some small differences caused by technical limitations of Windows 8 RT.

- **Office Mobile**

  Because smartphones have a much smaller display than a tablet or PC, a special version of Office 2013 has been created for them.

  Office Mobile is not the full version of each Office program, but a lightweight, cut-down version with limited features.

- **Office Online**

  Office Online will be discussed in depth in: *Lesson 8-4: Understand Excel Online.*

Office 2013 compatibility (at Dec 2013)

Device	Office 2013 Desktop	Office Mobile	Office Online
Apple Mac			X
Apple iPad		X	X
Apple iPhone		X	X
Android Tablet		X	X
Android Phone		X	X
Windows 7/8 PC	X		X
Windows 8 RT tablet	X		X
Windows 7/8 Phone		X	X

Note that not all Android devices are supported.

Lesson 8-4: Understand Excel Online

Excel 2013 desktop application

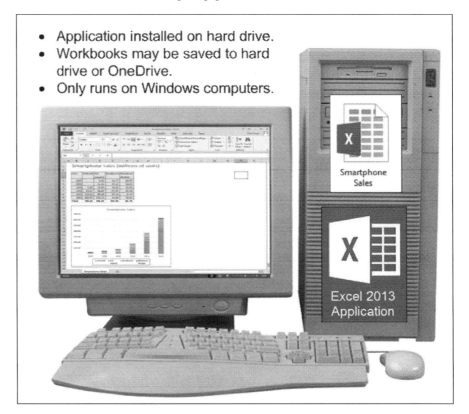

- Application installed on hard drive.
- Workbooks may be saved to hard drive or OneDrive.
- Only runs on Windows computers.

Smartphone Sales

Excel 2013 Application

The Excel 2013 desktop application is a conventional locally-installed application. This means:

- You need a license to use the Excel 2013 desktop application.

- You need to install the Excel 2013 desktop application software onto your computer before you can use it.

- The Excel 2013 desktop application will only run on a computer running the Windows 7, 8 (or later) and RT operating systems.

- The Excel 2013 desktop is the only Excel version that includes every Excel feature.

- Workbooks may be saved to (and opened from) either the local hard drive or a OneDrive.

Excel Online

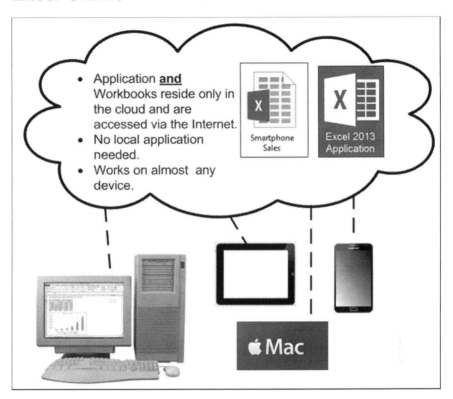

Excel Online is a cloud application that runs inside a web browser. This means:

- You don't need any license to use Excel Online.

- You don't need to install any software to use Excel Online.

- Because a cloud app doesn't directly communicate with the operating system, Excel Online will run on any device that has a supported web browser. This includes the Apple Mac, iPad and almost all recent tablet and smartphone devices.

- Excel Online provides only a limited-feature version of Excel 2013. The most commonly-used features are included.

Excel online makes it possible to share a workbook with just about anybody

If you e-mail a copy of a workbook to another user (as an attachment), you have to assume that the recipient has a Windows computer with a compatible version of Excel installed.

When you send a user a link to a workbook (that will open using Excel Online), you can be confident that the user will almost certainly be able to open the workbook. You'll learn how to share links that open using Excel Online later, in: *Lesson 8-6: Share a link to a workbook*.

The recipient of a link can have any type of device (such as a Windows PC, Windows 8 RT pad, Apple Mac, iPad, Android pad or even a smartphone) and does not have to have a copy of Excel 2013 installed.

note

Touchscreen gestures

Touchscreen devices (such as tablet computers and smartphones) do not usually have a mouse.

When using a touchscreen you can use the following gestures to work with Excel Online:

Left-click: Tap the touchscreen.

Right-click: Touch and hold your finger on the touchscreen.

Scroll: Touch a blank area of the workbook and slide your finger in the direction you wish to scroll in.

Zoom in: Touch two points on the touchscreen and then move your fingers away from each other. (This is normally done with the thumb and forefinger).

Zoom out: Touch two points on the touchscreen and then move your fingers towards each other.

Select text: Tap on the text to place the insertion point. If it is in the wrong place, tap again to move it. Drag the circular handles (called *grippers*) to select.

note

Excel Online automatic Save feature

Excel Online automatically saves changes as you make them.

In: *Lesson 8-7: Edit a workbook simultaneously with other users using Excel Online,* you'll discover how this feature enables multiple users to all edit the same workbook at the same time. This amazing ability does not exist in the desktop "full" version!

Smartphone Sales

Lesson 8-5: Open a workbook using Excel Online

Now that you have saved a workbook to your OneDrive, you can use Excel Online to open it from any device that has a supported web browser (see facing page sidebar). This includes most recent smartphones, tablet devices and personal computers. Even if the device does not have Excel 2013 installed, you will be able to view and edit the workbook using the free Excel Online application.

If you have a tablet computer (such as an iPad), or recent smartphone, you might find it interesting to use this device (rather than your Windows PC) for this lesson.

1 Open *Smartphone Sales* from a web browser using Excel Online.

   1. Open a web browser on your PC or (ideally) using another device.

   2. Enter the url: **www.OneDrive.com**

   3. If necessary, enter your user name and password to log in.

   4. Click the *Documents* folder. (If you are using a smartphone or tablet computer, see sidebar for the touchscreen gesture that simulates a left-click).

   5. Click the *Excel* folder. You created this folder in: *Lesson 8-1: Save a workbook to a OneDrive.*

   6. Click the *Practice* folder.

   You will now see the *Smartphone Sales* workbook that you saved in: *Lesson 8-1: Save a workbook to a OneDrive.*

   7. Right-Click on *Smartphone Sales*

   8. Click *Open in Excel Online* from the shortcut menu (or simply *Open* if you are using a device that does not have Excel installed upon it.

In a real-world situation you'd usually select *Open in Excel* (if it is available) because Excel has more features and is faster than Excel Online. For the sake of this lesson, you'll open the file using Excel

338

Online so that you can share the experience of users who do not have Excel installed on their device.

The *Smartphone Sales* workbook opens in Excel Online:

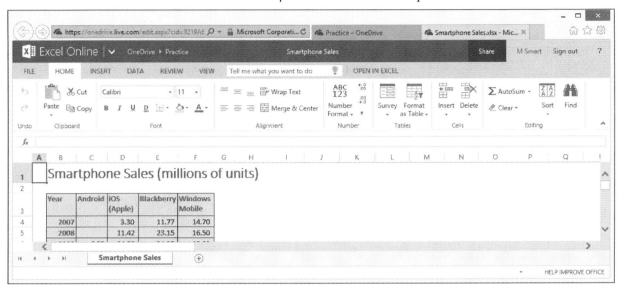

note

Supported web browsers

Excel Online is only supported on recent versions of the four most commonly used browsers: Internet Explorer, Chrome, Safari and Firefox.

Almost all recent devices (such as the Windows PC, Apple Mac, iPad, Android tablet, and most smartphones) can run at least one of the supported browsers.

Some early devices only supported older browser versions. Others (particularly early Android devices) had their own custom browser. You may find that the Excel Online will not run on this type of device.

Internet Explorer is always the best browser to use if it is available. If not use Chrome, Firefox or Safari. If you find that Excel Online does not work correctly with any of the supported browsers, try again using a different browser.

Excel Online looks very much like the desktop Excel application. Most (but not all) of Excel's features are now available from the ribbon.

2 **Expand and collapse the Excel Online ribbon.**

If you are using a SmartPhone or tablet device with a very small screen, Excel Online may open with the Ribbon minimized.

Just like the desktop Excel version, you can double-click on any of the Ribbon tabs to minimize or maximize the Ribbon.

Try minimizing and maximizing the Ribbon to see this working.

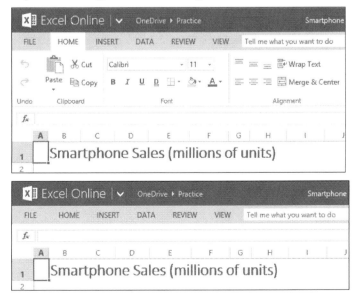

3 **Close your web browser.**

note

Other ways to share a link

A sharing link is the most versatile way to share a link as it can be copied and pasted to any destination.

Excel also provides faster ways to share a link when you know exactly what you will do with it.

When you click: File→Share you have options to:

Invite People

This option allows you to quickly send a nicely formatted e-mail to share a file:

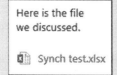

Here is the file we discussed.

📄 Synch test.xlsx

Email

This option enables you to share your workbook in several different ways:

- As an attachment.

- As a link (this is the method that you use manually in this lesson).

- As a PDF or XPS file. You learned about PDF and XPS files in: *Lesson 1-7: Understand common file formats.*

- As an Internet fax. You need to subscribe to an Internet fax service to use this option.

Post to Social Networks

This allows a link to be posted to popular social network sites such as Facebook, Twitter and LinkedIn.

Lesson 8-6: Share a link to a workbook

When your workbooks are stored on a OneDrive, it is possible to share them without sending a physical copy of the file to the recipients. This is done by distributing a simple hyperlink (via an e-mail, or by pasting the link into a Facebook page, Twitter tweet, blog or other web page).

As discussed in: *Lesson 8-4: Understand Excel Online,* you can be sure the the recipient will be able to open the workbook on almost any device, even if Excel 2013 is not installed. The workbook will automatically open using the free Excel Online application.

You can also use the technique taught in this lesson to share Word documents and PowerPoint presentations as there are also Word Online and PowerPoint Online applications available.

1   Open Excel.

The start-up screen is displayed.

2   Open the *Smartphone Sales* sample file from your OneDrive.

This is the file you saved in: *Lesson 8-1: Save a workbook to a OneDrive.*

3   Send an e-mail link to enable the recipient to open (but not change) the workbook.

1. Click: *File.*

2. Click: *Share* on the left-hand menu bar.

3. Click: *Get a Sharing Link* in the *Share* menu.

Notice that you can create two types of link:

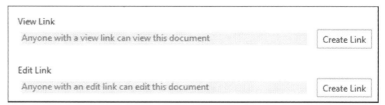

A *View Link* allows the recipient to view (but not change) the workbook. An *Edit Link* will enable the recipient to make changes to the workbook on your OneDrive. You'll use an *Edit Link* later, in: *Lesson 8-7: Edit a workbook simultaneously with other users using Excel Online.*

4. Click the *Create Link* button next to the *View* link.

5. Right-click on the *View Link* and then select *Copy* from the shortcut menu:

Smartphone Sales

trivia

How a Greek Wedding instantly travelled the world

One of my friends recently got married and decided to have the wedding on the Greek island of Rhodos.

The day after the wedding we all pooled our video footage (there were many cameras and SmartPhones recording the event). I edited all of the footage into a nice video.

The file size was just over 1Gb and it ran for a little over an hour.

I copied the video to the *Public* folder of my OneDrive. A simple hyperlink was e-mailed to friends and relatives and posted on social networking sites such as Facebook.

A few hours after the wedding had finished, the video was being viewed by relatives all over the world.

note

Users can save (and then edit) a local copy of read-only workbooks

When you send a *View* link, you can be sure that recipients cannot change the workbook stored on your OneDrive.

This does not prevent the user from making a local copy of your workbook. It is then possible for the user to make changes to the local copy.

To make a local copy the user can click:

File→Save As→Download

... from inside Excel Online.

It is then possible for the user to open and edit the local copy of the workbook.

6. Create an e-mail, addressed to yourself, with whichever e-mail application you normally use.

7. Paste the link into the body of the e-mail:

> Dear Mike
>
> Here's the workbook we discussed:
>
> https://skydrive.live.com/redir?page=view&resid=B182751730E7A45!151&authkey=!AIB2vchNRoeAbzw
>
> ... just click on the link above and you'll be able to see it.
>
> Best Regards
>
> Mike Smart

8. Send the e-mail to yourself.

9. Close Excel.

After a few moments you should find that the e-mail has appeared in your inbox.

4 Log out of your OneDrive.

While you are logged in to your OneDrive you will always have full access to your own files.

This means that even though the link is read-only (a *View* link) you will still be able to edit the file as if it were an *Edit* link.

To simulate a recipient that is not yourself, you will have to log out of your OneDrive.

1. Open a web browser.

2. Go to: **www.OneDrive.com** and sign in if necessary.

3. Click your name in the top right corner.

4. Click *Sign Out* on the shortcut menu.

5 Test the link.

1. Open the e-mail previously sent to yourself.

2. Click the link that you placed in the e-mail.

The workbook opens in Excel Online.

Notice that there is no *Edit Workbook* link on the ribbon. This is because you sent a *View* link that does not allow the recipient to edit the workbook.

Note that the user is still able to save (and then edit) a local copy of your workbook (see sidebar).

6 Close Excel Online.

Lesson 8-7: Edit a workbook simultaneously with other users using Excel Online

When working with Excel Online you never have to save

Excel Online has no save button.

While this seems strange at first, it is actually quite logical.

When you open a workbook using the normal Excel desktop application, the workbook is copied from your hard drive into the computer's memory. When you make changes they are applied to the copy of the workbook (in the computer's memory) rather than the workbook on the hard drive. If you don't save the workbook you will lose any changes that you make. The desktop Excel application always works like this, whether the workbook resides on your local hard disk or your OneDrive.

When you open a workbook using Excel Online, the workbook is not copied into the computer's memory. You work with the actual workbook on the OneDrive and not a copy of it. This means that any changes are instantly applied to the workbook, making a save button unnecessary (as any changes that you make are being instantly made to the actual workbook file).

This new way of working provides an unexpected benefit.

If several users are all working with the same workbook (and all are using Excel Online), any change made (by any user) will magically, and almost instantly, appear on every other user's screen!

This provides a completely new way of collaborating with other users.

<table>
<tr><td>

note

If you only have one device

If you only have one device you can still work through this lesson.

To do this, you will need to open two web browser windows.

You'll have to imagine that each browser window is a different user with a different device.

</td><td>

To get the most out of this lesson you will need two devices to simulate two different users. See sidebar if you only have one device.

1 Open Excel 2013 on your Windows PC.

The start-up screen is displayed.

2 Open the *Smartphone Sales* sample file from your OneDrive.

This is the file that you saved in: *Lesson 8-1: Save a workbook to a OneDrive.*

3 Send an *Edit Link* to yourself via e-mail.

This will enable the recipient to both view and edit the workbook via Excel Online.

You learned how to do this in: *Lesson 8-6: Share a link to a workbook.*

4 Close Excel.

It is important that you close Excel. If the workbook remained open in Excel you'd lock the workbook and prevent other users

</td></tr>
</table>

from editing it using Excel Online. File locking was discussed in more depth in: *Lesson 8-2: Open a workbook from a OneDrive.*

5 Use the *Edit Link* to open *Smartphone* Sales on your Windows PC using Excel Online.

1. Open the e-mail previously sent to yourself.

2. Click the link that you placed in the e-mail.

    If you do this on your Windows PC you will be given the choice of opening the link in either *Excel* or *Excel Online.* Choose Excel Online in this case.

    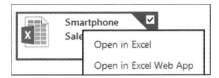

    The workbook opens using *Excel Online.*

    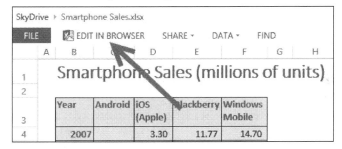

    Notice that there is an *EDIT IN BROWSER* link on the ribbon (*Edit Workbook* on some devices).

    This is because you sent an *Edit* link that allows the recipient to both view and edit the workbook.

6 Use the same *Edit Link* to open *Smartphone Sales* on your other device using Excel Online.

   Your other device may be a different Windows PC, an iPad, an Apple Mac, an Android device, or any other device that has a supported web browser.

   You now are now viewing the same workbook on both devices. This means that any changes made to the workbook on one device will (almost) instantly appear on the screen of the other device.

7 Put both devices into *Edit* mode.

   Click *EDIT IN BROWSER* on the ribbon (*Edit Workbook* on some devices).

8 Make a change to the workbook on one of your devices.

   Notice that the change appears (almost instantly) on the other device.

9 Close Excel Online on both devices.

   There is no need to save the workbook (there isn't even a save button in Excel Online). Your changes were automatically saved to the OneDrive as you made them.

Session 8: Exercise

1   Open *Broadband Speeds* from your sample files folder.

2   Create a new sub-folder in your OneDrive documents folder called: Exercise 8

3   Save the *Broadband Speeds* workbook into the */Documents/Exercise 8* folder.

4   Send a *View Link* and an *Edit Link* for the *Broadband Speeds* workbook to yourself via e-mail.

     (If you have a slow Internet connection you may have to wait until synchronization completes before you are able to do this).

5   Close Excel 2013.

6   Log out of your OneDrive.

7   Use the *View Link* to view the *Broadband Speeds* workbook using Excel Online.

     Note that it is not possible to make changes to the workbook.

8   Close Excel Online.

9   Use the *Edit Link* to open the *Broadband Speeds* workbook using Excel Online.

10   Enable editing within Excel Online.

11   Change the *Average Speed (Mbs)* for *Luxembourg* (cell B4) to: 75.00

12   Close Excel Online.

13   Open the desktop Excel 2013 application.

14   Open *Broadband Speeds* from your OneDrive.

     Note that the average speed for Luxembourg is now 75.00 Mbs.

15   Change the Average Speed (Mbs) for Luxembourg to: 100.88

16   Save the workbook.

Broadband Speeds

If you need help slide the page to the left

Session 8: Exercise answers

These are the questions that most students find difficult to remember:

Q 10	Q 6	Q 4	Q 2
1. Click: *Edit Workbook* on the ribbon (*Edit in Browser* on some devices). This was covered in: *Lesson 8-7: Edit a workbook simultaneously with other users using Excel Online.*	1. Open a web browser. 2. Go to: **www.OneDrive.com** 3. Click your name in the top right corner. 4. Click *Sign Out* on the shortcut menu. This was covered in: *Lesson 8-6: Share a link to a workbook.*	1. Click: File→Share. 2. Click: *Get a Sharing Link* in the *Share* menu. 3. Click the *Create a Link* buttons next to the *View* and *Edit* links. 4. Right-click on the *View* link and then select *Copy* from the shortcut menu. 5. Paste the link into the body of an e-mail. 6. Repeat the same operation for the *Edit* link. This was covered in: *Lesson 8-6: Share a link to a workbook.*	1. Click: File→Save As. 2. Click: *OneDrive* in the *Save As* menu. 3. Click: *Browse* in the *OneDrive* menu. 4. Double-click the *Documents* folder. 5. Right-click in the *Documents* folder and select: New→Folder 6. Type: **Exercise 8** as the name of the new folder. If you have difficulty doing this, right-click on the folder and select *Rename* from the shortcut menu. This was covered in: *Lesson 8-1: Save a workbook to a OneDrive.*

If you have difficulty with the other questions, here are the lessons that cover the relevant skills:

1   **Lesson 1-5: Download the sample files and open/navigate a workbook.**

3   **Lesson 8-1: Save a workbook to a OneDrive.**

5,9   **Lesson 1-1: Start Excel and open a new blank workbook.**

7,8   **Lesson 8-5: Open a workbook using Excel Online.**

11,12,13 **Lesson 8-7: Edit a workbook simultaneously with other users using Excel Online.**

14   **Lesson 8-2: Open a workbook from a OneDrive.**

15   **Lesson 2-1: Enter text and numbers into a worksheet.**

16   **Lesson 1-6: Save a workbook to a local file.**

Index

A

A4 size paper, 305
absolute references, 140
accounting number format style, 168
alignment
    horizontal, of cell contents, 172
    vertical, of cell contents, 176
android. *See* operating system
apple OS X. *See* operating system
apps
    content, explained, 49, 150
    downloading from the Office store, 49, 151
    task pane, explained, 49, 150
    uses of, 49, 150
arrange all, 68
AutoComplete
    formula entry using, 91
    text entry using, 120
AutoFill
    custom fill series, creating, 98
    date series, examples of, 96
    filling down, right, up and left with, 121
    formulas, using to adjust, 94
    smart tag options, using, 96
    text and numeric series, creating with, 92
AutoFit rows and columns, **83**, 129
automatic updates
    applying, 26
    switching on and off, 26
AutoSave, 42, *See also* versions
    draft versions, explanation of, 42
    time interval, changing, 42
AutoSum, 70
    AVERAGE functions, creating with, 86
    MAX functions, creating with, 87
    SUM a non contiguous range with, 84
AVERAGE function, 86

B

backstage view, 50
backup. *See also* AutoSave
    automatic backups, reverting to, 42
    RAID array, use of to improve resilience, 42
    time interval for automatic backups, changing, 42

binary workbook format, 36
borders
    adding to cells, 184
    draw border line tool, using to add, 185

C

cancel button, 66
cells. *See also* styles; comments; formatting
    active cell, 80
    aligning contents of, horizontally, 172
    aligning contents of, vertically, 176
    borders, adding to, 184
    color, adding to, 182
    conditional formatting of, 192
    copying one to another, 122
    copying using drag and drop, 124
    custom styles, creating, 188
    deleting, 86
    entering text into, 66
    entering values into, 66
    gradient fills, adding to, 182
    merging, 174
    selecting a range of, 73
    selecting all in a worksheet, 83
    styles, applying to, 180
    unique values, detecting with conditional formatting, 195
    wrapping text within, 174
chart source data
    adding series, 242
    assigning non contiguous, 238
    changing, 236
    changing using *select data source* dialog tools, 236
    deleting series, 242
    hidden and empty cells button, 245
    horizontal (category) axis labels, defining, 242
    horizontal (category) axis labels, editing, 247
    legend entries (series), 242
    non-contiguous source data, charting by hiding rows and columns, 244
    numerical axis labels, configuring, 246
    series, deleting, 242
charts. *See also* chart source data; visualizations; sparklines
    3-D elements, formatting in, 230
    activating, 219

axis title element, 225, 230

axis, formatting, 257

axis, maximum and minimum values, setting, 257

borders, formatting in, 228

category data explained, 240

color set, applying to, 226

combination, creating, 262

copying, 220, 226

creating quick charts with visualizations, 196

creating quickly with two clicks, 218

data labels, adding to, 250

data labels, formatting, 251, 257, 264

data labels, referencing a range from, 252

data series explained, 230

data table, adding to, 225, 230

deleting, 220, 226

deleting elements from, 232

element button, 226

elements, explained, 216

elements, formatting in, 228

elements, moving in, 232

elements, re-sizing in, 232

embedding in worksheet, 221

empty data points, dealing with, 248

fill color, changing of in elements, 254

filters button, 226, 235

filters, applying, 234

fonts, changing sizes in, 232

format shape task pane, working with, 228

gradiated fill, adding, 266

gridlines explained, 230

gridlines, major & minor, adding, 256

gridlines, major & minor, enabling and disabling, 257

hidden and empty cells button, 249

horizontal (category) axis defined, 225, 230

layout, changing, 224, 225, 230

layouts, explained, 216

legend, displaying in different places, 232

line with markers chart type, creating, 260

moving average, adding, 264

naming, 220, 226

numerical axis labels, configuring, 246

pie charts, 258

pie charts, pulling a slice out of the pie, 259

pie charts, rotating, 259

plot area, 230

quick analysis button, creating with, 219, 223

recommended charts feature, 222

re-sizing, 220, 226

rows/columns, switching, 240

secondary axis, adding, 261

selection pane, using to activate, 220

series data explained, 240

shadows, applying to elements, 230

shapes, inserting into, 255

sheet, moving to, 221

style, changing, 226

styles button, 226

styles, explained, 216

templates, creating from, 268

text box, adding to, 254

tips, 225

title element, 225, 228, 230

title element, linking to worksheet cell, 228

title element, re-positioning to dead center, 232

transparency, 229

trend line, adding, 264

type, changing, 262

types, explained, 216

values and labels, importance of selecting, 218

vertical (value) axis defined, 225, 230

vertical axis, creating chart with two, 260

x axis defined, 225, 230

y axis defined, 225, 230

check box, 48

clipboard

    copying and pasting multiple items with, 130

    described, 122

close button, 30

cloud computing. *See* OneDrive; Excel Online

collapse dialog button, 237

color sets, component of a theme, 179

columns

    deleting, 118

    freezing, 152

    hiding, 244

    inserting, 118

    making several the same size, 83

    resizing automatically, 82

    selecting, 76

    selecting non contiguous, 76

    unhiding, 244

    width of, manually changing, 83

comma style, 168

comma[0] style, 168

comments

    changing the user name shown in, 134

    displaying, one or more all of the time, 137

    hiding, 137

    inserting, 134

moving, 136

printing, 138

printing all at the end, 138

printing exactly as displayed on a worksheet, 139

re sizing, 135

showing all, 136

conditional formatting. *See also* visualizations

explained, 192

formula driven, 198

highlighting a complete row of data with, 199

quick analysis button, applying with, 192

rules manager, managing multiple with, 194

unique values, detecting with, 195

confirm button, 66

copying

one cell to another cell, 122

using drag and drop, 124

crash, recovering from, 42

currency

prefixes, 67

styles for, 169

cursor shapes, explained, 73

custom formatting codes, 165, **170**

custom lists, 99

cut, 122

D

dates and times

custom format, 165

difference in days between two dates, calculating, 167

formatting, 164

internationally safe formats, benefits of, 164

serial number, explained, 166

time value, containment within dates, 166

decimal places, changing number of, 126

delete, recovering work accidentally deleted, 42

dialog launcher, 49

documents. *See also* files

organization of, 38

pinning, 38

downloading the sample files, 13, **32**

draft versions, explanation of, 42

drop-down list, 49

E

editing cell contents, 66

effects, component of a theme, 179

Excel 97-2003 workbook format, 36

Excel Online, 336, *See* also OneDrive

browsers, supported, 339

edit workbook simultaneously with other users using, 342

open workbook using, 338

overview of, 336

ribbon, hiding and showing in, 339

save local copy of read-only workbook, 341

save, automatic, explained, 338

Excel workbook file format, 34, 36

F

files. *See also* workbooks; documents

default workbook file location, setting, 39

formats supported, 34, 36

opening with earlier Excel versions, 36

organization of, 38

recent workbooks list, increasing the number of entries in, 38

find and replace

formats, 290

look in option, 290

options, 290

using, 290

wildcard, searches using, 291

flash fill

autofill handle, using to apply, 102

automatic, use of, 100

examples, 106

extracting initials with, 100

formula based solution, compared to, 103

header rows, importance of formatting for, 100

manual, use of, 102

multiple examples, use of, 104

numbers, working with, 104

splitting delimited text with, 100

switching on, 100

telephone numbers, formatting with, 102

use of seperators with, 100

using to solve common problems, 106

font sets, component of a theme, 178

fonts

default, changing, 188

font sets, use in themes, 178

serif and sans serif explained, 179

formatting. *See also* themes

3-D Elements, 230

aligning cell contents horizontally, **172**

aligning cell contents vertically, **176**

borders around cells, 184

cell styles, 180

chart borders, 228
chart elements, 228
color, 182
conditional, 192
custom cell styles, 188
custom codes, **170**
dates, **164**
find and replace, replacing formats with, 290
format painter, copying with, 206
gradient effects, 182
numbers using built-in styles, **168**
rotating text, 208
shadows, 230
themes, changing, 180
themes, understanding, **178**
transparency, 229
visualizations, comparing values with, 196
formula bar
    expanding and collapsing, 174
    explanation of, 72
    graphic showing location of, 34
formulas
    absolute and relative references in, 140
    Autocomplete, creating with, 90
    AutoFill, adjusting with, 94
    AVERAGE function, creating using AutoSum, 86
    conditional format, driving with, 198
    cross-worksheet, creating, 286
    F2 key to display range addressed by, 87
    formula bar, viewing in, 72
    MAX function, creating using AutoSum, 87
    mouse selection, creating with, 88
    multiplication operator (*) using in, 89
    SUM function, creating using AutoSum, 70
    syntax box, understanding, 91
    visual keyboard technique, creating with, 89
fractions, entering into cells, 67
freeze columns and rows, 152
full screen view, 56
functions
    AVERAGE, 86
    MAX, 87
    ROUND, 169
    SUM, **70**, 84

G

gallery, 48
goto special, 81

H

hashes
    indication that columns are too narrow by, 164
help system, 58
    F1 key, accessing with, 59
    formula AutoComplete, accessing from within, 91
    help button, accessing with, 58
    ribbon, accessing directly from, 59
hide rows and columns, 244
hide values, using three semicolon custom format, 171
hiding and unhiding worksheets, 284

I

Intelliprint, 308
internet. *See* OneDrive; Excel Online
iPad, described, 334

J

justify, horizontal alignment option, 173

K

key tips, 52
keyboard shortcuts
    AutoSelect a range, 81
    AutoSum, 70
    bold, 53
    close, 31
    copy, 122
    create a mixed cell reference, 143
    cut, 123
    cycle through worksheets, 41
    fill down, 121
    find, 290
    flash fill, 102
    insert a comment into a cell, 134
    insert column, 118
    insert row, 118
    italic, 53
    make a relative reference absolute, 141
    move to cell A1, 152
    paste, 122
    redo, 132
    replace, 290
    ribbon, show/hide, 46
    save, 34
    select every cell in a worksheet, 82
    spell check, 156

underline, 53
undo, 132
workbook, create new, 68

L

landscape orientation, 298
letter size paper, 305
lines, adding beneath cells, 184

M

macro enabled workbook format, 36
marching ants, 70
marquee, 70
MAX function, creating using AutoSum, 87
maximize button, 30
menus
    rich, 49
    shortcut (contextual), 53
    standard, 48
merge and center button, 174
merge, cells, 174
mini toolbar
    shortcut (contextual) menu, 53
    using when entering text, 52
minimize button, 30
mixed cell references, 142
moving
    the Excel window, 30
multiplication operator (*), 89

N

name box, 32
negative numbers, entering into cells, 67
normal view, 54
number sign (#), 82
numbers
    changing number of decimal points displayed,
        126
    using built-in styles with, 168

O

office theme, changing, 28
OneDrive. *See also*, microsoft account; Excel
    Online
    advantages of using, 333
    alternatives to, 333
    link, sharing, 340
    lunchtime lock, problems caused by, 332
    open a workbook from, 332

save a workbook to, 330
save local copy of read-only workbook, 341
security concerns, 331
SharePoint, using in place of, 331
social networks, sharing links via, 340
subscriptions, 330
operating system
    android, 334
    apple OS X, 334
    checking version of, 16
    explained, 334
    iOS, 334
    Windows 7, use of, 16
    windows 8 RT, 335
    Windows 8, use of, 16
    windows phone, 334
organizing
    excel files, 38
    sample files folder, 32

P

page break preview, 54
page layout view, 54, **300**
paper sizes explained, 305
paste, 122
paste special, 127
paste values, 127
PDF, workbook format, 37
percentage style, 169
portrait orientation, 298
pound sign (#), 82
precision, changing to avoid rounding errors, 169
printing
    area, setting, 316
    autoheaders and autofooters, adding, 310
    cell comments, adding, 138
    column headings, showing on every page, 318
    comments, exactly as displayed on a
        worksheet, 139
    comments, printing all at the end, 138
    error messages, suppressing in printouts, 322
    graphical header, adding, 313
    headers & footers, adding custom, 312
    headers & footers, including an ampersand (&)
        in, 312
    headers & footers, specifying different first,
        odd and even, 314
    margin settings, changing the default, 301
    margins, adjusting using rulers, 301
    margins, custom, adjusting with page setup,
        302

over then down, page order, changing with, 320

page break preview, 54

page breaks, adjusting using *page break preview*, 308

page breaks, inserting and deleting, 306

page number, setting the starting value, 310

page order, changing, 320

paper orientation, changing, 298

paper size, setting, 304

paper sizes explained, 305

part of a worksheet, 316

previewing on screen, 50, **298**

row headings, showing on every printed page, 318

rulers, showing and hiding, 301

scaling to fit paper, 304

several worksheets at the same time, 320

protected view, potential problems when downloading sample files, 32

Q

quick access toolbar

adding commands to, 50

adding seperators to, 50

deleting commands from, 50

quick analysis

charts, creating with, 219

conditional formatting, creating with, 192

sparklines, creating with, 201

totals, creating with, 71

quotations

Aristotle, 48

Benjamin Disraeli, 297

Confucius, 21

Dr. Frank Crane, 17

Euripides, 23

Frederick R. Barnard, 215

Henry Ford, 275

Margaret Thatcher, 117

Oscar Wilde, 163

Robert Collier, 30

Steve Jobs, 329

Winston Churchill, 20

R

RAID array, 42

ranges

AutoSelect , selecting automatically with, 80

copying data across, 74

entering data into, 74

non contiguous, selecting, 78

select all button, to select a range containing every cell in a worksheet, 83

selecting, 72

selecting visually for formulas with the mouse, 88

transposing, 128

visualizations, comparing values with, 196

recommended charts, using, 222

redo, 132

relative references, 140

replace cell contents using *find and replace*, 290

reset to match style, 231

restore down button, 30

ribbon

benefits of wide screen with, 46

command groups on, 48

contextual tabs, explanation of, 46

controls on, 48

customizing, 46

default, resetting to, 46

font panel controls, explanation of, 46

overview, 46

showing and hiding (minimizing), 46

rotate text, 208

rounding errors, avoiding, 169

rows

conditional format, highlighting entire row with, 199

copying contents of one to another, 124

deleting, 118

freezing, 152

hiding, 244

inserting, 118

making several the same size, 83

manually setting height of, 83

resizing automatically, 82

selecting, 76

selecting non contiguous, 76

unhiding, 244

rulers, showing and hiding in page layout view, 301

rules manager

controlling conditional formatting with, 194

editing rules with, 196

S

sample files

downloading, 13, **32**

organizing folder, 32

potential protected view problem when downloading, 32
sans serif and serif fonts explained, 179
save, 34, 36
    AutoSave, using to recover work after crash, 42
select all button, 280
selecting cells, 72
serif and sans serif fonts explained, 179
shortcut keys. *See* keyboard shortcuts
smart method. *See* The Smart Method
smart tag
    explained, 72
    options, 96
    using to paste values, 127
SmartPhones, explained, 334
sparklines, 200
    column type, inserting, 201
    date axis, specifying for, 204
    deleting, 202
    empty cells, setting options for, 249
    formatting
        line thickness (weight), changing, 203
        marker (data point) color, 203
        markers (data points), 203
        single sparkline rather than group, 205
    group and ungroup, 205
    hidden cells, show/hide on sparkline, 249
    inserting group of into a range of cells, 200
    line type, inserting, 201
    quick analysis button, creating with, 201
    size of containing cell, changing, 203
    style, changing with style gallery, 203
    type, changing, 203
    ungroup and group, 205
    uses of, 200
    vertical axis, applying common scaling to sparkline group, 202
    win/loss type, inserting, 201
spell checking
    dictionary language, setting, 157
    using, 156
split button, 48
split, window into multiple panes, 154
start Excel, 24
styles
    accounting number format, 168
    applying cell styles, 180
    built-in, for numbers, 168
    comma, 168
    comma[0], 168
    currency[0], 168
    custom, 188
    importance of using theme colors and fonts, 182, 191
    master style book, using, 190
    merging, 190
    percentage, 169
    removing from cells, 180
SUM function
    creating manually using formula AutoComplete, 90
    creating using AutoSum, 70
switch windows, 68
synchronous scrolling, 278

T

tablet computers, explained, 334
tabs. *See* worksheets
telephone numbers, formatting with flash fill, 102
templates
    cloud, storing in, 144
    creating, 146
    custom, about, 145
    folder, organizing, 145
    folder, setting location of, 145
    potential problems when using samples, 144
    using, 148
the smart method
    avoiding repetition, 18
    informal summary, 19
    learning by participation, 21
    putting the smart method to work, 16
    session objectives, 19
    sessions and lessons, 16
    two facing pages rule, 20
themes. *See also* office theme
    changing, 180
    changing the default, 179
    color sets, 179
    custom, creating, 186
    effects, 179
    explained, 178
    font sets, 178
    importance of using theme colors and fonts, 182
times. *See* dates and times
title bar, 68
touchscreen, gestures, 338
transparency, 229
transpose, 128

U

undo, 132
unhide rows and columns, 244
unique values, detecting with conditional formatting, 195

V

values. *See also* Styles
    built-in styles, applying to, 168
    currency prefixes, using with, 67
    entering into cells, 66
    fractions, entering into cells, 67
    negative numbers, entering into cells, 67
    precision, changing to avoid rounding errors, 169
    rounding errors, avoiding, 169
version
    Excel, checking, 26
versions. *See also* AutoSave
    earlier versions, viewing, 44
    explanation of, 42
    recovering an earlier version of a workbook, 44
vertically align cell contents, 176
visualizations, 196
    color scale, 196
    comparing values with, 196
    data bar, 196
    icon set, 196
    rules manager, editing with, 196
    use of *show bar only* to create quick charts, 196

W

web browser. *See* OneDrive; Excel Online
wildcards, searches using, 291
windows
    arrange all, using to automatically size, 68
    closing, 30
    moving, 30
    resetting position of, 279
    resizing, 30
    restoring down, 30
    splitting into multiple panes, 154
    switching to view a different workbook, 68
    synchronous scrolling of, 278
    viewing two workbooks side by side in, 278

views, creating two of the same workbook, 276
Windows 7. *See* operating system
Windows 8. *See* operating system
workbooks. *See also* files
    changing default number of worksheets in, 40
    comparing side by side, 278
    creating new, 68
    duplicating worksheets in, 280
    open from OneDrive, 332
    opening, 32
    recent workbooks list, increasing the number of entries in, 38
    save to OneDrive, 330
    saving, 34, 36
    switching between open workbooks, 68
    synchronous scrolling, comparing with, 278
    viewing the same workbook in two windows, 276
    viewing two at the same time, 68
    views, 54
worksheets
    3-D creating, 288
    adding, 40
    changing default number of, 40
    chart worksheets, explanation of, 40
    copying from one workbook to another, 282
    deleting, 40
    duplicating, 280
    gridlines, switching off in, 184
    groups, 288
    hiding and unhiding, 284
    maximum number of rows and columns in, 32
    navigating, 32, 40
    non-contiguous, selecting, 288
    renaming, 40
    tab colors, changing, 41
wrapping
    splitting wrapped text into different lines, 177
    text in cells, 174

X

XPS, workbook format, 37

Z

zoom control, 108

Become an Excel Expert with our Expert Skills book

The next book in the series builds upon all of the foundation skills you've learned.

There's a whole lot more to Excel, and you'll learn it all with this book. Security, advanced functions and formulas, tables, macros, pivot tables, what-if analysis... and so much more.

Search for it at **Amazon.com** or **Amazon.co.uk**.

You can also find links to book resellers stocking this title at the **ExcelCentral.com** web site (click *Books* on the top menu bar).

ExcelCentral.com

For many years I have dreamed of creating an online learning resource that would provide the same experience as my classroom courses.

My books cover the same material as my classroom courses, but it is clear that some learners need more than can be delivered via printed media. In 2013 we completed an Excel Internet resource that aims to bring my classroom courses onto your desktop.

The site is available at: **www.ExcelCentral.com**

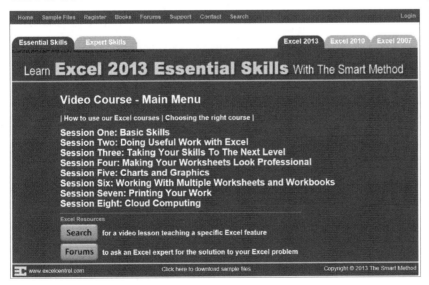

On the site I have recorded a video walk-through for each and every lesson in this book. The videos have also been indexed by keyword to provide a unique interactive Excel reference resource.

Lessons can be viewed without cost by using our *FreeView* facility.

Enhanced features can also be unlocked for a small annual subscription charge.

Use your new Excel skills to teach your own classroom courses.

If you've worked through this book carefully you will now have excellent Excel skills and if you progress to the *Expert Skills* book in the series you'll be a true Excel expert.

There is a huge demand, everywhere in the world, for Excel training at all levels. The skills you have learned in this books will enable you to teach an introductory Excel course (providing all of the skills needed by most office workers).

We can directly and rapidly supply books, at educational discount prices, to Excel instructors, corporate clients, schools, colleges and universities from our warehouses in the USA (also serving Canada), UK (also serving Europe) and Australia (also serving New Zealand).

Our books are also printed in Germany, Brazil and Russia so are instantly available in almost every country by simply quoting the ISBN number (shown below) to any bookseller or wholesaler.

Use our books to teach all Excel versions.

This book is available for all Excel versions in common use (Excel 2007, 2010 and 2013). This means that you'll be able to teach Excel classes even if the client uses an earlier version. You can use the books as courseware during your classes and then give each student a copy of the book to take home as reference material when the course is over.

| 978-1-909253-07-0 | 978-1-909253-06-3 | 978-0-9554599-8-6 | 978-0-9554599-7-9 | 978-0-9554599-3-1 | 978-0-9554599-2-4 |

You can quote the ISBN numbers shown above to any book retailer or wholesaler. All major distributors have our books in stock for immediate delivery.

Order 10+ books and we'll offer you an educational discount!

If you live in the USA, Canada, UK, Europe, Australia or New Zealand we can rapidly deliver books to your doorstep at a discount price. You only need to order ten books or more (you can mix titles if you wish).

For a fast no-obligation quotation, fill in our online form here:

http://www.excelcentral.com/discounts

We'll usually get back to you the same day via e-mail with a quotation.

Obtain a fast solution to any Excel issue using our support forum

Now that you have mastered Excel you will need to apply your skills to real-world business problems.

Sometimes the correct solution to a specific Excel-related problem is not immediately apparent. Our online support forum enables you to ask any Excel-related question. One of our staff members will solve the problem – usually within 24 hours of posting.

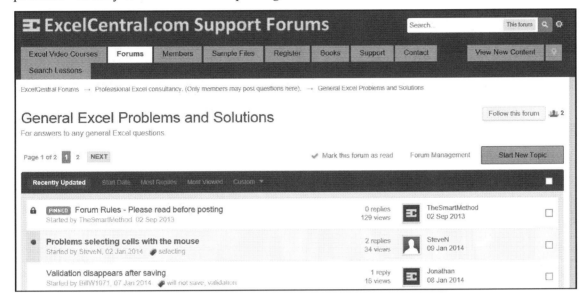

Here's an example of a support request and reply:

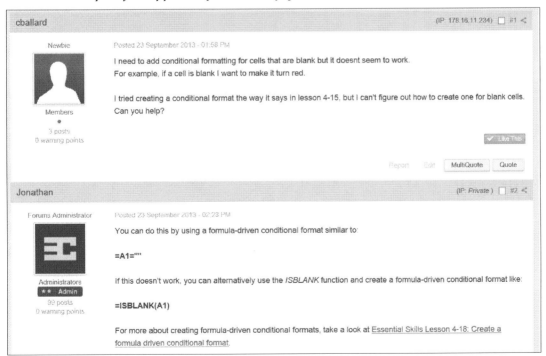

You need to be a member to post questions but you can view all previous questions and answers completely free of charge at:

http://forums.excelcentral.com/

Made in the USA
Middletown, DE
11 February 2015